INSIDE STORY

INSIDE STORY

THE POWER OF THE TRANSFORMATIONAL ARC

DARA MARKS

THREE MOUNTAIN PRESS

THREE MOUNTAIN PRESS

Publishers Cataloging-in-Publication Data

Marks, Dara.
   Inside story : the power of the transformational arc / Dara Marks. --
1st ed. – Studio City, Calif. : Three Mountain Press, 2007.

      p. ; cm.
      ISBN-13: 978-0-9788129-0-4
      ISBN-10: 0-9788129-0-5
      Includes bibliographical references and index.

   1. Motion picture authorship--Handbooks, manuals, etc.
   2. Screenwriters--Handbooks, manuals, etc. 3. Plots (Drama,
   novel, etc.) I. Title.

PN1996 .M37 2007   2006932223
791.43/7--dc22   0701

ACKNOWLEDGMENTS
With gratitude for permission to reproduce the following. Sony Pictures Entertainment for the use of excerpts from the screenplays *The Fisher King* written by Richard LaGravenese © 1991 and *A Few Good Men* written by Aaron Sorkin © 1992. Warner Bros. Entertainment, Inc. for the use of excerpts from the screenplays *Goodfellas* written by Nicholas Pileggi and Martin Scorsese © 1990 and *Casablanca* written by Julius J. Epstein, Philip G. Epstein, and Howard Koch © 1942. MGM for the use of excerpts from the screenplay *Rocky* written by Sylvester Stallone © 1976. Twentieth Century Fox Film Corp. for the use of excerpts from the screenplay *Romancing the Stone* written by Diane Thomas © 1984. Paramount Pictures for excerpts from the screenplays *Ordinary People* written by Alvin Sargent © 1980 and *American Beauty* written by Alan Ball © 1999.

Printed and bound in the United States of America
Cover and Book Design: Patricia Bacall
Author Photograph: Xaque Gruber
Editing: Brookes Nohlgren

Published by Three Mountain Press, 11054 Ventura Blvd., Suite 205, Studio City, CA 91604, SAN 851-6758, www.threemountainpress.com, 800-313-1345

To my mother and father,
who encouraged me to try my wings and fly.

To my husband,
who inspired me to soar.

ACKNOWLEDGEMENTS

All great stories are about relationships; my own is no exception. In gratitude:

To my mentor, Dr. Linda Seger. Her wisdom and generosity of spirit have been a guiding influence throughout my life and career.

To all of my extraordinary teachers who have helped illuminate the path that has led to this book, especially: Dr. Ginette Paris, Dr. Dennis Patrick Slattery, Dr. Gilles (Zenon) Maheu, and the amazing staff and faculty at Pacifica Graduate Institute.

To those who gave hands-on support, wise counsel, steadfast commitment, and relentless prodding: Robin Haney, Julie Wellings, Heather Hale, Tinker Lindsey, Carol Abbott, Eugenia Bostwick-Singer, Raymond Singer, Lisa Loomer, Joe Romano, Dino Audino, Deborah DeFuria, Bess Armstrong, Catherine Hart, David Huff, Dana White, Constance Welsh, Donie Nelson, Janis Cohen, Barbara Nussbaum, Ellen Reid, Patricia Bacall, Ghislain Viau, Brookes Nohlgren, Xaque Gruber, Laren Bright, Robert Menna, Wanda Webster, Richard Marcus, and my extraordinary family: Libby, Tim, Jane, Jeff, Vicki, Fred, Zachary, Lauryn, and Eleanor Marks.

To my students and clients, who continue to teach me everything I know about the art and craft of screenwriting.

To all of my extended family and friends, who show me how to live and who keep me focused on what is important.

To Randy and Justin, who make it all worthwhile.

And always to the Muses, who forever guide me to the truth, though I sometimes forget to listen.

We are lonesome animals.
We spend our life trying to be less lonesome.
One of our ancient methods is to tell a story
begging the listener to say
– and to feel –
'Yes, that's the way it is,
or at least that's the way I feel it.
You're not as alone as you thought.'

~ JOHN STEINBECK

CONTENTS

PART II
BUILDING THE ARC OF CHARACTER

INTRODUCTION

O ver the years in my work as a script consultant, I've found that notes telling writers to *"write what's in your heart," "add more depth," or "find your authentic voice"* aren't especially useful. It's not that these problems don't exist; in fact, they are often the primary reason a story feels flat and is un-involving. But, achieving depth in any artistic endeavor isn't just a *thing* you do; it's the totality of the experience. It's the result of an "in-*depth*" process that grows with the story as opposed to something that is tagged on in the end as an afterthought.

No one questions a writer's need to have a strategy or technique for developing the physical, external plotline of a story (e.g., catching the killer, solving a crime, making it to the altar on time). Most serious writers study the basic elements of story structure and learn how to organize a film script, novel, or play in a manner that resembles the form and serves the dramatic function. However, when it comes to expressing inner values and establishing a personal perspective on a story, writers are often guided only by their instincts or intuition and a little luck.

Instinct and especially intuition are absolutely essential for getting to the more meaningful, authentic aspects of a story, but they can easily degenerate into random guesswork if they're all you have to rely on. The starting point for any artistic creation is *always* at the level of intuition because it's where new ideas are conceived. However, new ideas, even great ones, seldom rise to the level of consciousness fully formed. They often begin as a jumble of thoughts, impressions, feelings, and images that can be as confusing and contradictory as they are inspiring and compelling.

The method for getting to the emotional heart of a story is not a divine secret bestowed only on the anointed. All writers have a well of valuable feelings and insights; it's just a question of knowing how to tap into them. *Inside Story* offers techniques and methods to help writers identify and stay focused on the deeper thematic and emotional dimensions that are necessary to create a more natural or organic story structure.

Crossing to the Borderland

I have a problem with the notion that writers must suffer for their art. I do believe, however, that we have to *live* for it. Living, of course, includes suffering as well as disappointment, disillusionment, and rejection, but it also includes joy, enlightenment, and even contentment. Ultimately, every one of the stories we tell tells our *own* story. Though a story seldom reflects the direct autobiographical chronology of our lives, it *always* reflects what we know to be true. It has to; we don't *know* anything else.

A young client of mine recently completed a high-wire action thriller, but from what she shared of her background it was apparent that she had also turned the rage she felt toward her domineering father into a story about the heroic pursuit of independence. Of course, that was hardly her plan when she first sat down to write, but that's the power of the creative experience: It opens up the space for a new piece of our own truth to be revealed—to us.

The writing experience is often described as a journey because, although it may physically shackle us to our desks, it does fulfill the primary mandate of a true journey: It takes us to someplace new. Even if we end up right back where we started—we will inevitably see where we are with new eyes.

Inside Story is intended to be a traveling companion on the storyteller's journey. It will help you explore and navigate the rugged, unpredictable, and often harsh landscape that lies in every writer's path. It will serve as a translator for the complex metaphorical language of story and will guide you to the outposts of your known world, helping capture in your stories a glimpse of the wild new thing that lies just beyond everything you thought you knew. This is the true destination of all stories. At their best they take us to the space that lies just outside what we know about ourselves and introduce us to a new piece of personal knowledge that enhances our connection to others, to nature, and to the divine. Most importantly, stories can transform our painful and even blissful life experiences into higher consciousness.

The place that lies between what we know and what we are coming to know about ourselves and others is sometimes referred to as the *borderland*. It is the place where new consciousness is beginning to dawn, the place where we emerge from darkness into light. A writer who relies entirely on intuition rarely makes it to the borderland because what comes from the unconscious will generally stay there *unless* it is confronted and examined. This is why so many films today lack cohesiveness, substance, and relevance even though they may have an interesting central idea. A story that never makes it to the place where new consciousness, illuminating insights, and fresh perspectives are birthed will merely recycle worn-out clichés that trivialize and marginalize the true heroic quest for wholeness.

This quest for wholeness, for connection to all the undiscovered parts of our true nature, which includes our relationship with nature itself, is the model around which this theory of the transformational arc is formed. It embraces the principle that *any* living thing that isn't growing and evolving can only be moving toward decay and death. That we are either moving toward life or away from it is the heart of the human drama. To stand up and fight through the conflicts, confrontations, and disappointments we all encounter is the heroic challenge. To run away, disregard, dismiss, or avoid these challenges isn't merely benign or cowardly, it's tragic. It destroys the opportunity to grow and evolve. Ultimately this path leads only to the death of hopes, dreams, ambition, love, and all forms of interconnectedness.

Furthermore, if stories themselves avoid this internal challenge, they aren't simply harmless or shallow: They are tragic as well. A story that lacks any real reflection of a character's inner struggle can only portray the human condition in an idealized state. This means that characters who are "good" were born good and characters who are "bad" or "evil" were born that way as well; neither have any capacity to grow and evolve. This communicates to the audience that virtues like courage, kindness, and compassion aren't choices, but birthrights. Likewise, for those characters aligned with dark forces, there is no way out nor any hope of redemption. If only an occasional film lacked this dimensionality, it probably wouldn't matter too much, but when stories that undervalue the complexity of human drama dominate film, television, and all other manner of popular fiction, they become the standard by which we inevitably see ourselves—and each other. This is not only tragic, but the implication of its dehumanizing influence on the culture is catastrophic. The only way around this fate is for modern storytellers to make the journey inward themselves and share with audiences what is discovered there.

Twenty-five hundred years ago, a Chinese general named Sun Tzu wrote a collection of essays on military strategy known as "The Art of War," in which he offers this sage advice:

> *If you know the enemy and know yourself,*
> *you need not fear the result of a hundred battles.*
> *If you know yourself but not the enemy,*
> *for every victory gained you will also suffer a defeat.*
> *If you know neither the enemy nor yourself,*
> *you will succumb in every battle...*

While the art of writing is certainly not an act of war (for most people) and a script is not your enemy (most of the time), Sun Tzu's wisdom in regard to successfully facing a great challenge is also the foundation for developing a winning strategy as a writer.

If you *know* your story and *know* yourself, your writing can't fail. This doesn't necessarily guarantee that film studios will have a bidding war over every script you write, but it does promise that something of great value will be achieved by the experience. However, if you know yourself and you don't express that knowledge in your story, your script will fail creatively—no matter how much money a studio pays you. But most assuredly, if you refuse to look inward to know either yourself or your story, nothing of any value will ever come of your efforts—regardless of how "big" the film hits at the box office. Video store shelves are littered with the corpses of life-*less*, ineffectual films that no one remembers and no one ever really cared about because nothing of any emotional substance was ever invested in the story.

Invest in Yourself

All literary theories arise principally through observation. As far back as the time of ancient Greece, Aristotle observed that *drama imitates life* (he called this *mimesis*). Even if a theatrical situation appears to be more outlandish than any known human experience, it will always be grounded in some physical, emotional, or spiritual aspect of our reality, or we simply won't comprehend it. This means that writers are observers and interpreters of life. Therefore, it can be said that *everything you need to know about dramatic writing—you already know!*

However, most of what we *know* is unconscious, which makes getting to this information difficult, especially if all we have to rely on is accidental or inadvertent moments of insight and clarity. A successful writer must, therefore, develop and hone an effective process to gain access to the knowledge that lies within. When I'm teaching a course and I notice that a student has suddenly abandoned my lecture and is furiously scribbling in a notebook, I know that the person has just consciously connected with a piece of his or her own process. It's as if the synapses in that person's brain have just forged a new pathway, resulting in a stronger ability to communicate the story that is pulsating through the heart to the brain.

Because writing is a struggle to get to the new, undiscovered place, it will always be a mystery. But it is of little value to a writer if the process of unraveling this mystery is a mystery itself. Therefore, this book is intended to lead you to the discovery of your own inner process. When you, too, become excited and sidetracked by something you have read that solves a current script problem, stimulates a new story idea, or suddenly makes you realize that you have a lot more in common with your characters than you thought, you have just added a new page to your own personal writing manual. In the end, that's the only technique on writing that really matters. You have found your way inside your own story—and it is from here that a more organic or natural story structure will begin to form around your own unique and original story idea.

A natural story structure is one that reflects the true nature of the human experience. At its core, this structure demonstrates that the conflicts and problems in our outer, physical world do impact our internal reality. When problems of great magnitude arise, our own personal character is tested and often strengthened or diminished by the encounter. I know this to be true because it's how my own character has been formed, and I would ask you to consider how yours was formed as well. To some degree, we are all influenced by the attributes with which we were born: looks, intelligence, strength, and aptitude. However, these traits alone don't determine the *quality* of our character. Characteristics like integrity, compassion, ambition, courage, and resiliency only manifest themselves when something challenges their existence. None of us are born brave or cowardly, considerate or neglectful, benevolent or intolerant: These are personal choices we make when faced with situations that demand our involvement. If we choose to rise to a challenge, then we will inevitably engage a new part of our inner being in the struggle. As a result, we expand and grow toward the fullness of our true nature. However, if we run from or avoid the challenge, we will remain stuck at the same level of existence—doomed to continually re-engage the same challenges until we finally rise above them or are destroyed by them altogether.

In story terminology, this challenge to grow and evolve as we face the trials in our life is referred to as the *transformational arc of the character*. In the film industry and in other literary disciplines, this concept is widely used to indicate the need for interaction or interrelatedness between plot and character development. However, as the theory in this book demonstrates, the transformational arc has much greater significance and value. In effect, it is a second line of structure that is wrapped within the structure of the plot. It is, quite literally, the story that is found *inside story*. When it is well used, it is the driving force of the entire drama. When it is poorly applied or absent, a story will feel shallow and one-dimensional because there is no internal development of character to give meaning and significance to the conflict of the plot.

What's Inside the "Inside Story"

The process in this book begins, "*In the Beginning…*" with Chapter One. It's difficult to get to "meaning and significance" in a story unless we understand where those values originate, how to tap into them, and—for that matter—why they're even important.

Chapters Two, Three, and Four set the groundwork or foundation for the development of the transformational arc by defining its three primary building blocks: plot, character, and theme. These chapters are *not* a remedial review of story fundamentals, but rather a reevaluation or, more accurately, a re-*valuing* of the core elements that compose a story. If stories are to have more substance, it's important that they are built of only the finest construction materials.

Chapter Five defines the *fatal flaw of character*. This is the primary element that sets up the internal value system or *theme* of a story. In the writing process, there are only two substantial ways in which the theme can be expressed: either a character gives speeches about it, or the protagonist is forced to grow toward the thematic value as he or she struggles to resolve the conflict of the plot. Obviously, the second option is far more potent. Defining the fatal flaw of character is the starting point for integrating the development of plot, the movement of character, and the thematic voice of the writer throughout a story.

Whereas Part I of *Inside Story* lays the foundation for the transformational arc, Part II is the construction phase. Chapter Six begins by laying out a blueprint for the arc that will be built upon throughout the remainder of the book. The arc itself is shown to be an organic phenomenon. It expresses the natural rise and fall of a dramatic structure, which always begins with an escalation of tension and is resolved as the tension

de-escalates. In a story that fully utilizes the power of the transformational arc, this tension serves not only to solve the conflict of the plot,
but also to pull the protagonist toward internal renewal and higher
consciousness—which is the essence of the transformational process.

Chapters Seven through Ten illustrate how plot, character, and
theme need to move in unity throughout a storyline. Each of these chapters breaks the structure of a script into one of four essential parts: Act I,
first half of Act II, second half of Act II, and Act III. As Aristotle
described, drama imitates life; therefore, embodied in every movement
of the protagonist throughout each of these quadrants is a representation of the archetypal pattern of transformation. These chapters serve
as a very powerful guide for writers, providing clear information about
what is required at every stage in a story in order to complete the arc
and fulfill a *natural* dramatic structure.

A Final Note before You Begin

Keeping the flame of inspiration alive and using it as a guide
throughout the writing process is the underlying basis for the techniques
and strategies detailed in this book. Most writers have experienced
moments of sublime connection with their stories when both the prose
and images poured forth perfectly. But if no deliberate process was used to
help facilitate that experience, there is no way to retrace those steps and
repeat them. The real function of all artistic technique is to make conscious in the artist his or her own innate process. Too often, access to our
personal treasury of wisdom and insight is buried under the complexity of
the writing process itself. Therefore, what is needed in the way of writing
tools are instruments of excavation that can unearth the bounty of self-
knowledge that lies beneath the surface of our own stories.

But there is an obvious trap implied in any technique because *technique is not art;* it is only a device that can be used to help the artist
maximize the communication of his or her own creative expression. In
teaching a method like the one found in these pages, there is always a
risk that what is meant to assist writers in understanding and manifesting

their own unique vision will be interpreted as "rules" that must be followed. Rules convey a certain authority that presupposes that if you follow them, you succeed—that if you don't follow them, you fail. Clearly, nothing could be more destructive to the creative process. Therefore, the techniques in this book are meant to be extremely expansive. They invite you to play with established boundaries and push them to new limits. And for those of you who are willing to do the soul-excavating work, you will find that your stories will grow and thrive beyond anything you ever imagined.

Writing is a tool of transformation and can shine the light on the inside,
dispelling darkness, taking us through external layers,
bringing us closer to our souls.[1]

~ HILLARY CARLIP

---

[1] Hillary Carlip, *Girl Power: Young Women Speak Out* (New York: Warner Books, 1995).

PART ONE

LAYING A STRONG FOUNDATION

Fill your paper with the breathings of your heart…

~ WILLIAM WORDSWORTH

CHAPTER ONE

IN THE BEGINNING
The Word…

There is no wealth that could buy these words of me,
and the meaning that belongs to them. Once cast away as idle breath,
no wealth or power can bring them back. I mean them; I have
weighed them; and I will be true to what I undertake.

~ CHARLES DICKENS

It Was the Best of Scripts, It Was the Worst of Scripts…

A few weeks ago I received a frantic phone call from a screenwriter, in anguish because his project was teetering on the brink of collapse at one of the major studios. "I gave them everything they asked for," he moaned. "Now all they can tell me is that the script is flat and unmoving. Can you believe one producer even suggested I add a chase scene and a car crash?"

It didn't make him feel any better, but I assured him that anyone who's seen a Hollywood movie in the past thirty years could believe that. Somewhere along the way our modern cinematic stories have lost contact with the *quality* of the content, refocusing their attention instead on the *quantity* of the activity. This leaves only physical motion in place of real emotion, and without real emotion we simply don't *care*. We may feel momentary excitement, terror, horror, and even awe, but these emotions are relatively superficial and transitory. Nothing deeper can be felt because no authentic view of our own humanity has been exposed in the story.

This is why my client's movie was falling flat. Looking over his draft, I found that the studio's notes were pretty much correct. I, too, was unmoved by his script, but it wasn't because of a lack of action, as they had indicated. The plot was smart, fairly well structured, and full of complex twists and turns. What the story did lack, however, was a *connection* between all that **external** activity and the **internal** life of the characters. The internal needs that motivate a character to take action relate to our own inner needs. The stronger and more well developed this connection is, the greater the ability for the audience to connect with and care about the outcome of a story.

External actions are always driven by internal need. Our conscious existence is based on two distinct yet simultaneous realities: There is an *external world* where activity occurs, and there is an *internal reality* where we process what has taken place and give value to it according to our own individual perceptions. In a film, if this relationship between outer experiences and inner value is undeveloped, then we're only being told half the story. We observe movement without meaning, ultimately rendering the activity value-*less*, which makes the element of *caring* difficult to achieve.

This lack of a strong and well-defined internal/external reality is extremely common in modern films. While there may be a keen understanding of the need to make drama compelling by creating a profound sense of urgency, that sense of heightened importance is seldom applied to anything beneath the surface of the action.

Houston, We Have a Problem

For better or worse, the interlunar catastrophe around which the 1997 film *Apollo 13* was developed pretty much epitomizes the standard view of *dramatic tension*. Apollo 13's "problem" set up a profoundly urgent and compelling conflict that propelled the film toward an exhilarating and pulse-pounding climax. Leaving the theater, most of us felt like we just stepped off an "E" ticket ride at Disneyland. Emotionally our chests heaved with pride at the knowledge that heroes like Jim

Lovell still walk among us. Of course, a week later the thrill was relegated to an off-handed review at the water cooler of, "Good flick," and the hero of the ill-fated rocket ship would forever be emblazoned in our memories as "ole-what's-his-name," should the topic of doomed space travel ever come up again.

So, ultimately, even though this film was a good flick—meaning it was well produced, well directed, well acted, well attended, and well developed around a very big and exciting event—as do too many modern movies, it left little lasting impact. This may be an indication that it might not have been so dramatically urgent after all.

In contrast, the original *Star Wars* still holds audiences so enthralled that it has the rare distinction of twice becoming a box office mega-hit. In fact, it has become such a cultural phenomenon that the names *Luke Skywalker, Obi-Wan Kenobi*, and *Princess Leia* are permanently inscribed in our modern lexicon. The comparison here is not one of size and scope, for certainly the critical failure of the more recent prequels to the *Star Wars* trilogy demonstrates that a glut of interstellar pyrotechnics and quirky alien Muppet creatures isn't enough to make us care or to leave any lasting impact.

Trust the Force Within

What made audiences care and gave the original *Star Wars* its enduring urgency was simply that for Luke to fulfill his mission (like Jim Lovell), he had to learn (unlike Lovell) to trust a force greater than himself. This doesn't mean that *Star Wars* came up with a better cliché or slogan than *Apollo 13*; it means that for Luke the experience was *internally* transformative. On the other hand, there was little evidence that for the Lovell character his experience amounted to much more than a really, really bad day at the office. This isn't to imply that this is how Jim Lovell actually internalized these events in his real life, but that's precisely the point—*there was no meaningful life experience occurring in this film.*

If this sounds questionable, we need only look just below the surface of *Apollo 13* to realize that despite the enormity of the catastrophic events that happened to Lovell, they appear to have had very little impact on his internal reality. In the cinematic version of what occurred on his way to the moon, he is portrayed as a strong, brave, confident man who handles the disaster in outer space with strength, bravery, and confidence. Even though the situation gets exceedingly tense—especially when Lovell doesn't know if his spacecraft will bounce off the stratosphere and float off into oblivion—we, the audience, are pretty secure in our feelings that even if the worst happens, Jim will have died like a good soldier: strong, brave, and confident.

Therefore, when all the stardust clears, the net effect of what happens *internally* to Lovell on his way to the moon isn't much. Physically, he may have gone where few men have gone before, but emotionally and even spiritually his character never leaves terra firma. What we see of his experience in this film is, indeed, analogous to the "E" ticket ride because, even though there is the sensation of a wild, untamed adventure, he never sets foot into the uncharted regions of his own capacities. In other words, what he achieves by the end of the film, he is fully capable of achieving before it even starts. Therefore, no *real* transformative journey has taken place.

In contrast, at the climactic moment in *Star Wars*, Luke manages to save the entire galaxy from the clutches of the Evil Emperor *only* because he ventures internally to a place where he has never been before. Even though Luke is a fairly brave and confident kid when the story begins, it's a different, deeper kind of courage that is demanded of him in the climax. Like all the other young fighter pilots, Luke is on a mission to destroy the Death Star planet. With explosives blazing around him, he flies over the target and takes aim through his radar screen at the single, vulnerable point that can obliterate the deadly enemy. Luke will have only one opportunity to achieve his goal, but just as he is about to fire off his lasers he hears the voice of Obi-Wan Kenobi, reminding him to *trust the force within*. He has a split second to decide whether to be rational and shoot at the Death Star in the traditional way that has so far failed all the other fighter pilots, or to trust something completely intangible—his own instincts. Ultimately, Luke chooses to remove the radar screen from his view and he demolishes the malevolent planet, using only his own internal guidance system.

The subtlety that should not be missed here is that if Luke had stayed with the known, safe, and familiar and had opted to shoot at the Death Star using conventional radar, it's highly likely that he, like the other pilots, would have missed his target and they all would have been destroyed. Therefore, encoded in this simple fantasy/adventure is an essential piece of our humanity that is far more encompassing than the value of simply *trusting the force within*. By stepping into the unknown, Luke is moving toward the unknown aspects of his own being, toward the energizing connectedness of life, which we may call *soul*. For Lovell's character, this principle is impossible to attain because, as he is portrayed in the film, he exists only in an idealized state, which we intuitively know is inauthentic. Therefore, even though *Apollo 13* looks on the surface to be grounded in reality, it is really the more fantastic fiction of *Star Wars* to which we instinctively respond.

This concept elevates the nature of what is dramatic or urgent in a story to a much higher level. If the protagonist is like Jim Lovell's character, who internally faces the uncertainty of the adventure with the total capability of overcoming any adversity, it's not much of a challenge. To achieve the goal of saving his spacecraft, he has no need to go to new heights (or depths). Making contact with the *other* unknown aspects of his true nature is a non-issue, because it isn't necessary. As a result, this greatly minimizes the audience's emotional involvement in the story because no personal identification can be made with what it takes to achieve this type of heroism and personal greatness.

However, if the protagonist in a story has yet to test the internal limits of his or her ability to face the uncertainties of an adventure, then survival, on many levels, is an unknown. This draws the audience into the adventure right along with the protagonist, because the internal uncertainties that the character faces and must confront are part of a struggle that exists within everyone.

Therefore, it isn't the fate of the spacecraft Apollo 13 or the Death Star planet that hangs in the balance in these films; neither of them is real to us. Obviously, neither is Jim Lovell nor Luke Skywalker. The life we're concerned about saving is our own. **Story is not the passive experience we perceive it to be. Instead, it is as essential an activator of our internal development as any experience we have in real life.**

If our stories are to be potent they must contain the same dynamics that we know to be true about our own internal reality, even if the external factors are completely outlandish and unfamiliar. Few of us will ever fly in a spacecraft and have to fight for interlunar survival. But at some point in each of our lives we will be called upon to fight for what is right, to defend our personal boundaries, to overcome great obstacles, and to persevere against injustices. How will we know that these goals are even attainable if our stories tell us that the road to heroic achievement is reserved only for those who come with their heroic attributes already intact?

If we examine the development of our own character, it is the challenges we are forced to face in life that provide the opportunity for self-discovery and personal growth. Through the challenges Luke faced, he made contact with an internal part of his nature that proved to be more powerful than an arsenal of laser-guided missiles. As Jim Lovell's character was presented to us, however, it was impossible for any such connection to be made.

Stories teach us through symbolic experiences *how* to be human. Therefore, this book will illustrate that when the dramatic tension is focused on the internal conflict, the external action becomes much more powerful and significant because it reflects what we know to be true about our own lives: **We (and our characters) grow and evolve internally in direct relationship to the conflicts and obstacles that we face and overcome in the external world.**

No More "Mr. Nice Guy"

The idea that writers want their stories to have more depth and internal value is certainly not a revolutionary concept. As vacuous and crassly commercial as so many films are today, I'd like to believe (perhaps optimistically, if not naively) that most filmmakers generally aspire to make more significant movies. However, judging from what we see at our local theaters, too often there seems to be an enormous gap between this desire to tell a great story and the ability to do so.

The most damaging by-product that results from idealizing the heroes in our stories is that these characters tend to be stripped of the human qualities that make them interesting and even relevant. Although it was unsettling for my client to be told he needed to beef up his screenplay with gratuitous car chases, the real reason his script was lethargic stemmed from something far more subtle and insidious than a lack of explosive action. At the studio's insistence, he had been directed to *"Make the lead guy more likeable."*

Ultimately, it was that little word *likeable* that had become a flesh-eating virus that was about to destroy his project. On the surface, this idea of likeability may sound perfectly reasonable, but from my perspective as a story analyst it may be the single most destructive force in all of modern cinema. Concern for marketability and for attracting major star power often leads film executives, producers, and sometimes the stars themselves to insist that writers create leading characters with whom it is *easy* to spend a couple of hours. Certainly, if it's an action film, they don't mind if you scruff up the hero around the edges or make him a little arrogant and sullen. Likewise, in a romantic comedy, it's downright essential that the female lead be quirky and offbeat. But these are pretty much the far reaches of where character complexity is permitted to go with the exception, of course, of the occasional gender switch, allowing the female the rough edges and the male a little quirk or two.

There's nothing intrinsically wrong with the concept of likeability. In fact, I'm sure that most of us prefer our friends and loved ones to have that quality. However, when it comes to drama, likeability is about as important as hair color. It's only *one* of many character possibilities and it should be applied where appropriate, but not with lavish abandon.

For example, in Frank Capra's Christmas perennial, *It's a Wonderful Life*, it is essential that George Bailey be a kind-hearted, considerate man, not because it would sell more movie tickets, but because those are precisely the traits that are at the core of his conflict. His constant acts of selflessness have nearly driven him over the brink (or into the drink, as it were), leaving him in despair and questioning, "When is it *my* turn?" But that same character design could hardly be applied to the likes of Ebenezer Scrooge in another yuletide favorite, *A Christmas Carol*. In this story, the conflict of the plot demands that Ebenezer be mean-spirited, selfish, greedy, and unkind, specifically because the *internal* journey that he takes in the story will lead him to the discovery that kindness and generosity are the sources of his true happiness. Clearly, a character can't **grow** toward kindness and generosity if he already has those qualities when the story begins. In reality, it is Ebenezer's inability to love and to connect with the rest of humankind that invites the audience into the real conflict of the story.

While this concept may seem self-evident when applied to an obvious example such as Ebenezer Scrooge, too often modern storytellers tend to see complex characterization as a necessity only in stories that are driven by character. Stories that are driven by intricate plotting—such as action adventures, capers, who-done-its, and even romantic comedies—tend to utilize the central character more as a ringmaster, who serves the function of moving the plot pieces around, rather than as the actual subject of the drama. "Likeability" or "presentability," therefore, feels like a reasonable character trait in the role of a host. But is that *ever* really the role of the protagonist?

If the leading character in a story is nothing more than the inoffensive person moving the action along, what meaning or value does he or she bring to the story? As seen in *Apollo 13*, if the protagonist is already good, brave, and confident, he becomes nothing greater from an experience that calls for those same traits. If the only thing he needs by the end of his terrifying and death-defying ordeal is a clean change of clothes and a shave, why would anyone truly care?

The single most important connection authors make with their audience is forged through the protagonist. In effect, **the audience enters the story through the protagonist; as the protagonist encounters conflict, hardship, and obstacles, the audience encounters those same problems right along with him or her.** This is how we become engaged in a story.

As the protagonist makes choices, we in the audience make choices, too. However, this doesn't mean we make the same choices. As observers rather than as actual participants, we often have a clearer perspective on the events. This gives us the advantage of having more objectivity and insight into the situation. Hence, the story becomes more and more compelling as we watch the characters make emotional decisions that go one way when we *know* they should go another.

In the beginning of both *It's a Wonderful Life* and *A Christmas Carol*, the audience *knows* that George Bailey's life is already valuable and that Scrooge would be happier if he were kinder. But the characters don't know this yet because they are both *stuck in old patterns of behavior* that distort their perceptions. The drama, therefore, is designed around knocking down those old barriers.

When writers make characters "likeable" for the sake of being liked, it is almost inevitable that character traits will become idealized. For example, if solving the goal of the plot necessitates vanquishing a villainous foe (or landing an errant spaceship), then the protagonist will probably be the bravest and most courageous. If it's a mystery that needs to be solved, then it's likely the hero will be the smartest and the cleverest. If it's love he or she is after, then the character is not only the best looking, but also kind, compassionate, and remarkably tolerant toward annoying house pets. Success is attributed to the most superficial qualities: beauty, brains, and brawn. Victory tends to go to the smartest, fastest, strongest, and most attractive. In real-life terms, however, that would exclude most of us. Therefore, if our own lives are not succeeding with the ease of the heroes in our stories, then there must be something wrong with us— we're not pretty enough, strong enough, smart enough, and so on.

In contrast, look at how audiences respond to a character like Forrest Gump. In spite of his huge intellectual imperfection, he is still considered heroic. This doesn't mean that as we watch this film we suddenly come to desire a marginal IQ. But the story does remind us that what we perceive as our own imperfections can be the source of heroism as well. Even the most unlikely of champions, such as Oskar Schindler, can rise to the level of heroic, not by being the bravest man who ever stood up to the Nazis, but by simply opening his heart to others.

In essence, this reveals that there is another way to define the **heroic journey.** Instead of attributing success to victory over an external foe using only external devices, triumph is measured against the struggle within. Swords, shields, and AK-47s are useless here. *The only viable weapon is internal growth.* The adversary, who sometimes—but not always—takes on the physical form of an antagonist, is really a reflection of an internal weakness of character or spirit found in the protagonist.

Therefore, even though in the external world Forrest perseveres over his limitations, Schindler outwits the Nazis, Rocky prevails against impossible odds, and Harry and Sally attain the love they've been seeking, the real triumph is the victory over their own internal limitations. It is from this accomplishment alone that they gain the strength to fight their battles in the outer world. Audiences cheer for them, love and care about them, specifically because their imperfections are real, which informs us that our own inner obstacles are conquerable as well. And it is in the conquering of these inner limitations that we, too, are able to do battle with the dragons we encounter in our own external reality.

The Eternal Story

As William Shakespeare so eloquently put it, *"To be or not to be…"*[1]—that is the essential question of the human condition. It asks if we have the courage and fortitude to face the challenges that life hurls in our

[1] William Shakespeare, *Hamlet* (III, i, 56-61).

path, or if we'll just succumb to the sirens of fear and complacency that beckon us to stay awhile as we deteriorate and decay.

We all know people whose spirit died long before anyone threw dirt on their coffin. And the question, *How do I avoid this tragic fate?* is at the core of nearly all great drama. From the depths of our mythic lore in stories about Oedipus, Achilles, and Ulysses to the legends of King Arthur, the fables and fairy tales of ugly ducklings and sleeping princesses, to the simple parable of a boy who cried wolf, we find that our stories reverberate with the single, undistilled message: *What's it going to be—life or death?*

There is no condition of stasis in nature. Every living thing is either moving toward growth, change, and development or it has begun to decay and die. No matter how far-ranging a writer's imagination may roam, a great story will always have its roots in this elemental question of life and death. This is the universal common denominator found in the human experience. Audiences don't have to make a direct connection with the age, gender, race, or life experience of the central character in order to connect with and internalize the essence of what the story is revealing about their own human experience.

This implied struggle of choosing between life and death—on some level—is the single greatest source of dramatic tension that can be found in a story. Although Rick Blaine (Humphrey Bogart) in *Casablanca*, Michael Dorsey (Dustin Hoffman) in *Tootsie*, and Celie (Whoopi Goldberg) in *The Color Purple* are three distinctly different characters who exist in highly diverse circumstances, their stories share this single common thread. Consider, for example, where each of these characters will be physically, psychologically, and emotionally in five or ten years if nothing in their nature evolves or changes. Rick's cynicism has already choked the life out of what's left of his dismal existence in an isolated corner of the world. Michael's chances of sustaining a successful acting career are dying on the vine, and the odds of Celie finding even a single shred of love or happiness are slim to none.

As each of these stories begins and the central characters are introduced, it is not a physical death sentence that looms over their lives.

However, on some level it's made clear that a far worse fate may await them. This includes the death of hopes, dreams, desires, spirit, relationships, and creative potential. Their stories are important, not because of complicated plot contrivances, death-defying stunts, or heart-wrenching sentimentality, but simply because these characters are given the opportunity to become truly heroic by transcending their own internal limitations.

This is not to say that there is only one way to tell a great story. In our daily existence, as reflected in storytelling, the ability to take a risk and struggle to meet the challenges of life does not always guarantee physical survival. If that were the case, it wouldn't be a risk and it wouldn't be very dramatically interesting. We don't always get what we want or what we think we deserve in life. So, what's the payoff?

Stories, even if based on true events, are never the real experience, only a *representation* of that experience. Because of this limitation, stories don't relay direct information about every individual's life; instead, they reflect information to us about the life process in general. This means that the characters and situations are symbolic. The payoff, therefore, is something that a writer can interpret in many different ways. Most often a story will show us how hard work pays off with the success for which the protagonist has been striving. Sometimes, however, the struggle for internal transcendence can lead to great sacrifice and, on the surface, the protagonist may not directly receive the justice, recognition, or liberation he or she deserves. But, on the symbolic level, the value of his or her experience comes through with complete clarity.

A great example of this is seen in Lawrence Hauben and Bo Goldman's adaptation of the Ken Kesey novel, *One Flew Over the Cuckoo's Nest*. In this classic film, the central character, McMurphy, struggles to outwit a witless system: the mental institution. By confronting the choice between life and death, McMurphy not only chooses life, but he also tries to instill the need to make this choice in the other defeated inmates. Ironically, even though he does succeed at inspiring others, he is lobotomized and dies thereafter. But his death gives rebirth to The Chief, who seizes the moment and escapes his captivity. It isn't necessary to use an interpreter to understand the life-affirming symbolism of this story. Even though McMurphy dies before he gets to the Promised Land, he is victorious over the mediocrity that threatens to enslave us all. The story of McMurphy begs us to take a look at our own lives and ask: *"Do I want to settle for being an inmate?"* We know the answer, and our spirit springs through the window to our freedom right alongside The Chief.

There are also stories that demonstrate how the protagonist can completely fail at the struggle between life and death. He doesn't get it. He doesn't choose life. In Martin Scorsese's masterpiece *Goodfellas*, the protagonist, Henry Hill, begins his story by telling the audience that he always wanted to be a gangster. He covets the good life and likes the idea of getting something (money, respect, women) for nothing. And he gets it—the best seat in restaurants, wads of cash, and loads of fun. In fact, for the first half of the film it looked so appealing, I wanted to be a gangster, too. Then the first toll gate appears. A young kid, not unlike Henry himself, is brutally shot to death by one of the gangsters (Joe Pesci) because he had the temerity to ask to be treated with respect. It's no longer a free ride, but Henry is cruising downhill at such velocity that jumping off seems imprudent. Even when he crashes and burns, he doesn't realize that he's ended up with nothing. All things considered, he tells us in the end, it was more fun being a gangster. He doesn't get it. He doesn't see how everything around him has turned to dust—but the audience does. That's all that matters.

Whether or not a character becomes greater or is diminished by the challenges that he or she faces in a story, audiences will garner what is needed from the tale to help put the trials in their own lives into perspective. Though we do not think of ourselves today as primitive or superstitious, when our stories tell us only that the external forces of beauty, brains, and brawn will succeed, we tend to worship at their altars, afraid to value our individuality, our uniqueness, and our need for connection. Stories such as *It's a Wonderful Life*, *Goodfellas*, and even *Pulp Fiction* tell us mutually that we don't have to settle for being mere victims of chance and opportunity. While none of us has any real ability to control what destiny hurls in our direction, we do have the internal capacity to navigate those challenges and use them to make of our lives something great.

The Why Factor

It is vitally important for writers to seize the opportunity in the writing process to make contact with these internal challenges themselves. It is only from this inner place of personal truth that stories take on any real depth or significance. But mastery of the deep doesn't occur accidentally, inadvertently, or without effort. While it is true that creative impulses do seem to bubble up quite unexpectedly and unpredictably from the unconscious, they will pretty much remain only raw material unless they are examined and processed. I have yet to encounter an accomplished writer who doesn't have some sort of a purposeful and intentional method that helps him or her sort out and understand what the images from the creative imagination are expressing. Without some insight into what is going on in the depths of our stories, it's almost impossible to communicate anything of substance to others.

Gaining access to these inner regions is tricky; in order to get to the deep end, we must first learn how to navigate through the shallows. What lies on the surface of a story for a writer is the *idea*. This is usually a "what if…?" notion that begins to bring some sort of character or characters into contact with an obstacle. **Without any effort, the moment that character engages with conflict a natural story structure begins to form around the need to resolve the problem.**

The three most basic elements that contribute to the standard view of story structure are: **Plot, Character,** and **Theme.**

- Plot reveals *WHAT* the problem is and *WHERE* the action takes place.
- Character focuses on *WHO* is trying to solve the problem.
- Theme leaves the audience with some understanding of *WHY* this problem and the actions of the characters are relevant.

Commonly, *WHAT, WHERE*, and *WHO* are the most obvious indicators of *HOW* to proceed in the beginning phases of building a story. Deed by deed, encounter by encounter, exploit by exploit, the actions of the characters escalate around the conflict and shape a BEGINNING, MIDDLE, and END to a story. While this simple architectural form has many variants, it is the basis around which most theories on classical and modern story structure have developed.

What has not been as thoroughly or clearly developed is the *WHY* factor. Theme is the most intangible and subjective aspect of a story and, therefore, it can be very difficult to identify and develop. As a result, we often disregard theme altogether or merely give it lip service. **But it is the *theme* that makes our writing meaningful. It opens up the story's inner value system, so that writers can make *conscious* connection with what the story *really* wants to communicate to them and through them.**

For example, in its most simplified and objective form, the **plot** of *Casablanca* is really just a story about how a renowned World War II freedom fighter, Victor Laszlo, escapes the Nazis. Victor is set up as an important figure in the underground war effort and he is needed to help lead the Resistance, but the Germans are hot on his trail. Even though a lot of people need to escape the Nazis, Victor's plight is magnified in importance because he is such a brave and intrepid leader. As important as he is to the war effort, however, Victor is not the central character of *this* film. Neither is his wife, Ilsa, who will help provide the means for him to escape through her contact with an old lover. Instead, the writers chose to focus their attention on that old lover, Rick Blaine, a cynical expatriate, who is really just an un-involved saloon keeper trying to sit out the war as unobtrusively as possible.

Why did the writers choose to focus on Rick for this story? For that matter, why did Shakespeare choose to focus on Hamlet instead of his mother, Gertrude, or his gal-pal Ophelia? Or why didn't Mario Puzo choose to tell the story of Tom Hagen instead of Michael Corleone in *The Godfather*? Because we can't possibly get into these writers' heads, we may never know the specific answer to these questions, but we can presume to know one thing for certain: **All writers express the conflict through the characters they choose simply because that perspective means something to them.**

The reason *Casablanca* has left an indelible imprint on audiences has little to do with Victor's escape, even though it is the lynchpin of the action. Likewise, it isn't Rick's ability to outwit the Nazis that makes anyone truly care about this story. It is Rick's *internal* struggle to help his former girlfriend and her husband that makes us actually feel something.

The writers' perspective in *Casablanca*, their **thematic point of view—** *that the problems of a few little people do "amount to a hill of beans,"* that war and all aspects of the human condition *are* personal—is what ultimately determined the focus of how this **plot** and these **characters** were developed. Looking *deeper* at the obstacle that keeps Rick from achieving the goal of the plot (to help Ilsa and Laszlo escape), makes it clear that the real impediment is not an external foe but Rick's own internal demons. The Nazis may be sly, treacherous, and potentially deadly, but in *this* story their heartless nature is really just an external manifestation of what is internally destroying Rick's soul. In the beginning of the film, Rick is portrayed as a lonely, isolated man whose own heart is just a beat or two away from turning to stone. So the *external* conflict, to help the woman he loves escape with another man, is really an *internal* opportunity to soften and redeem his heart and make it human again.

When our stories define themselves through these *internal/external, life/death* factors, finding value and meaning becomes inescapable. For the writer, working with theme is an opportunity to explore personal truths. Most importantly, what evolves from this approach is that structural elements that once seemed random and arbitrary begin to take on profound significance. **The plot of a story becomes the external *context* in which the internal *value* of the character is lost or redeemed. This exposes the writer's value system as a thematic *point of view*.** Thus, a writer's existing relationship to story and structure is opened to more expansive and meaningful possibilities.

Getting to the Gold—The Transformational Arc

Once the *who*, *what*, and *where* of a story are assembled into a *beginning*, *middle*, and *end*, a **line of action** is formed that pushes the plot forward from conflict to resolution. This movement is the primary element that composes the *STRUCTURE* of the plot. All of the outward, physical movement of a story will fall somewhere along this line of action, which is why it is so important. But there's definitely more to a story than just moving action forward. In our own lives, *all* outward movement is motivated by inner necessity. We make dinner because we're hungry and we argue with our spouse because we don't feel that our needs are being met. If a story is to be well told, it must meet this same condition.

As you write, always keep in mind that *there is no action, activity, motion, or movement that has any meaning or value to us whatsoever, except for how it is internalized.* This means that there are always two sides of a story to tell: One side follows the external line of action; the other side expresses how a character internalizes and processes that action. This concept is the basis for the development of the *TRANS-FORMATIONAL ARC OF THE CHARACTER.*[2] While the line of action tracks the protagonist's engagement in an external conflict, **the transformational arc tracks the protagonist's internal struggle to rise to meet that external challenge by overcoming internal barriers.** Ultimately, this reveals whether or not these challenges will serve to renew the protagonist's life or destroy it altogether.

The transformational arc expresses the single most consistent pattern that defines the nature of a great story. It reveals how:

- A person [**character**] succeeds or fails...
- to grow and change [**arc**]...
- within the context of the conflict that is unfolding [**plot**]...
- from the writer's point of view [**theme**].

---

[2] The *transformational arc of character* is also referred to as the *transformational arc*, the *arc of character*, or sometimes just the *arc*.

The goal of the following chapters is to rebuild our notion of story structure from the inside out. This will help you develop a stronger connection to the internal movement of the characters in your stories and perhaps provide a better understanding of your own character as well. Inevitably, all anyone ever really writes about is himself or herself—because that's all a person can truly know. As long as our stories are disconnected from this reality, they will remain superficial, underdeveloped, and never meet their full potential.

CHAPTER TWO

PLOT
Lights, Camera, Action!

A good story cannot be devised, it has to be distilled.

~ RAYMOND CHANDLER

Conflict, Action, and Goal

As important as internal character development is to the making of a great film, when the director yells, "Action!" there better be some great movin' and shakin' going on. Without it, there's nothing to see, nothing to feel, and, most importantly, nothing to hold our interest. If stories are to reflect the human experience, they must rely on activity and movement just as we encounter it in everyday life. Actions get us from one place to another and they also provide direction.

Conversely, action alone carries no intrinsic value. The activities of going to the store, getting out of bed in the morning, baking a cake, making love, or losing a job take on meaning and significance only when given a specific context.

In the simple story that follows, notice at what point you begin to feel involved with the characters and actually *care* about the outcome.

Story	*Emotional Reaction*
John goes to the store…	DON'T CARE
to buy some milk…	STILL DON'T CARE
for his baby…	CARE A LITTLE
who is sick…	CARE A LITTLE MORE
and who hasn't eaten in days.	CARE A LOT

As a story, the action of John going to the store means absolutely nothing to us. Even when we learn that he's going to buy milk for his baby, it doesn't amount to anything that would hook us into the tale. However, when the action of going to the store becomes connected to the need to feed a sick, hungry baby, our perception of the activity shifts and we suddenly begin to care about the outcome. What's at stake for John's little trip to the store is now attached to the survival of his child.

This is the simple nature of the **PLOT** of a story. It is formed around the motion and activities that are generated by a **CONFLICT.** But that conflict must be of a great enough size and scope to produce a sense of **JEOPARDY** or there will not be enough *momentum* to drive the story forward. Once conflict has reached the level of jeopardy, it automatically establishes a need to get to a **RESOLUTION.** This need to get to a resolution forms a **GOAL,** and it is the struggle to get to that goal that produces the **DRAMATIC TENSION,** which keeps audiences connected to the outcome of a story.

Heightened CONFLICT creates JEOPARDY.
JEOPARDY creates a need for RESOLUTION.
Getting to the RESOLUTION establishes a GOAL.
The struggle to achieve the GOAL generates DRAMATIC TENSION.

As obvious as this concept may seem, the lack of a strong, clear conflict that sets a story into motion is a surprisingly common problem in modern screenplays. Writers have a tendency to bring the conflict in slowly and even covertly, believing that the mystery surrounding what's going on is sufficient to hold our interest. This is seldom effective. Until it's clear what the problem is, there is no way to *care* about whether or not the conflict of the plot will be solved. If the need to get to the resolution is not established, there will be very little tension holding the story together. A lack of tension means there is no momentum.

The most important thing to remember about the plot is this: **Where conflict leads, action follows...**

On the other hand, if action were the only thing that connected the audience to a story, then great plots would rely solely on great, big problems (such as terrorists vaporizing entire cities, planets colliding, and giant meteorites falling out of the sky). But contrary to what many Hollywood producers seem to believe, *bigger isn't always better.*

Our connection to conflict is not limited to the size and scope of the external activity. In fact, most great stories deal with external problems that are much smaller and far more intimate than the destruction of the universe. While there have been recent Academy Award–winning blockbusters such as *Lord of the Rings, Gladiator, Titanic,* and *Braveheart*, there also have been much more introspective winners such as *Crash, A Beautiful Mind, American Beauty, Shakespeare in Love, Forrest Gump,* and *Schindler's List.*

There is no consistent level of "bigness" in the external conflict that drives the plot of any of these award-winning films. Some of them battle for the soul of an entire culture, while others fight to overcome a single broken heart. What is consistent, however, is that each of these stories made us care about something big. The plots of these films, both grand and intimate, served the function of conducting audiences on a journey that brought them into contact with *big* and important human emotions. This is where size does matter. Even though the plot of *Lord of the Rings* is driven by a great need to save the world from the clutches of evil and *A Beautiful Mind* is driven by a relatively small need to save a single man from falling into the abyss of insanity, both films find their real power in something that lies beyond the external conflict. Audiences may become drawn in by the external activity, but they identify with and become involved in the film through the struggle that the characters face within themselves.

Take a look at how the story of the man and his sick baby intensifies when some personal, emotional details are added.

Story	Emotional Reaction
John has gone to the store to buy milk for his sick, hungry baby **but** he doesn't have any money…	BECOMING CONCERNED
He drank up every nickel of his unemployment check before ever making it home.	BECOMING INVOLVED

With the addition of the father's drinking problem, the goal becomes multi-dimensional. No longer is there just the singular, external drive to get milk for the sick baby. To achieve that goal there is now an internal obstacle of getting the father sober. This makes the stakes go way up because as long as the father is putting his drinking needs ahead of everything else, we *know* that his baby will continue to be in jeopardy. This creates a supplementary goal that is formed around an entirely separate, but interrelated plotline, called a SUBPLOT.

It's a common misconception to consider the subplot of a story to be a lesser or secondary plotline. This couldn't be further from the truth. **Whereas the plot carries the line of action, the subplot(s) carry the emotional and thematic content.** This means that when the film ends and audiences reflect on what they've just seen and experienced, it is the subplotting that often leaves the biggest impact.

For example, when we think of the original *Rocky* film, it's easy to forget that Rocky didn't actually win the fight in the end. It's not that the plot of defeating the heavyweight champion isn't important; it's just that the most compelling and memorable parts of the story are found in the subplotting. This is where Rocky has to battle his most formidable opponent—himself.

Both plot and subplots are vital to the development of a great story. Think of the plot as a train moving down a railroad track and the subplots as the cargo. The train has no real purpose without the cargo and the cargo can't get where it's going without the train.

Deepening the Plot

In the last chapter, I described the underlying pattern that defines the transformational arc.

- A person [character] succeeds or fails...
- to grow and change [arc]...
- within the context of the conflict that is unfolding [plot]...
- from the writer's point of view [theme].

The plot, which is the line of action, represents *the **conflict** that is unfolding*. People do not grow and evolve by simply willing it to be so. Great stories reflect how development and progress in life occurs as a result of dealing with and facing the obstacles life throws in our path...*or not*.

Therefore, it can't be emphasized enough that the conflict in the plot provides the opportunity for the growth of the character. This approach offers a very different perspective on the construction of a story. Instead of devising a plot that merely moves the action forward and takes a character along for the ride (e.g., *Apollo 13*), the plot is developed instead around the needs of the protagonist to mature and evolve (e.g., *Star Wars*). As I've stressed, *the external challenges in life shape the internal value of who we are and what we are becoming.* When a character wallows in self-pity, blames others for ill fortune, or denies a problem altogether, the conflict that unfolds will ultimately drive that life into a tragic, downward spiral. However, if the challenges and fears are faced and the problems are worked through, then the character's life will grow and expand.

Developing a plot that serves the internal development of a character begs writers to consider his or her story choices in a very different way. **The conflict that is introduced and the events that unfold must serve a specific function: *to push the inner nature of the character toward maturity and wholeness.***

A client of mine agreed to let me share the following story:[1] Several years ago she sent me a script about a sixty-year-old woman whose four-decade marriage ended abruptly when her husband not only ran off with another woman, but also absconded with their entire life savings. The central character was a very pleasant, middle-class lady who had devoted her life to providing a clean, comfortable home for her husband. Needless to say, she was left emotionally and financially devastated by his departure.

As I read the first draft of this script all I really felt for the poor woman was a little pity. As the events in the plot unfolded, they merely revealed how a callous world, dominated by callous, unfeeling men, had taken advantage of, and then discarded, an aging woman whose beauty and economic usefulness had ebbed.

From what I knew of my client's age and background, I assumed that this story might be somewhat autobiographical. But it turned out that I was wrong, at least in part. During our first consultation she told me that she and her husband had just returned from a romantic cruise to Alaska, where they had celebrated their thirtieth wedding anniversary. She gave me no indication that her husband made her feel, in any way, inadequate or insignificant. Yet as I probed deeper into what was really motivating this script, I learned that my client harbored a lot of anger and resentment toward the way society treated aging women. She felt that as she grew older she was becoming increasingly disregarded, especially in the workplace, where she felt more and more invisible and undervalued.

From this conversation, I began to sense that it was a kind of cultural victimization that she was really trying to communicate in her story, which is a pretty interesting topic. However, the script wasn't working very well because all it really had to say on this issue was: *Isn't it terrible what that bad man did to that poor woman?* The external events in the conflict of the plot were actually quite strong and did indeed pose very serious and heart-wrenching problems for the protagonist. But because

---

[1] Details have been slightly altered to protect the identity of my client and the particulars of her story.

her character faced no inner challenges from the circumstances, she never developed past the point of being a victim.

This insight caused my client to recognize that while she had tried to deal with the politics of aging, her story didn't really explore the personal side of the issue. In fact, she came to realize that her story wasn't as much about getting old as about self-empowerment. The terrible things that occurred to the woman in her story were neither nice nor fair, but they forced her to survive on her own. Survival, therefore, was the external goal of the plot. The character had no control over her husband's lack of caring, the bank's unwillingness to help save her home, or the job market that refused to value her experiences as a homemaker. Without an inner agenda that would push this character to overcome these obstacles, the only thing the story could tell us of her plight was that she was a victim of circumstances. However, with an inner goal, she had the possibility of influencing her fate. Even though her husband was a jerk, the bank treated her impersonally, and the job market demanded she have modern skills, the character could potentially rise above all these problems if she could meet her internal goal of self-empowerment. This would not only help her survive, but in doing so the character would be able to redefine herself in a greater way than she had ever imagined and move on with her life.

It's important to note that as the scope of the story expanded to include an internal conflict, the scope of the story's appeal to a larger audience also greatly expanded. In its original form, this film would have primarily attracted other older women who also felt abandoned and victimized. However, once the story focused on an internal quest, it had more potential to draw in anyone struggling with issues of self-empowerment—which could include most of us.

It's a Wonderful Life is a great example of how **a story can transcend a common, if not overused, plotline to become something truly unique by developing a strong internal conflict.** In the plot of this film Mr. Potter is set up as a greedy, mean-spirited banker who conspires to undermine the town's confidence in the local savings and loan so that he can take control and assume ownership of the entire city of Bedford Falls. The only one standing in Potter's way is George Bailey, the owner of the savings and loan, who refuses to sell his company to Potter. But Potter is relentless and he seizes upon an unfortunate moment when George's addled uncle misplaces bank funds. Potter secretly pockets the found money so that he can ruin George and drive him out of the savings and loan business.

Thus far, all of the events that have been described are external, which means they are happening outside of George's control. Notice how similar this external conflict is to the basic plot of many old westerns. The town is under the maniacal grasp of a selfish, old tyrant who wants to run the good, honorable deputy out of town and take over. There's usually only one solution: The good, honorable deputy must stand and fight. This leads to a shoot-out where the inevitable outcome is for good to defeat evil.

However, in *It's a Wonderful Life*, other dimensions to the story open up different possibilities for the resolution. The goal of the plot doesn't change—it's still necessary to defeat the tyrant, but this is only one aspect of the story. Stopping Potter is merely the great obstacle that has been placed in George's path to push him toward internal growth.

Unlike the deputy in the typical western, George is not a superhero who will simply put on some spurs, grab a lasso, and go shoot up the bad guys. George is a real human being with real imperfections. As the defender of the town, his battle with old Mr. Potter is his unwanted legacy. The long-running feud has forced George to sacrifice all his dreams of seeing the world in order to remain in the cocoon of Bedford Falls, taking up the mantle of protector where his fearless father left off. But when Potter's final, lethal blow strikes, George can't fight anymore; he is simply used up. He is not his father; he is not the savior of Bedford Falls. And because he has exhausted his life's energy fulfilling everyone else's needs, at the crucial moment when George Bailey is needed to stand and fight, there is no George Bailey left. *It is like he never existed.* This is George's internal *conflict*. His internal *goal*, therefore, is to reclaim his own value before the external goal of saving the town is lost forever.

Ultimately, in this deeper type of storytelling *it is the attainment of one's internal goal that allows a character to achieve the external goal.* But as in our own life experience, the rewards are not always what we think they should be. With the help of an angel, George reviews his life and retrieves his spirit. As a result, he does return with a renewed sense of identity, but something else truly remarkable happens to him as a by-product. Instead of coming home reinvigorated, with the strength to put on his spurs and go fight the good fight, George comes home to something he never thought possible. The good townspeople, whom he always thought he had to protect and defend, have gathered the money on their own in order to help George defeat Potter. In his absence they, too, have been forced to grow up. Symbolically, this gives George what he's always searched for— his baptism into life. He is no longer alone; he does not have to carry the false burden of taking responsibility for everyone else. Instead, he can now make the connection to others as equal to equal, each capable of caring for the other. And through this life-affirming bond with others he will now get the care he needs to fill the emptiness inside that he had always mistaken for wanderlust. The external goal of stopping Potter is met only because George found the courage to meet his own internal needs. **When a story has a strong arc of character, the plot forms the container in which the inner journey of the character is made possible.**

There are, of course, variations in the relationship between internal and external goals. A character may achieve his or her outer goal of becoming rich and powerful, but fail at the inner challenge of finding personal value. That was certainly the tragedy of *Citizen Kane;* however, in the film *Rocky,* we find the opposite result: Rocky loses the prize fight but wins the greater battle of gaining self-esteem. Notice that for the audience the interpretation is the same. Whether a character succeeds or fails at finding the courage to achieve his or her inner goal, the audience has the greater perspective of understanding what success really means.

In *The Godfather* trilogy, Michael Corleone, like George Bailey, is a man who carries the false belief that he has to sacrifice his own needs in order to fill his father's shoes. But Michael's story reaches a tragic conclusion because he never confronts the issues of self-abandonment to which this leads. Unlike George, whose life becomes full and robust, Michael ends up with nothing but desolation and emptiness. Notice, however, that it doesn't really matter whether this story is told tragically or heroically, it still leads the audience to the same understanding.

When trying to distinguish **plot** from **subplot**, there are three primary things to remember:

- **While both plot and subplots are parts of the same story, they are not both parts of the plot.**
- **A *plot* only represents the action or activity of the protagonist in the outer, physical world.**
- ***Subplots* represent the motivations and consequences for the protagonist in his or her inner, emotional, psychological, or spiritual experience.**

Even though the action and conflict in *The Godfather* and *It's a Wonderful Life* are vastly different, the internal values their characters are challenged to attain are similar to each other and to the kinds of challenges we all are forced to face.

One Story, One Plot

Because the plot of a story expresses the physical line of action, it must comply with the basic law of nature that governs all physical activity: *You can't be in two places at once.* Just as it's impossible for a train leaving Boston to end up in New York and Philadelphia at the same time, two completely unrelated conflicts cannot be set into motion and end up at the same climax at the same time. This doesn't mean that the action of a plot can't move the story in many different directions, or track several different avenues leading toward the single resolution of a conflict. **The line of action in the plot can be as wide as the Rio Grande and include a lot of divergent activity. But all of this**

action must ultimately flow in the same general direction. If the action runs on two divergent and unrelated plotlines, the audience's focus will become split as well. Stories with two separate plots have two separate goals. If more than one plot is initiated, then the focus of the action will jump back and forth between the different goals, confusing the audience about which story they are tracking. Because you can't end up in two separate places at the same time, at some point the stronger of the two plots will start to dominate and the other will fall by the wayside. This is not only distracting, but also unsatisfactory, as it tends to leave the audience disengaged from the central conflict (because they don't know what it is).

However, don't confuse the concept of a single plotline with dramatic devices that intentionally and effectively use multiple lines of action to lead to a single destination or goal. An excellent example is found in the Japanese classic *Rashômon*, in which the same story is told from several different points of view, allowing the audience to arrive at a single place where they must draw their own conclusion. Another format is Woody Allen's *Hannah and Her Sisters*, or Tom Schulman's *Dead Poets Society*, where ancillary plotlines feed like tributaries into a single stream. The use of seemingly different storylines that are woven into a single fabric is an especially powerful approach to understanding the complexity of contemporary life, as we see in the Paul Haggis film *Crash*. There is also the traditional device found in films such as *Fried Green Tomatoes* or *The Hours* where a story is told within a story, leading to separate, but similar goals that enhance, reflect, or otherwise illuminate the singular theme or meaning of the story. Shakespeare, Dickens, Hugo, and other classic writers have all used these devices well, but never to divide the story into separate, unrelated pieces—only to enlarge the scope or perspective of the plotline itself.

One potentially good film that suffered from the problem of divergent plotlines is the 1995 movie *Heat*, starring Robert De Niro and Al Pacino. Pacino portrays a cynical, world-weary cop who is chasing a cynical, world-weary thief, played by De Niro. Even with its flaws, this film rises above most police thrillers because it attempts to get personal in its use of the action genre, taking an introspective look into the psyches of the hunter and the hunted. Where it falls short, however, is that each of these characters is involved in separate stories with separate goals, leaving their plotlines to run on separate tracks that never really intersect. The plot conflict for the cop is his need to catch the thief; the plot conflict for the thief is to avoid being caught. In the end, even though both cop and thief end up in the same place at the same time—engaged in direct combat—the climax is ambiguous and confusing because the plotlines are mutually exclusive. If the story ends by focusing on the cop's victory or defeat, it takes the focus off the thief's victory or defeat, which suddenly makes his story irrelevant, and vice-versa. So, the writer is left with a real dilemma. He can give the climax to one character over the other, which completely undermines his need to tell both stories. Or, if he decides to leave the climax vague and unresolved, he will undermine the value of the film altogether, which is basically what happened.

Creatively, there is no question that looking into the lives of both the cop and the robber is a very interesting approach to a police thriller. However, because there is no overarching conflict that drives both storylines toward the same goal, there can be no clear resolution.

Problems like this, especially in films that are as well developed and thoughtful as *Heat*, are very fixable. Essentially, all a writer must do is re-define the conflict in a way that aims both characters toward the same goal. An excellent example of how this can be achieved is seen in *The Fugitive*. This film uses a similar device that parallels the storylines of both the hunter and the hunted. When Dr. Richard Kimble (Harrison Ford) is wrongly convicted of murdering his wife, he escapes from custody and eventually attempts to track down the real killer for himself. But his plans are thwarted at every turn by a U.S. Marshal named Sam Gerard (Tommy Lee Jones), whose job is to catch the escaped convict, whether he is guilty or not.

Throughout the course of the film, the focus of the action jumps back and forth between Kimble running and Gerard chasing, but it never feels like these are separate storylines. Even though the lead characters appear to have opposite goals, there is a very real place where their goals actually intersect and become one. The greater goal sought by both men is *justice*. It doesn't matter that they are committed to this goal for different reasons, or that they go about finding it in different ways. This expanded view of their goal makes it a singular, not a plural, destination. A shared goal allows for the separate pieces of the story to come together in the climax, and it brings about a powerful and unambiguous resolution.

Not only do multiple plotlines splinter our attention, but because the plot contains the external obstacles against which the internal growth of the character is challenged, having more than one plot fractures this inner goal as well. Because a writer expresses the thematic point of view in a story through the internal conflict, when the goal of that conflict is divided by opposing plotlines, as in *Heat*, the writer's perspective tends to get lost or become neutralized altogether.

If, in the writing process, two separate plotlines are developing, there are several options for resolving this problem. The obvious one is to simply eliminate the weaker of the two plots. In many cases, this is a good choice. It helps get rid of excess material, which will strengthen and focus the work. However, often the second plotline exists because it is an intrinsic part of the story. Sorting out the issues that are causing the plot to split may create a connection that pulls both plotlines toward the same goal. Sometimes this link is so significant that it will open up your entire artistic vision.

Naming the Plot

At some point in the development of a story, it is essential to name the plotline. This name should contain only the key elements that describe the plot. In *Schindler's List*, for example, the plotline might be called: *Schindler defies the Nazis and risks everything in order to save Jewish lives.* Notice how the reductive quality of this single phrase tells us the three most basic elements that define a plot and move the external line of action forward: **CONFLICT, ACTION,** and **GOAL.**

CONFLICT	*Schindler defies the Nazis*
ACTION	*He risks everything*
GOAL	*To save Jewish lives*

There are absolutely no details involved in this statement of purpose. The conflict is described in the broadest possible terms: Schindler is going to take on the Nazis. The action revolves around the increasing risks he is forced to take in order to achieve his goal of saving the lives of thousands of innocent people.

To construct a powerful arc of character, a writer must have the ability to make conscious, purposeful choices. In the early stages of development, plot details can only be intuited and are therefore relatively random. But at some point it will be necessary to gain a conscious understanding of what the story is really about. **By naming the plotline in these simple, basic terms, a writer is able to see with clarity the nature of the obstacles that are challenging the protagonist.**

Don't be concerned if there is a generic quality to the name of a plotline. *Art is in the details* and, eventually, as flesh is put on the bones of a simple storyline it will become a unique and personal vision. In fact, the more familiar a plotline sounds on the surface, the greater the chances the story is striking a strong, universal chord.

When I first began working with my client on the story of the wife whose husband had run off with another woman, she was very concerned that her story was unoriginal and overdone. I asked her, *"How often is too often to tell a story about overcoming powerlessness?"* Have we already told too many stories about greed, love, or any other human frailty?

Based on her story elements, she determined this was the basic plotline:

*A middle-aged woman is **left with nothing** and must **rebuild** her life in order to **survive.***

After reducing it to its essence, my client began to understand that this was indeed a timeless story of courage and survival. While it was neither the first nor the last time this type of story would be told, it was her opportunity to tell it her way. What other purpose is there for writing?

When trying to sort out the basic elements of the plot in order to give it a name, **it can sometimes be difficult to distinguish plot from subplot. The difference is basically *action* versus *reaction*.** In *It's a Wonderful Life*, the plot is defined by the story elements that create the context (plot) in which George Bailey is forced to face his emptiness (subplot). His suicide attempt, therefore, is a basic element of the subplot because it is a *reaction* to the *action* taken by Mr. Potter when he finds the money George's uncle has misplaced. By attempting to take his own life, George is internally reacting to external events that are out of his control. These external events form the container in which George's inner journey through the netherworld of nonexistence is made possible and necessary because of Mr. Potter's actions. Therefore, the plot is defined as:

To save the town, George must try to stop Potter from taking over the savings and loan.

CONFLICT   *Potter tries to take over the savings and loan*
ACTION   *George tries to stop Potter*
GOAL   *To save the town*

Notice that the goal of this plotline once again revolves around issues of *survival*. Anytime a goal can be described in these terms it automatically implies that, on some level, this is a struggle between life and death. This is the language of the transformational arc because, in reality, we are most often pushed onto the path of transformational change by a need to survive. (Much more about this in Chapter 5.)

Here are a few additional notes on the technique of defining a plotline:

- Don't try to be too clever when defining the simple line of action. This isn't a sales pitch. Using only a single buzz word such as "betrayal" or a phrase like, "A man, a gun, and a blonde who done him wrong," is not enough information to appreciate the scope of the activity that is essential to move the story forward. Though eloquence is unimportant, precision is.

- As easy as it may appear, reducing your story to a single statement that defines the **conflict, action,** and **goal** can be a complex and time-consuming task. Don't get frustrated. This process is worthy of whatever time and effort it takes, because the outcome is clarity.

- *However*, please note, the line of action that defines the plot isn't chiseled in stone; at some point you must take a deep breath and commit to a plot idea for the sake of moving forward. **Trust that the process itself will begin to reveal to you what works, what doesn't, and where to make adjustments.** For some reason, there is a general belief that if you're good, you must be fast and also accurate. Neither of these assumptions are true. In life, maturing and developing continues to reveal the right path throughout a person's lifetime. So it is with writing; as you process the material, more will be revealed.

Case Studies

To help illustrate the concepts put forth in this book, I have completed each chapter with case studies. The three films I have chosen to follow exemplify and expand on the basic theories discussed, especially as they pertain to different genres. One of the great benefits of working with the transformational arc in a story is that it's very *genre* friendly. The general principles that govern the protagonist's movement throughout the arc can be applied to any type of story because all stories are based on the human story—the story of transformation and growth. This is not to say, however, that there is a one-size-fits-all formula for every genre, which is why it's important to see how different types of stories are developed within the framework of the transformational arc.

Two of the films we'll be looking at are the romantic comedy *Romancing the Stone* and the action-thriller *Lethal Weapon*. My general criteria for selecting these particular movies is that they needed to be well known, easy to access, and have a strong, clear structure that is simple to see and track. Even though these are older, classic examples of two very popular genres, the romance and the action-adventure, they are both worthy of examination because of their strong use of internal subplots in the development of the transformational arc. This is something that many of their more recent counterparts in the romance and action-adventure genres (including their own sequels) have neglected or failed at altogether.

My third case study is director Robert Redford's Oscar-winning film *Ordinary People*. It, too, is an older film, but is one of the finest examples of a character-driven story in modern cinema. By "character-driven" I am referring to a type of story that *seems* to gain its momentum more by the internal needs of the character than by heavy plotting. However, what this film will demonstrate is that even though it is a character study, it still relies on a deceptively well-developed line of action in the plot. As a result, this story is propelled forward with great energy, but it is done in a way that does not overwhelm or detract from the intimate, personal nature of the film.

(If you've never seen these films, or haven't watched them recently, I strongly suggest re-watching them in conjunction with reading these case studies.)

1) *ROMANCING THE STONE*: SCREENPLAY BY DIANE THOMAS

Romancing the Stone is an excellent script to analyze because it contains a very simple, straightforward plotline. The story revolves around a lovely, though lonely, woman, Joan Wilder, who's capable of finding love and passion only in the pages of her highly successful romance novels. She has cloistered herself in a small, Manhattan apartment with her cat, Romeo, where she lives in a world that's safe and protected, yet isolated. Her sense of security is breached one day when she receives a phone call from kidnappers in South America, who are holding her sister for ransom. In order to save her sister, she is told she must go to Cartagena, Colombia, to deliver a treasure map that has fallen into her possession. This demand instantly forces Joan to venture out into the world of risk and peril in order to bring her sister home alive. As in Joan's novels, the road to adventure leads her into the arms of love, but the knight in shining armor who rides to her rescue turns out to be someone quite different from the ideal man she's been writing about in her romance novels.

So, what is the plot?

If you determined that the action is being pushed forward by Joan's need to save her sister, you would be correct. If your answer included her quest to find love, you'd be headed in the wrong direction. Even though this is a love story and it's clear that Joan desperately wants to find her true love, there is no quest to find love in this story. In fact, that's a big part of Joan's problem; as much as she wants to find the man of her dreams, she has no clue that the fortress she's built to protect herself from pain and disappointment is likewise keeping him at bay. Even though this is a romantic adventure, the source of the activity that puts love in Joan's path is her need to save her sister. Her foray into the land of love is a consequence of her goal to save her sister, which makes it a subplot rather than a plot.

The simple action line of this film is:

Ruthless kidnappers take a woman's sister, and she must risk danger and peril to bring them a treasure map in order to save her.

CONFLICT	*Kidnappers have taken a woman's sister*
ACTION	*She faces danger and risk to deliver a map*
GOAL	*To save her sister*

2) LETHAL WEAPON: SCREENPLAY BY SHANE BLACK

Lethal Weapon is a great example of how confusing it can be to separate plot from subplot. The most memorable aspect of this classic action flick is the riveting portrayal of a cop, Martin Riggs (Mel Gibson), who is so tormented over the death of his wife that he constantly puts himself in harm's way, hoping one of the bad guys will just shoot him and put him out of his misery.

The darkness of this subject matter is mitigated by the comic pairing of Riggs with an older cop who's completely his opposite. Roger Murtaugh (Danny Glover) has a wonderful family and he is nearing retirement, which causes him to play it so safe that he's become timid about using a gun. While this relationship is undoubtedly the most interesting part of the movie, *it is not plot*—it is subplot. The plot actually involves a very *un*memorable drug cartel fiasco, which is what forces Riggs and Murtaugh to work together. It also keeps the line of action moving forward.

Here's how the plotline is described:

> **Two policemen must risk their lives pursuing deadly drug dealers** in order **to destroy a dangerous cartel.**

CONFLICT	*Two policemen must risk their lives*
ACTION	*Pursuing deadly drug dealers*
GOAL	*To destroy a dangerous cartel*

Notice that in defining this plot, there is no mention of the contentious relationship between the cops, or of Riggs' death wish. The drug cartel plotline provides the *action* against which Riggs and Murtaugh *react*. It is in their reaction, found in the subplots, that they develop the bonds of mutual support that enables them to grow past their fears in order to survive and stop the drug dealers.

3) *ORDINARY PEOPLE:* SCREENPLAY BY ALVIN SARGENT

Clearly, the storyline of *Ordinary People* is more complex than the first two examples. There is no obvious, outward activity that is pulling the story forward such as stopping drug dealers or rescuing a sister. The story's momentum comes from the inability of a young man, Conrad, to reconcile his own survival with his older brother's untimely death in a boating accident. This conflict is severely aggravated by his mother's obvious contempt. She says she doesn't blame Conrad for his brother's death, but her actions betray her words. Prior to the beginning of this story, it becomes clear that Conrad had attempted suicide because of his inability to cope with this tragedy. Even though his survival is still tenuous, his family is so eager to get things back to "normal" that they don't realize that it is their false sense of "normal" that is not only killing Conrad, but destroying the family as well.

Compared to most films, this story appears to be driven more by character development than by external situations. Yet, on closer examination, we see that the brother's death is the driving force of the drama. The accidental drowning was an external event over which the family had no control. What they do have control over is the denial of their own emotions and that has rendered them, as individuals and as a family, extremely vulnerable.

Very few films are made, and even fewer succeed, that are pulled along by what appears to be the inner needs of a character. Because there is often no obvious external goal (such as catching a killer, saving the kingdom, or righting a wrong) in films that are referred to as *character driven*, the storyline is always in peril of meandering if it is not attached to some sort of physical consequences. If you are committed to writing this type of script, be aware of this critical pitfall by keeping the external stakes high enough to keep the story moving forward. Study a film like *Ordinary People* to observe how the conflict of the plot stems from external conditions and the goal has to do with survival (physical, emotional, spiritual). Used well, this can create enough dramatic tension to keep the momentum strong.

Don't assume, for example, that *Ordinary People* is merely an intimate portrait of a dysfunctional family in crisis. At its core, this is a war story. Mother, father, and son are locked in a lethal battle for the soul of this family. Mom's weapons are propriety and seduction. The son's weapons are truth and the courage to face his own darkness. Dad appears to be the arbiter and the peacemaker, yet his ambivalence provides much of the fertile terrain on which the battles are being waged. Ultimately, whoever wins this war will determine whether or not this family gets real or will forever remain bound to its delusions.

The name of the plotline is:

To overcome their grief from the death of a son, a family struggles to survive.

CONFLICT	*To overcome their grief from the death of a son*
ACTION	*A family struggles*
GOAL	*To survive*

Even though Conrad's suicide attempt is the event that brings the family's problems to the surface, it was the death of his brother that created the grief from which the family cannot seem to recover. The attempted suicide is a manifestation of that grief, and although it appears motivated by his brother's accidental drowning, it may really be a result of something much bigger—the death of the illusion that this was once a happy family.

CHAPTER THREE

CHARACTER
Getting to the Heart of the Matter

What is character but the determination of incident?
What is incident but the illustration of character?

~ HENRY JAMES

The Myth of the "Hero" Myth

Probably the greatest symbol of the hero in Western culture is the character of Hercules (Heracles) found in Roman and Greek mythology. From our earliest recollections most of us heard stories, saw movies, and even watched cartoons that celebrated his heroic exploits. He was the righter of wrongs, defender of the weak, champion of the oppressed, and just all-around good guy, who made women swoon and men tremble. However, what's become obscured in our modern interpretation of this archetypal hero story is that in the actual myth (according to all those old Greeks) Hercules was a much darker, more insufferable fellow. Even though he was unquestionably the strongest and the bravest, he was also a big bully who was prone to fits of rage, during which he once even murdered his own children. In fact, what contemporary stories have lost track of altogether is that it was this little psychotic temper tantrum that forced him into the penance that has become celebrated as the Twelve Labors of Hercules.

Because of this slight omission or "spin" that's been applied to this classic hero model, not only has our view of this icon been sanitized, but it's similarly lost its complexity and relevance. Without his need for atonement, all of the trials and labors of Hercules take on the appearance of being exceptional and extraordinary, rather than being the reasonable cost of redemption for the wreckage he'd made of his life.

As a result of this perspective, modern stories tend to bestow the title of "hero" only on characters who achieve great, uncommon feats of valor, such as scaling tall buildings in a single bound or saving an errant spacecraft from its collision course with oblivion. But if *hero* were to be defined the old-fashioned way, by characters who earned it through the service of redeeming their self-worth, then not just astronauts and superheroes would get the accolades. Little old ladies who struggle to raise themselves from the ashes of a failed marriage could be considered heroic as well. In fact, any human being—young or old, weak or strong, timid or brave—would be a contender for this honor because the potential to be heroic lies within everyone.

The potential for failure exists within everyone as well, and herein is found the drama. Wanting to achieve things like redemption, self-acceptance, love, and honor are all worthy aspirations, but as Hercules himself discovers, it takes a lot of hard work and uncompromising resolve to achieve these goals. In this context, then, the opposite of heroic is not cowardly or despicable, but **tragic.** Therefore, it is essential for writers to always be aware that *what makes characters tragic is not just the result of what is done to them, but the result of what they fail to do for themselves.*

The basis for the internal development of character, or the transformational arc, found in great stories is that **the internal goal for a protagonist is *always* to become heroic.** This means that **the protagonist will be challenged by the conflict in the plot to transcend personal limitations in order to become someone greater in the end than who he or she was when the story began.** But the heroic outcome for the protagonist is not a foregone conclusion. There is always the possibility of failure, which brings about the *tragic* possibility of becoming diminished or destroyed entirely by the circumstances of the conflict.

In this book, the terms *heroic* and *tragic* will **not** be used as a character description or trait, but instead they will define the goal for the internal development of character. If our stories are written presupposing that the protagonist *is* a hero, then where's the drama? Without the possibility of failure lurking around every corner, it would only be a one-sided story. As in the modern version of the Hercules tale, all this says about the human condition is that winners are born, not made.

Identifying the Protagonist

Traditionally, *protagonist* is defined as the leading character in a drama. But to build a strong arc of character, it's important to emphasize that the protagonist is also the *heart* of your story, which means that he or she *must* be the central focus of everything that is going on.

- **The protagonist is the person or being who is primarily impacted by the action and conflict of the plot.**

And:

- **The protagonist is the person or being around whom the primary goals of the plot are formed.**

Therefore:

- **The protagonist *must* carry the goal of the plot.**

For example, if the conflict of the plot is concerned with a murder, then the protagonist must somehow be involved with that crime. He or she might be responsible for catching the killer, or for trying to get away with killing someone, or even for trying to clear his or her name of a false conviction. But one way or another, the protagonist's presence in the story must have something very significant to do with the goal attached to the murder, or this isn't his or her story, which means this isn't your protagonist.

Most of the time documentaries, and especially news reports, aspire to relay a story without a protagonist, by communicating events from no particular point of view. However, the moment a point of view is established, there is an implied central character with a personal investment in the outcome of the story. When this occurs, even a news story becomes more personal and feels more accessible. This may be one reason Michael Moore's documentaries are so popular: He's turned them into a storytelling experience. His quest to find the truth or to hold people accountable for their actions makes him the protagonist in his own films, with a clear and crucial goal that needs to be resolved. While his political views may be highly controversial, his *I'm-just-a-confused-guy-trying-to-figure-things-out* persona invites the audience to enter his story and react to the events in the movie right along with him.

It is through the protagonist that the audience finds their way into a story. This makes the conflict of the plot personal. As a result, the audience is able to *feel* the emotional impact of the events as they unfold. One of the greatest assets a writer must never underestimate is: ***The audience enters a story through the protagonist.*** Stories that attempt to be told from some neutral, unbiased perspective will pretty much sideline the audience, inviting them to observe voyeuristically rather than fully participate in the story.

In most storylines, the protagonist is fairly easy to distinguish. Many good plot ideas evolve out of the supposition: *What would happen to a person if...?* But there are also story ideas that do not automatically identify the central character or focal point.

I recently consulted with a writer on a historical drama about a gang of young men who rose to infamous distinction. All the facts of their rise and ultimate decline were extremely fascinating, but the story was told in a very one-dimensional style because there was no central character. Each of the members of the gang had a different motive (goal) for participating in a series of crimes over many years. This meant there was neither a specific event nor a primary player around whom the plot developed. The result was that the story felt sluggish and un-involving in spite of a lot of explosive action sequences. Without any definite direction or focus, there was nothing to engage me or hold my interest. Once a singular goal was attached to the plot, it became relatively easy to see who the central character was. From this point on, many of the script's problems began to solve themselves.

Secondary Characters

To a greater or lesser degree, most of the characters in a story will be involved in one or all three of the primary aspects of the plot: *conflict, action,* and *goal*. Unlike the protagonist, **the primary function of all secondary characters in a story is not specifically to achieve the goal of the plot, but to serve the protagonist in attaining it.**

Achieving the goal of the plot always belongs to the protagonist. It doesn't matter whether he or she fails; it is his or her goal to aim for. This doesn't mean that there aren't people to cheer the protagonist along or lend a helping hand, or even to give assistance over the finish line. But if your protagonist doesn't accomplish or attempt to accomplish the goal of the plot, then it's necessary to reconsider who your protagonist is.

Even in a film like *It's a Wonderful Life*, where the townspeople collect the money in the end to pay George's debt, the goal still belongs to George. While paying the debt is an essential part of stopping Potter from taking over the town, it is George who inspires the townspeople to stand up for themselves. This creates a defensive line that Potter is incapable of crossing. As the story reviews George's life, it reveals that without him the townspeople would never have learned to stand up for themselves. George is the one who accomplishes the goal of the plot, and having the townspeople raise the money only reinforces George's complete victory over Potter.

Although some characters assist the protagonist in achieving the goal in a positive way by teaching, caring, loving, mentoring, and so on, the story gets its biggest boost from the characters who stand in the protagonist's way. Those who are *antagonistic* to the protagonist serve perhaps the greatest function because they create the obstacles that give the story its momentum. This is especially true of the characters who incite the conflict in the first place. By making things hard for the protagonist, they likewise create an environment in which transformation can take place.

Without problems and conflicts in our lives, very little would ever change. Think about the conflicts and upheavals you've experienced in your life. Notice that there were really only two kinds of people involved:

those who were *for* you and those who were *against* you. It's hard to recall a neutral person who neither helped nor hindered nor influenced your progress. Especially when caught up in the tumultuous undertow of the transformational experience, we tend to see others as either part of the problem or part of the solution.

Defining the protagonist separately from the other characters in a story is essential, but it can be quite confusing when a story has a strong secondary lead who moves a great deal of the action forward. The title of *The Godfather*, for example, might lead to the assumption that Don Corleone (Brando) is the protagonist. However, the focus and point of view of the story instead tracks the impact that the actions and lifestyle of the old Don have on the future of his son, Michael (Pacino). While the old Don is a prominent character, his actual function in the story is to create many of the internal obstacles that Michael must face and hopefully overcome.

Secondary characters create an orbit around the protagonist, either providing assistance or resistance to the attainment of his or her goal. Friends or mentors serve the protagonist by providing counsel, wisdom, safety, and sometimes a strong shoulder to cry on. Antagonists traditionally thwart, undermine, deceive, harm, or betray the protagonist, which ultimately defines the challenge he or she must face in order to achieve the goal.

Not only did the townspeople in *It's a Wonderful Life* help George meet his goal, but every person in that story had a relationship with George Bailey that served to help him identify his own value, which was the primary obstacle he had to overcome. But it was the loathsome old Mr. Potter who created the environment that forced George to stop and face his darkest demons. George could never have evolved as a human being without that challenge.

Co-Protagonists

- **The protagonist is the character who carries the goal of the plot.**
- **A strong story has only one plot.**
- **Therefore, a strong story has only ONE protagonist.**

If the goal of a police drama is to catch a killer and two officers are assigned to the case, who is the protagonist? Because a plot has only a single goal and it is the protagonist who carries that goal, then there can only be a single protagonist. UNLESS…**two or more characters share the *same* goal. Then they *share* the role of the protagonist. I refer to these characters as *co-protagonists,*** meaning that, in terms of story function, they are a single entity even though that entity is expressed with multiple characters.

If a story has more than one protagonist, each with a separate goal, then it's imperative to find a creative way to link their goals into one. This is similar to the principle in mathematics that requires a *common denominator* in order to add two unlike fractions into a single number.

$$\frac{1}{2} = \frac{3}{6}$$

$$\frac{1}{3} = \frac{2}{6} \quad \text{Common Denominator}$$

$$\frac{5}{6}$$

In storytelling, the audience can't easily follow various leading characters if their actions are scattered in different directions with no common purpose. However, a story can certainly be layered with multiple tracks that follow different protagonist characters, *if* they are all linked by a clear, common goal.

The popular television series *Sex and the City* is an excellent example of how this can be achieved. Each episode tracks the exploits of four different women and their amorous escapades around Manhattan. The common link in all of their storylines is that they are each searching for romantic fulfillment. Their differing definitions and visions of romance don't detract from their common goal. If anything, these differences add dimension and expand the scope of what the writers have to say about sex and love.

Another great example of how complex the use of co-protagonists can be is found in the film *Fried Green Tomatoes.* On the surface, the goal for the exuberant character Idgie Threadgoode is to conquer life on her terms. She's not going to settle for her piece of the pie; she wants the whole thing. Conversely, the goal for the dowdy Evelyn Couch is to get through life as unobtrusively as possible, wanting to gobble down every last morsel of the pie yet settling only for mere crumbs to feed her vast emptiness. The two women lived in different eras and there was nothing conspicuous that paralleled their two experiences. But as the writers (Fannie Flagg and Carol Sobieski) expanded these two women past their individual goals, they were able to link the experiences of the two characters into a mutual goal of survival through self-discovery. This opened the door for each of them to find love and connection.

If a writer can't find a common goal for multiple leading characters, then he or she needs to consider the possibility that the diverse protagonists do not belong in the same story or that one of them will serve a stronger function as a secondary character. More often than not, however, the discovery of a connection between multiple protagonists is easy to spot, because the very thing that ties the characters together will often amplify and clarify the thematic meaning of the story for the writer.

There's More to a Protagonist Than Meets the Eye

As the protagonist has been defined so far, there's an uneasy gray area that can undermine the definition altogether. If the protagonist is identified as the character or characters who carry the goal of the plot, then is *anyone* and *everyone* who is trying to resolve the conflict a protagonist? If this is so, then in some stories the role of the protagonist could even include background characters. This, of course, would make the definition somewhat meaningless.

For example, in the beginning of *Speed*, two cops (Keanu Reeves and Jeff Daniels) are assigned to stop a deadly bomber. However, shortly into the film, Daniels' character is injured and sidelined, only to be replaced by Annie Porter (Sandra Bullock), who is coerced into helping Jack Traven (Reeves) drive an out-of-control bus that is rigged with a deadly explosive. Are all three characters co-protagonists? Going strictly by the definition that the protagonist carries the goal of the plot, the answer could be yes, because they each want to stop the bomber. But what about the police commander and all of the supporting patrolmen, who likewise assist in stopping the deranged bomber? Are they protagonists, too? It doesn't really *feel* like it. The focus seems to be set squarely on Jack Traven because he gets the most screen time. So the writing is tailored to fit the *feeling* that Traven and possibly Annie Porter are the protagonists. But depending on a "feeling" is a rather vague and unreliable way to define a story element as essential as the role of the protagonist. *There must be a better way…*

To further define the protagonist role so that there is no ambiguity, the definition needs to become more specific. However, it's difficult to get more specific if the only thing going on in a story is the external quest to resolve a conflict. *Jack Traven wants to stop the bomber* pretty much sums up everything that is happening in *Speed*.

On the other hand, if a story has both an *external* and an *internal goal* for the protagonist (as defined in the last chapter), then who the protagonist is will instantly become more precise. The protagonist is not only distinguished from the other characters because he or she is the focus of the external activities, but also because he or she is the focus of the internal quest as well. Therefore, **the protagonist is the character who not only carries the external goal of the plot, but also the internal goals in the subplots.**

Like *Speed*, the film *Sea of Love*, written by Richard Price and starring Al Pacino, is also a police action thriller, but, unlike *Speed*, there is a great deal more going on in this story than just the need to catch the bad guy. Pacino plays a cop, Frank Keller, assigned to track down a serial killer who is responsible for the deaths of several men. The link between all of the victims is that they each placed personal ads, looking for companionship. Because of Keller's own inner feelings of desperation and loneliness, he is unwittingly drawn into the killer's web when he begins a passionate and possibly dangerous love affair with a potential suspect. But in the end it is Keller's internal goal, *to risk everything for love*, that ultimately puts him in a position to catch the killer.

Sea of Love does not have to rely on guesswork to clarify who the protagonist is. Even though Frank has a partner and there is an entire police force trying to catch the killer, there is no doubt that he is the protagonist. The focus is always on Frank because his internal and external goals are completely interdependent; they push each other forward and one can't be resolved without the other. The result in the end is that Frank not only proves himself to be a great cop, but he also becomes a greater human being for having had the life-altering experiences in the story.

Linear, one-dimensional storytelling that relies on no inner development of character leaves the protagonist with only external means of achieving the goal of the plot. In *Speed*, the good, honest cop can only stop the evil terrorist from blowing up a bus full of innocent people by using the guts, brains, and muscle with which he is already well endowed. But in a more complex film such as *Sea of Love*, just being a good cop is not enough. The protagonist is challenged to find the deeper kind of strength and courage required to defeat all types of enemies, within and without.

Defining the protagonist as the character responsible for both the external and internal goal also applies to the use of co-protagonists. If the story has a well-developed internal subplotline, it is still quite possible to utilize co-protagonists. But instead of just vaguely designating two main characters to mutually share the external goal of the plot, **co-protagonists must likewise share the internal goal.**

The wonderful old film *The African Queen* has an excellent co-protagonist structure. The shared *external* goal for both Charlie (Humphrey Bogart) and Rose (Katharine Hepburn) is to sink a German warship. This goal provides a clear and well-focused escapade for this highly mismatched couple, who are forced to make their way down a treacherous jungle river on Charlie's dilapidated old steamboat, the *African Queen*. *Internally*, it becomes evident that even though Charlie and Rose are opposites in behavior, background, and breeding, they are both similarly damaged souls who have hidden themselves away from both life and love. With each other's help, the perils of the voyage give them the opportunity to individually revive their broken spirits. What starts between them as aversion and distrust blossoms into love and devotion, and it is through their belief in each other that they come to believe in their ability to carry out their implausible mission to sink the boat.

Remove either Rose or Charlie from the story and the German ship would still be afloat. Charlie had the experience and the know-how to guide the steamboat, but he was also a cynical drunk who had no ambition or belief in their crazy scheme. Rose, on the other hand, had an overly optimistic view of their ability to do battle with the Germans, but had no skills whatsoever to execute the plan on her own. As the relationship between Rose and Charlie flourishes, so does her confidence in him. This inspires Charlie to become a better man, one who could fulfill her impossible dream. Similarly, as Charlie gets to know Rose, she becomes more beautiful in his eyes. This makes her more confident in her femininity and enhances her ability to open her heart to love, which is the guiding force of their story. These two people were otherwise lost to the world, but together they complete each other, which enables them to complete the mission of sinking the German ship.

Casablanca, another romantic classic from that era, also has two very memorable lovers, but they are *not* co-protagonists. While Rick (Humphrey Bogart) and Ilsa (Ingrid Bergman) share the same *external* goal—to get her husband out of the country—their *internal* goals are not the same. Rick is a man whose essence has been nearly devastated by the disappointment and disillusionment of love. To regain his footing in life, he needs to transcend his immature and self-serving view of love and open his heart to its greater potential. This internal goal for Rick is one that Ilsa has long since attained. Therefore, it is Rick's internal change that is the focus of the story. If he does not learn to love without condition or reward (*internally*), he will not agree to help get Ilsa's husband out of the country (*externally*). This makes Rick the singular protagonist, which is not to say that Ilsa's role is unimportant. She is essential to the story because, without her influence, Rick would never have agreed to get involved in the war again and help the Nazi resistance—nor would he have been given the opportunity to redeem himself.

When Harry Met Sally is another great example of a story that fulfills the dual requirements for a co-protagonist structure. The central driving question of this is: Will they fall in love with each other? This defines Harry and Sally's *external* goal as mutual, and is indispensable to the telling of the story. However, in order to achieve love, they both need to grow up and open their hearts to true intimacy through the bonds of their friendship. This is their shared internal goal, and if either Harry or Sally had had a separate internal goal the story wouldn't have worked.

For example, if Harry's internal storyline had focused on his need to find his true professional calling, or if Sally's inner goal were to overcome dysfunctional family ties, then they could not have shared the co-protagonist structure. Even though they were both looking for love, if their inner journey to get that goal was different, it would have created alternate rather than mutual paths.

At the beginning of this film, Harry and Sally are both in their early twenties and appropriately naive and unrealistic about their requirements for love. She wants the perfect guy with chiseled features, a six-digit income, and social acceptability. He wants a great-looking babe and hot sex. Even though their romantic ideals are vastly different, they both share a view of love that is completely superficial. As a result life conspires to give them exactly what they believe they want, and they each come up empty. Similarly wounded from these parallel experiences, they meet again at a moment when their romantic defenses are so high that they are mutually resistant to falling in love at all. The only pathway for intimacy left open for either of them at this time is friendship. And it is through the healing bond of that friendship that they are both able to recuperate and reopen their hearts to the possibility of finding true love, which they happen to find in each other. Thus, a singular protagonist goal has been achieved both internally and externally in two separate people.

A good example of a film that attempted to utilize this identical co-protagonist structure, but did not succeed nearly as well, is *Sleepless in Seattle*. While finding true love is the mutual external goal for the two leading characters in this story, they have very different internal goals. Sam (Tom Hanks) is deeply grieving the death of his wife, and his internal goal is to learn to love again. Annie (Meg Ryan) is about to enter a loveless marriage and has as an internal goal the need to learn to trust her inner voice and not settle for anything less than true love. Even though they both recognize that they are looking for the "magic," there is no parallel in their inner stories to define what that magic is.

Because Sam and Annie don't actually get together until the end of the film, the story bounces back and forth from one character's journey to the other's, with nothing more in common than the writer contriving to thrust them together in the climax. The problem with this, as we are about to explore in the next chapter (on theme), is that the inner journey of the character represents the writer's point of view. Therefore, **when the protagonist's journey is split in two by having two separate protagonists with two separate internal goals, the point of view is also split.** This means that the thematic focus of the film is very unclear and confusing. As this film jumps back and forth from character to character, the audience not only has to constantly readjust to being in separate storylines, but they must also continually reorient themselves as to what the writer is trying to say about love. *When Harry Met Sally* contains a clear, simple theme that is easy to internalize about the importance of friendship in finding true intimacy. *Sleepless in Seattle* has no such clear theme; therefore, there isn't a lot of depth to either of the main characters, nor to the film itself.

As powerful as the beginning of *Sleepless in Seattle* is, when we first encounter Sam mourning his wife's death, the issue of grief is virtually dropped by mid story. The reason Sam's character is lured to the Empire State Building in the end is not to take a risk and learn to love again, but to retrieve his wayward son. This demonstrates no inner change at all because flying across the country to find his son is something he would have easily done at the very start of the movie.

In *Dead Poets Society*, the co-protagonist format is a little more complex. Because Robin Williams is such a big star, it's easy to assume that his character is the protagonist. But upon closer scrutiny it becomes apparent that it is really his students who are being pushed along by the external events in this story toward the possibility of internal transformation. Even though each of the boys has a very different response to the conflict, their internal challenge is the same—they are each struggling with the adolescent tug-of-war between the safety of conformity and the excitement of the call to individuality. John Keating (Williams) is their mentor, and with his help they are able to make the leap to manhood by learning to stand up for their convictions.

It is extremely important to distinguish the protagonist from the other characters, because the story is formed around the protagonist's need to complete or at least encounter his or her transformational challenge. Always bear in mind that secondary characters, whether a help or a hindrance, are there to serve the movement of the protagonist along on this journey. Although in the end of *Dead Poets Society* Keating is forced to leave, it is clear that he has helped the boys make the transition to a more authentic life.

Case Studies

Just as it was important to keep the definition of the plot simple and clear, it is also essential to identify your protagonist without much detail. As you will see in the next chapter, character details will begin to form naturally and effortlessly around a writer's thematic intentions.

1) ROMANCING THE STONE

Even though *Romancing the Stone* is a story with two strong lead characters, the protagonist role is not divided into a co-protagonist structure. It is Joan Wilder alone who has the external goal of saving her sister, which is the central conflict of the plot. Jack Colton (Michael Douglas) has a lot of influence over Joan in the external storyline, but it is ultimately she, not Colton, who is responsible for achieving the goal of the plot. This distinction makes Colton's character much more pliable in terms of how the writer can use him. Instead of only being directed toward the goal of the plot, his character is also used to challenge Joan and push her past her safe and untried boundaries. For this purpose, Colton is actually antagonistic toward Joan when they first meet. While her goal is to save her sister, his goal in the beginning is to take advantage of Joan and abscond with the stone. This provides the story with excellent comic tension between these two memorable characters, but it does not make them co-protagonists.

On the other hand, both Joan and Colton have internal goals that are mutual. They are both people who have hidden away from life and intimacy, and their adventure to recover the stone offers them both the opportunity to grow toward love and intimacy—together.

In addition to clearly defining the line of action that forms the plot, it is also now apparent which of the characters exclusively carries the goals of resolving both the external and internal conflicts.

CONFLICT	*Kidnappers have taken a woman's sister*
ACTION	*She faces danger and risk to deliver a map*
GOAL	*To save her sister*
PROTAGONIST	***Joan Wilder***

2) *LETHAL WEAPON*

In *Lethal Weapon*, because the Martin Riggs character is so prominent, it is often assumed that he alone is the protagonist. But is that really true? On the surface it's easy to see that both Riggs and his partner, Roger Murtaugh, are trying to achieve the same external goal of the plot: *to stop a dangerous drug cartel.* But internally they at least *appear* to have very different agendas.

Riggs has recently lost his wife and can't face the emptiness of living without her. His grief is so severe that he seems intent upon putting an end to his miserable existence, either by his own hand or by recklessly exposing himself to the line of fire. This not only makes him a danger to himself, but also to anyone else unfortunate enough to work at his side. At least that is the perception of his reluctant partner, Murtaugh, a genial family man who is fast approaching retirement and pension status. Unlike Riggs, Murtaugh has everything to live for, which makes him a little too cautious and hesitant to use a gun—also a very perilous trait for a cop.

So perhaps these two have a lot more in common internally than it at first appears. While neither of them lacks the physical courage to be a good cop, on the inside they both seem very afraid of life. Riggs' fear of living and Murtaugh's fear of dying are two different sides of the same coin. The net effect is that it has rendered them both a danger to themselves as well as to others.

Because they have similar internal and external goals, Riggs and Murtaugh are co-protagonists. Many writers have tried to replicate the success of this film (including the endless sequels to *Lethal Weapon* itself) and have failed, primarily because they didn't capture the depth of this alter-ego relationship between the two men. They are each one-half of the same whole. Like Rose and Charlie in *The African Queen*, Riggs and Murtaugh must learn to trust and value in each other what they most dislike and fear in themselves. Ultimately, what the story demands is that they either merge as one or fail altogether. And, in this case, failure means death.

In addition to understanding the goal of the plot, it is now also clear that this is a co-protagonist structure.

CONFLICT	*Two policemen must risk their lives*
ACTION	*Pursuing deadly drug dealers*
GOAL	*To destroy a dangerous cartel*
CO-PROTAGONISTS	***Martin Riggs, Roger Murtaugh***

3) ORDINARY PEOPLE

Ordinary People is interesting to analyze because defining its protagonist is deceptively complex. Conrad, the suicidal teenage boy, seems to be the obvious choice for the protagonist, and his cold, unyielding mother appears to be the antagonist. Yet the story reaches a much broader climax than merely resolving the conflict between these two. In fact, the father and the choices he makes also have a great impact on the resolution of this film. All three of these characters are integral to the family's struggle to survive—*as a family*. Therefore, it's not just the individual actions of each family member that matter; it is their struggle, as a group, that ultimately determines the outcome of the story.

If this family chooses to work toward an honest relationship with themselves and one another, they will achieve the goal of survival. However, if they don't, it's clear they will fall apart. Conrad and his mother stand out so distinctly in this story because they represent the two opposing directions in which the family can develop. Conrad is pulling the family toward change, intimacy, and growth, and Mom is trying desperately to hold on to the way things have been. Dad, on the other hand, represents the ambivalence that has led this family to the point where their only remaining son has attempted suicide. This is a clear indication that their fragile emotional barricades are about to come crashing down. The actions they take and the choices they make in this story will either lead them to wholeness or destroy their family system altogether.

In *Ordinary People* it is, therefore, not an individual but the *family* as a group or an entity that serves as protagonist. This is yet another interesting demonstration of how expansive the protagonist function can be. **As long as the criterion is met—that the protagonist holds the goals of both the plot and the subplots—then the creative possibilities for how this role is configured can be vast.**

CONFLICT	*To overcome their grief from the death of a son*
ACTION	*A family struggles*
GOAL	*To survive*
PROTAGONIST	**The family**

CHAPTER FOUR

THEME
Defining Intention

Do you not see how necessary
a world of pains and troubles is
to school an intelligence
and make a soul?

~ JOHN KEATS

Making Meaning

I was recently flipping through the television channels and happened to catch the last few minutes of Steven Spielberg's Academy Award–winning film *Schindler's List.* In the final scene, the actual descendants of the concentration camp survivors quietly placed stones of tribute on the grave of Oskar Schindler. While I've always felt this is an incredibly powerful epilogue, I was still caught off guard by how strongly I reacted to watching just these final moments. A lump formed in my throat and my eyes moistened (okay, I started to cry). It was as if no time had passed since I first saw this film, and I was instantly overwhelmed by feelings of profound *connectedness*. The image of descendants acknowledging Schindler's life-affirming legacy stands as an emotional reminder of how much we all need each other in this world—and how every person can make a difference.

The film didn't leave me with a sense that I wanted to be Schindler, but rather that I wanted to be Schindler-like. This indicates that it succeeded in telling a story in which the journey of the protagonist portrays something so meaningful that it takes on symbolic value.

Conversely, when I saw *Saving Private Ryan* (also a Spielberg film), I had a very different reaction—which was to have almost no emotional response at all. Even though this film also ended with descendants gathering at the graveside of a very brave soldier who had helped save the lives of others, I barely felt even a slight tug on my heartstrings. When the elder Ryan said to the headstone of the long-dead Captain Miller that he hoped he had earned the life that Miller had sacrificed for him, I thought to myself: *Oh, that's what the movie was supposed to be about.*

The story of a man questioning the success he's made of the life he's been given through the sacrifice of another man's life is such a powerful idea that it's literally of biblical proportions. Unfortunately, this isn't the story on which this film chose to focus. While *Saving Private Ryan* certainly can be considered a riveting, action-filled war adventure, it never achieves enough internal clarity to give any real meaning to the value of this kind of self-sacrifice. In fact, some of its images are so conflicting that they jeopardize the possibility of making any meaning at all.

In the extended opening sequence, as the Americans land on the beaches of Normandy, the filmmaker goes to great lengths to paint a vivid portrait of the nightmarish hell our soldiers had to endure. In contrast to many other war films that emphasize the clean and untarnished heroics of the proud American liberators, *Saving Private Ryan* portrays D-Day as a grim, bloody, horrifically chaotic, and terrifying experience. The opening scenes seem to imply that human life is sacrificed wantonly, even recklessly, because of poor planning and a lack of well-coordinated, skillful leadership.

While hard to watch, the scenes are very compelling—with a raw, honest edge. It feels as though this is going to be a film that attempts to demystify war by making the characters and situations real instead of idealized or romanticized. But when the conflict of the plot is introduced—*a group of men are ordered to the frontlines to bring back Private Ryan so that he can be sent home to his family*—the entire tone of the film abruptly changes. Suddenly, the view of war shifts from uncompromising and critical to traditional and somewhat sentimental.

There's nothing wrong with either of these perspectives—separately—but they are so disparate in their points of view that combined in the same story they tend to negate each other. This is why when the film reaches its conclusion and old man Ryan asks if his life has been worth saving, it seems as though a third and more personal perspective has just opened up. However, since almost nothing substantial has been revealed in this film of Ryan's existence before or after the war, there is really no way to know or care about how he's spent his life. Ryan's inner journey is a completely undeveloped fragment of the film. It is Captain Miller who carries the goal of the plot—to save Private Ryan—and he is, therefore, the most obvious candidate for the role of the protagonist. Technically, Ryan is just the object of the conflict, not its principal subject.

Confusion over the themes that give meaning to a film is not uncommon. In too many of our modern stories the issue of *theme* gets relegated to the category of "runner up." It's not that writers don't have a high regard for a good theme, it's just that there isn't a lot of understanding of how to actually integrate theme into a story. Whereas working with plot and character are relatively easy and straightforward, theme can be complex and challenging. But learning to work with the theme is the greatest tool a writer can develop. To attempt to build a great script without it is like excavating a mountain with a teaspoon.

Some Assembly Required

Defining theme by its physical characteristics is difficult. Theme is an enigma. It is not visible, yet somehow it's terribly prevalent. It is subtle, yet also remarkably significant. It is colorful, intense, expressive, potent, powerful, and at the same time it can be described as nothing more than a notion. Yet a story has no real impact without it because **theme is what gives *meaning* to the activity of the plot and *purpose* to the movement of the characters.**

In everyday life, all of our actions have meaning and purpose. People don't just get up in the morning and go about their daily routines for no reason. Certainly no one endures hardships, suffering, disappointments, and loss for the sole purpose of merely existing. Consciously and unconsciously, a value is placed on every action we take.

The origin or starting point for most story ideas springs from a writer's experiences, observations, beliefs, and assumptions. Ideas capture the imagination because they mean something to the writer. This can be as profound as exposing an injustice, as personal as revealing a human frailty, or even as self-serving as exploiting our worst fears.

The problem with this as a starting point for developing a theme is that too often it is the ending point as well. Clutching the thematic meaning close to their hearts, writers will use it to create a backdrop or to incite a conflict that sets the story into motion, hoping that plot and character development take theme along for the ride. At best, this leaves a lot to chance and it certainly doesn't guarantee that the thematic purpose behind the story will become fully and clearly expressed. Many well-intentioned scripts find themselves swimming in long speeches at the end, because they try to cover thematic ground that just didn't happen to fall into place by itself. Used this way, theme is hardly a *tool* that can move a mountain. It is still not much more than a vaporous notion and, unless the theme becomes a lot more *tangible*, it may easily fall by the wayside.

The key to developing a theme is to make it tangible, which means that it must become visible, discernible, and understandable. The only way to achieve this in a story is to give the elusive idea of a theme some sort of physical expression. In a screenplay, the primary means of physical expression are found in the *action* of plot and the *movement* of the protagonist. So, **for the theme to manifest itself, it must become attached to the *actions* of the *protagonist*. It can, therefore, be said that: *The actions of the protagonist serve the function of expressing the theme.***

When the protagonist's actions express the theme, the writer's story choices are no longer arbitrary and random, but directed and purposeful.

The inner purpose or theme can only come from one source: *what a writer knows to be true.* I can't emphasize enough that this kind of truth is not a religious, moral, universal, or even a politically correct truth. While a theme can certainly coincide with any of these belief systems, it must come from the writer's own experiences, observations, and perceptions or it will feel superficial and false. In other words, a writer can't write someone else's theme. **Theme is based on what a writer believes and believes in. This is the writer's unique *voice*, distinctive *point of view*, and, above all, what is personally *valued*. Therefore, personal beliefs form the cornerstone of a theme, and it is from the theme then that a writer can come to understand the true *intention of his or her story.***

Regardless of whether a story is told as an intimate psychological drama, an action thriller, a murder mystery, or even a romantic screwball comedy, *all decisions for the actions of the protagonist can be derived from the writer's thematic intentions.* By defining these *intentions*, a writer can move past relying solely on random, arbitrary choices and begin to construct a story that is purposefully and intentionally told. Remember: **Random choices will lead to random results; intentional choices will lead to intentional results.**

Even if a script is not meant to be particularly deep or laden with powerful thematic substance, it is still necessary to give it a *point of view* that encompasses the writer's *vision, passion,* and *values.* These are the qualities at the heart of a theme, and without them the writing will almost certainly be insignificant and even meaningless.

For example, if you were to write something as lightweight as a thrill-packed adventure about an action hero who infiltrates and destroys a South American drug cartel, what are *your* thoughts and values about this activity? You must feel something, because nothing exists in a void. How do you feel about drugs? How do you feel about the "war" on drugs? Has it been effective? Is there some hypocrisy involved? Do the good guys always wear white hats? Does it take a criminal mind to catch a criminal? Does society have a double standard about the people it employs to do our dirty work for us?

There are no perfect answers to these questions. Every individual has a right to his or her own feelings, but it is a writer's job to explore these feelings and express them. Therefore, **in order to make intentional choices, writers must define their intentions.**

In this example of an action hero stopping a major drug cartel, there is certainly something worn and weary about the plotline. As it is with most action-adventure plots, there isn't much left that hasn't been bombed, blown up, crashed, or vaporized. The best way to find a unique angle into a story like this is to explore your own perceptions about what the circumstances of the plot mean to the characters involved. Instead of randomly devising a tough-guy character to fulfill the function of merely defeating the bad guys, creating character through thematic intention will make the story much more complex, interesting, and emotionally honest.

For example, if the writer has a personal belief that the justice system has set up good men to become corrupted by living undercover in a world of depravity and immorality, then the protagonist will evoke that complex duality. He lives one way and yet thinks another. He's committed to a job that tries to save lives, yet he must behave as if human life has no value. He observes "bad people" being vastly rewarded for immoral behavior, and "good people" being destroyed for incorruptibility. In order to survive, therefore, it's clear that his own behavior must be somewhat duplicitous.

This clue to the design of a very significant character trait evolved logically and non-randomly, directly from thematic intention. As soon as the writer determined that the point of view was that the "war on drugs" makes victims of its own foot soldiers, any character choice that follows becomes an offshoot of that intention.

The writer's perspective on the war on drugs not only affects the design of the character, it also triggers issues around the development of the plot. If duplicity is part of the personality of the protagonist, then this could inspire a plotline that will ultimately force the protagonist to examine who he really is. In order to accomplish this, it may be necessary to drive the protagonist to a point where he finds himself taking the fall for the drug dealer, or he may even succumb to the lure of easy money and start dealing drugs himself. There are an infinite number of ways to develop this line of thought, but notice that all of the ideas flow from a single source—the thematic intention. What was once only an inner feeling or a strongly held belief has been transformed into a *tangible*, understandable, trackable story-line that expresses the writer's point of view. Story choices have ceased to be random or arbitrary and are now guided by intention.

Write What You Know

There's a familiar notion that writers should always write what they know. If this were entirely true, then a writer who has never ridden a horse would be unable to write a good western. Or, if a writer hasn't personally witnessed a brutal homicide, he or she wouldn't be able to conceive a realistic crime drama. Of course this is absurd; if writers can only write about what they have physically experienced in life, there would be no film classics like *E.T.*, *Star Wars*, or even *Amadeus*. Imagination and a little research are the primary tools a writer needs to create intriguing plots and unique characters.

It's only in the realm of theme that writers must write what they know to be true. As already described, this may be a point of view, a passion, an observation, or a perception, and *no facts are required*. A writer's view of the world is his or her own, and that is indisputable. Whether or not anyone else is interested in what the writer has to say is another subject entirely.

Objectivity is of very little value in creative writing. Writers cannot write from the heart unless they are willing to open their heart and search within to find the connection between themselves, their characters, and the subject matter. For example, in the classic films *Casablanca* and *The African Queen*, there is clearly a strong thematic point of view on the issue of war. Both movies emphasize patriotism and heroism; both utilize themes of redemption to demonstrate man's innate ability to rise above his own complacency and "fight the good fight." This theme is not only effective from a literary perspective, but it also connected strongly with audiences of its time.

Several decades later, *The Deer Hunter* and *Platoon* similarly dealt with issues of patriotism and heroism, but from a completely different point of view. Times and attitudes toward war had changed considerably, especially since the development of nuclear weapons. Instead of depicting the rise out of complacency to "fight the good fight," these films tended to take a more cynical, pessimistic view on the value of war.

Whereas the themes in *Casablanca* and *The African Queen* moved the central characters from a position of cynicism to patriotism, the central characters in *The Deer Hunter* and *Platoon* tended to move in the opposite direction, from patriotism to distrust and skepticism. But this apparent contradiction is not an indication that one of the themes of war is correct and the other is incorrect. **A theme is a point of view— and there are no incorrect points of view.** Whether or not a writer's particular vision of life and reality is popular or highly regarded at any given time is not really relevant. There will always be detractors from any thematic position a writer holds. Artistically, that's just a risk that must be taken. To only write what is safe and acceptable renders the writing less than honest and seriously diminishes its significance.

It's interesting to note that other film classics, such as *It's a Wonderful Life* and *Citizen Kane*, weren't the resounding hits in their day that they have since become. Artists are visionaries, and sometimes it takes awhile for the views of society to catch up to and understand what a writer has to say.

On the other hand, sometimes a story reaches such a deep level in the human experience that it can withstand cultural mood swings by finding new relevance and meaning in every generation. It's noteworthy that *The African Queen* and especially *Casablanca* have never fallen out of favor with the public, even though perspectives on war have shifted in and out of social acceptance. This is because there is a *layering* effect to the use of theme in a well-crafted story. Layering allows for a subject like patriotism to be invoked as the *external* thematic vehicle (or metaphor) that carries the audience deeper into more profound human issues, such as self-acceptance and unconditional love. While the public's perception of patriotism will ebb and flow with popular opinion, themes of self-acceptance and unconditional love are timeless and always relevant. Therefore, the real journey of Bogart's characters in both *The African Queen* and *Casablanca* wasn't simply from cynicism to patriotism, but from valuelessness to self-worth. This concept also explains how films like *The Deer Hunter* and *Platoon*, which are nearly opposite in their external points of view from *The African Queen* and *Casablanca*, share a kindred link to these two earlier war movies. Once again, the inner journeys of the protagonists lead to a greater internal sense of personal value.

The Language of the Heart

Because the central characters in *The African Queen* and *Casablanca* move toward making patriotic decisions, it's reasonable to assume that the theme of both films is *patriotism*. On the other hand, these aren't just war stories; they are also love stories. So the theme then might also include something about love. Perhaps the theme is *patriotic love*, or how about *sacrificial patriotic love*, or even *love of sacrificing patriots*?

If this sounds a little ridiculous it's because the words *patriotism*, *love*, and *sacrifice* carry no implied value. They are certainly all worthy topics for a theme, but until a writer infuses them with a vision, a perspective, a point of view, or a personal value, they will remain just words.

According to Webster's dictionary,[1] *patriotism* is defined as "love for or devotion to one's country." The dictionary doesn't claim that love for or devotion to one's country is something we all must have. It doesn't tell us that we can't survive without it, nor does it say you're a better or worse person for believing in it. Even though the word *patriotism* may stir up deep feelings in many of us, it does not intrinsically contain a point of view. This is something the writer must subjectively bring to a topic,

---

[1] *Merriam-Webster's Collegiate Dictionary, Tenth Edition* (Springfield, MA: Merriam-Webster, Inc., 1999), 853.

because a concept like patriotism will have a somewhat different meaning for every person who writes about it. **A theme only becomes viable when a writer attaches personal meaning to the subject matter.**

To define a theme, it is helpful to begin by defining the subject or topic that is most pronounced in the story. Then ask yourself what you have to say about these topics. For example, if the thematic subject of a story is *family*, you must decide what you believe to be true about family. One point of view might be that family is the solid foundation from which everything else is made possible. Simplified, the theme could be: *put family first*. That's certainly one perspective on family; however, there are many others. In *The Godfather*, for example, "putting family first" is what destroys Michael.

This implies that there are at least two separate and contrary views about the same subject, *but* they both have value. We need family *and* we need a separate, personal sense of our own identity. If these values are held in balance in a family there is no conflict. But if one value severely dominates the other, then the part that's being ignored is going to cause big problems for the family.

Theme really speaks to an aspect of our human reality that is somehow *out of balance*. The theme of putting family first, for example, is only relevant in a story in which the bonds of support and caring are so obscured or nonexistent that an individual is left feeling isolated and disconnected. Conversely, if a family's sense of belonging is out of balance relative to the needs of an individual, that individual's self-identity can become so damaged that he or she suffers from disconnection and isolation as well. Always look below the surface to understand the true source of the imbalance.

Somewhere rooted in most thematic ideas is a core human value we all share. However, nearly every value we hold has an opposite and equal value that is just as important. For example, we need each other *and* we need a sense of personal autonomy. Sometimes we need to sacrifice for the benefit of others *and* sometimes we need to make sure that our own needs are met above all else.

The basis of all conflict is that something is out of balance. To understand the theme of a story, it's good practice for a writer to step back and assess what is out of balance in the human condition. A married couple doesn't get divorced simply because someone leaves the cap off the toothpaste. An incident such as this can be the final straw that pushes a bad relationship over the edge, but this couldn't happen unless it was already tipped too far in one direction.

Even with strong social issues such as racism, it's not enough to show that bigots are bigots. Hatred is such a strong emotion that it certainly indicates there is a great imbalance in the emotional perspective of a character. If a writer doesn't look deeper into the source of this imbalance, what's the point of the story? The purpose of this sort of introspection is not to make hateful characters more sympathetic, but to offer some insight into the tragic reality behind their behavior and their life choices.

When we watch powerfully thematic films like *The African Queen* and *Casablanca*, we hardly think of patriotism or heroism or any other kind of "ism." The language of theme transcends external realities and confronts us with the reflection of our own heart. In these depths, what we know to be true is that **none of us invents what it means to be human; we are all the same except in the details.** Therefore, the war that is being fought in both of these stories reflects a battle that rages inside all of us: to defeat alienation and isolation in order to become more fully human.

Finding the Thematic Goal

In essence, theme is a sort of *mission statement*. Narrowing the thematic intention from a subject or a concept to a singular point of view automatically pulls the story into clearer focus. It reveals what the writer is trying to achieve through telling the story.

This *singular* thematic point of view is akin to the *one-train-can-only-arrive-at-one-destination* principle discussed in the chapter on plot. A story can't tolerate more than one theme because dissimilar themes will pull the story in different, unrelated directions. This doesn't mean, however, that a single theme can't have many secondary ideas related to it. In fact, as a writer pulls back the layers of a theme, he or she often discovers that what's on the surface is not what the story is really about. This is also true if we examine our own lives. The real conflicts that demand our attention are often buried under superficial distractions that draw our attention away from the real issues. When couples argue over money, money is seldom the source of their actual problems. Liquor is only what overwhelms the alcoholic on the outside; it is often a lack of self-esteem that is calling for attention. Poverty doesn't create violence; ignorance, isolation, and lovelessness are the real culprits. And we can't stop racism with just placards and rhetoric; it will be healed when we heal our own hearts.

Theme is often found in an interrelated group of ideas. In *Dead Poets Society*, the writer, Tom Schulman, makes a strong and simple thematic statement of purpose a few minutes into the film. John Keating, the teacher, tells his young, impressionable students: *Carpe diem...Seize the day*. Go forth and make something great of your lives.

It's a good theme, clearly set up, but what specifically is a writer supposed to do with that concept besides preach about it? How does something so large and philosophical become integrated into a story so that by the end of the film the audience is feeling, not just acknowledging, its meaning? Thematic poignancy is established through the audience's identification with what a character is experiencing and feeling. While *seize the day* is a fine thematic concept, it's not really an activity—but in this film it becomes one.

Remember, **in order to become *tangible*, a theme must become material, visible, discernible; for that to happen, it has to take on qualities that can be expressed *physically* in both plot and character.** Therefore, the writer's challenge is to give a notion like *seize the day* an *interpretation* that will make it a physical challenge for the protagonist.

Because *Dead Poets Society* is about a group of boys who are struggling to grow up, it's reasonable to assume that *seize the day* is meant to be a sort of prescription for manhood. On the most basic level, "seize" means "to take hold of," but it also implies a sense of forceful-ness or urgency. "The day" can certainly be interpreted as a metaphor for this moment or every moment that collectively forms a *life*. From this sort of introspective examination of a thematic idea, a writer can begin to pose interesting questions for him- or herself. For example, why is it so urgent for a young man to take control of his life? The answer that seems most obvious, considering the situations in *Dead Poets Society*, is that if he doesn't take control of his life, there are other forces poised and ready to take control of it for him.

Isn't this what Luke Skywalker battles for, as well? His father, Darth Vader, tries to bend him to his will, but Luke's resistance to his father is the very thing that ultimately makes him discover the strength of his own manhood.

The simple idea that we must take control of our own lives adds dimensionality to the theme of *Dead Poets Society* and brings the physical expression of *seize the day* more clearly into focus. The boys aren't going to randomly go out into the world and vaguely start seizing things. Instead, they are challenged to take control of their lives by defending and fighting for who they are—*their own true nature*—which must be honored and valued above all else.

Through the development of the theme, tangible goals start to come into focus that will determine the conflict of the plot and the internal struggle in the subplots. What started as only an admonishment to "seize the day" is transformed into a line of action that the story will follow: *To become men, the boys must learn to be true to their nature in order to TAKE control of their own lives.* Their challenge is to discover who they are apart from their fathers' vision of what they "should" become. This sets up the conflict of the plot, and **where there is con-flict, action follows.**

It's important to see the relationship between *plot* and *character* development not as a random or accidental occurrence, but as one that is purposely designed to express the writer's thematic perspective.

Setting Up a Thematic Structure

The plot may be the first thing the writer intuitively creates, but as the story is processed, it is the needs of the character that must ultimately define the journey. Therefore, defining the nature of that journey is vital to making non-random choices in the development of both character and plot.

As we have seen with *Dead Poets Society*, thematic intention produces the motivation for the protagonist and defines the **internal** quest. But this represents only half of what the theme is capable of providing the story. Theme also helps establish the **external** issues that will drive the conflict of the plot. Remember, it is the external obstacles that force the protagonist to look inward. The greatest of all obstacles is the *antagonist*, who has an agenda that usually opposes both the internal and external goals of the protagonist. For example, if the theme of a story has to do with trust, then the antagonist may be untrustworthy or irrationally suspicious of the protagonist. If the theme expresses the need to stand up for what you believe in, the antagonist may be a repressive force that demands conformity and blind allegiance. **The theme sets up the obstacles that the protagonist must overcome in the outer world in order to achieve the internal goal of** *transformation.*

In *Dead Poets Society*, the boys cannot *seize the day* or take control of their lives if they allow their individual spirits to be held hostage by their fathers' fears and offered as a sacrifice to the gods of privilege, security, and conformity. What they need from the external world (plot) is a validation of their individuality, which of course may not be possible at their school. But this need for validation sets up a goal that defines the primary conflict of the plot. It tells the writer specifically what the antagonists are like, because they represent the force against which the boys must struggle. This repressive force does not value their individuality or their creative spirit, and the young men are going to be compelled to make a choice: become like their fathers and follow in their footsteps, or have the courage to carve out their own unique path in life. One of these choices is life-enhancing; the other is not.

Even though all of the specific details of character and plot have not yet been detailed, the theme has so far defined the internal and external needs of the protagonist. The big picture—which tells us what the story is really about—is starting to come into focus.

In the big picture, *Dead Poets Society* is becoming a story about finding the courage to choose between living your life in all its pain and all its glory on your own creative, authentic terms, or withering into the inauthentic nothingness of obligation, respectability, and conformity. The theme *seize the day* is *internalized* in the characterization of the young students, who are challenged to discover and honor the calling of their own **true nature.** The theme is *externalized* in the movement of the plot by creating a conflict around which the boys will be forced to stand up for themselves against powerful forces that refuse to value their individuality.

Utilizing intention to define plot and character enables us to begin to break down the organic structure of a story in broad, thematic terms. In *Dead Poets Society*, the subject of the theme is **manhood.** The thematic perspective or point of view on manhood seems to be that it can only be accomplished by **seizing the day,** which, in the context of this story, means that the boys must **take control of their lives.** In order to achieve this control, the plot is designed around a struggle for **individual value.** This tells us that the antagonists, who represent the obstacle the boys must overcome, will de-*value* their individualism. To defeat this repressive force, the boys will have to transcend their youthful dependence on parental and social approval, and learn to stand up for their own needs. In other words, they can't demand to be valued as individuals until they learn to **value their own authentic nature** themselves.

Here's how the theme begins to break down:

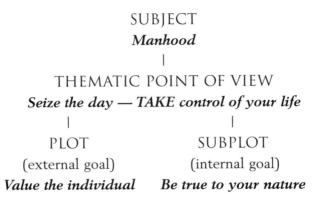

Through theme, the foundation or bone structure of the script has begun to form. When you are at this point in the development of a story, don't worry if the values that start to emerge sound unoriginal. In fact, a strong theme is usually one that is an essential part of our life experience, which means that we have a great need to hear it expressed over and over. Originality isn't dependant on what you have to say, but how you say it.

A film that has a similar thematic bone structure to *Dead Poets Society* is *The Piano*, beautifully written and directed by Jane Campion. The outer metaphors within which these two stories are told are vastly different, yet the thematic structure is very much alike.

The plot of *The Piano* places the protagonist, Ada, in a society that likewise encourages conformity and disdains acknowledging that which is authentic and unique in the individual. Ada is an exceptional woman who is considered odd because she refuses to speak and is subsequently shuttled away to a remote corner of the world to enter into a loveless, prearranged marriage. If the only thing the film centered on was the *external* theme of intolerance (represented in the plot as society's inability to accept her as an extraordinary individual), then the story would simply observe the downward spiral of a wounded soul who is further diminished by her experiences. However, because there is a powerful *internal* theme to this parable that has to do with the responsibility of the individual to fight for one's authentic identity, Ada must seize the opportunity, like the boys in *Dead Poets Society*, in order to transcend her environment and flourish, which she does. Therefore, instead of her languishing as a victim, we see Ada transform into a heroic figure.

Case Studies

In the following three films, I've attempted to demonstrate different ways to break down the thematic structure. Bear in mind that this is a very subjective and personal process, for which there are no right answers. If you find yourself disagreeing with my analysis, use it as an opportunity to play with the theme and see what resonates with you and where that takes you. In areas where you have a strong reaction to a theme—positive or negative—be especially conscious that you may be dealing with something much more important to you than you realize. Therefore, always approach theme work with caution and immense respect.

1) ROMANCING THE STONE

It's helpful to begin processing the theme of a story by looking at what is obvious. In *Romancing the Stone*, it isn't necessary to search any deeper than the fact that this is a *love* story in order to identify the primary topic of the theme. By their very nature, all romances fall into this category because "love" is what you're writing about. However, love is such a vast subject that the next step, to define what you have to say about love, demands a lot more work and personal reflection.

To proceed with the process of identifying a theme, don't ignore any other obvious symbolism or imagery. For example, in *Romancing the Stone* the most obvious characteristic of this particular romance is that it is an *adventure*. But what exactly is an adventure? Words can be great keys to unlocking a story's meaning. Look them up in a dictionary, make a list of their similes, and reference them with some of your favorite literary passages, especially mythological or other archetypal sources. Meditate and pray upon them, if you like, and discuss them with friends, associates, therapists, or clergy who can help you gain personal insight. Most importantly, ask yourself how any of this connects with personal experiences and insights that may reveal why this topic is inspiring to you.

For me the word *adventure* brings up the idea of stepping off into the unknown. If I know exactly what I'm in for, it's not much of an adventure. An adventure opens up the possibility of encountering something or someone new, and perhaps even discovering a hidden treasure. But the word also provokes thoughts of darker possibilities.

I returned to Webster's dictionary[2] and found that it defined "adventure" as:

1. *An undertaking involving danger and unknown risks*

2. *An exciting or remarkable experience*

I thought about how natural it is to want to have experiences that are *exciting and remarkable*, because they renew and energize our spirit. After all, energy is the food of all life; without the renewal of our energy supply, we die. Therefore, I would think we'd all want to run headlong into the arms of an adventure to be revitalized—but we don't. This is probably because the *danger and unknown risks* that also lurk around an adventure could potentially harm or kill us.

What's a girl like Joan to do?

If taking an adventure means that Joan will go where she has never gone before, then to stay out of the adventure means that she will stay only in the same place she's already been. There is nothing fresh, stimulating, invigorating, or remarkable about that place; it's life*less*—without renewable energy. And where there is no energy, there is no life. It's an interesting paradox: We fear leaping into the adventure of life because it *may* kill us, and we opt instead to embrace the familiar and the secure that contains no renewable energy, which means it *will definitely* kill us. Joan clearly needs the adventure.

The next step in developing the theme is to complete the link between love and adventure. Here again, don't avoid the most obvious connection. Even if a phrase like "Love is an adventure" sounds a little simplistic, it very likely carries a lot of potential and is exactly on target in terms of what the story wants to communicate about love. Clichés

---

[2] *Merriam-Webster's Collegiate Dictionary, Tenth Edition* (Springfield, MA: Merriam-Webster, Inc., 1999), 17.

only tend to get stuck at the trite and hackneyed level if no real substance is developed around them.

As an adventure, love does indeed take us to places we have never been before. It is exciting, thrilling, exhilarating, and remarkable, and yet even in the best of circumstances there are no guarantees for the outcome. With love, danger and unknown risk are not only possible, but the deeper you love, the more you have at stake. Here's an interesting quote I came across in Erica Jong's book *How to Save Your Own Life:*

> *Do you want me to tell you something really subversive? Love is everything it's cracked up to be. That's why people are so cynical about it... It really is worth fighting for, being brave for, risking everything for. And the trouble is, if you don't risk anything, you risk even more.*[3]

A strong theme is clearly starting to emerge. As a theme, *love is an adventure* is rich with dramatic potential because it aims right at the heart of the fear that keeps so many of us from taking a chance on love. There's no question that *Romancing the Stone* is a light-hearted romp, but it's a nourishing romp. And fortunately or unfortunately, it has spoken to a wider audience than all the great romantic poets ever could.

The final step in the process of creating a thematic structure is to convert the theme into something that the protagonist can *act* upon. Remember: **Theme is expressed through the *actions* of the *protagonist*.** If Joan Wilder is heading into an adventure, where possible danger and risk lies in wait around every corner, she's going to have to make some sort of internal shift in order to leave the safety of her apartment and venture into the great unknown. To do this she has to acquire some courage—*the courage to face the adventure that leads to love.*

But courage is not a physical substance that a person can simply consume or wear; it's an aspect of our character that implies strength of the heart and spirit. The two essential qualities that Joan will need in order to develop this kind of courage are: *trust* in the path that opens before her, and *faith* that it

---

[3] Erica Jong, *How to Save Your Own Life* (Austin, TX: Holt, Rinehart and Winston, 1977).

will lead to someplace great. The need to acquire *trust* in the road ahead tells us that the antagonist of the plot must be untrustworthy—full of danger and peril. But Joan can stand up to this terrifying force if she learns to have faith and accept that her heart will take her where she needs to go.

The need to acquire trust and faith not only gives dimension to the theme, but it also adds the substance from which plot and character can be developed (which will be the focus of the next chapter). Joan now has *goals* she can *act* upon that will bring the theme to life.

With this information, the thematic structure is beginning to form. The subject of the theme of *Romancing the Stone* is **love**. The writer's point of view on this topic is that **love is an adventure.** To keep this perspective from becoming corny and overly sentimental, deeper aspects of the theme are integrated into the plot and subplots. In the conflict of the plot, Joan is called upon to save her sister, but she can only achieve this goal if she learns to **trust the adventure.** Trusting the adventure is something that Joan is incapable of doing when the story begins, so it will take an internal *transformation of character* for her to accomplish this goal. Joan's transformation is expressed in the subplot, where she is challenged to find the courage to **follow her heart.** Only her heart can keep her on course as she faces the peril and danger of the unknown that leads to true love—the treasure at the end of the adventure.

This is how the theme begins to break down:

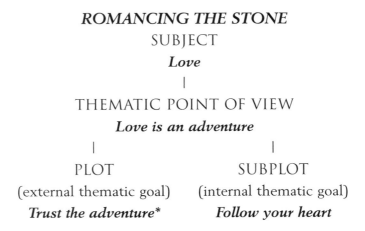

ROMANCING THE STONE
SUBJECT
Love

|

THEMATIC POINT OF VIEW
Love is an adventure

| |

PLOT   SUBPLOT
(external thematic goal)   (internal thematic goal)
Trust the adventure*   ***Follow your heart***

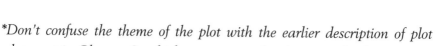

Don't confuse the theme of the plot with the earlier description of plot development in Chapter 2, which was to save Joan's sister. The theme represents the personal value that lies inside the conflict of saving Joan's sister.

2) LETHAL WEAPON

Because the plot of stopping a dangerous drug cartel is so generic, it's probably safe to assume that the writer's inspiration for *Lethal Weapon* came from the more interesting idea of a "bad ass" cop with a death wish. Regardless, this is definitely the most prominent feature of the story and, therefore, the best place to look for thematic subject matter. Here again, begin with what is obvious: This is an "adventure" film and the protagonist is obsessed with "death."

Whereas most heroes have to duel with death, what's particularly interesting about Martin Riggs is that he, instead, dances with her. Why is Lady Death so alluring to him? What does she offer? Taken literally, she offers *nothing*—as in nothingness, oblivion, the great void. For Riggs, this kind of nothing is better than the unendurable pain he's had to live with since the loss of his wife. Death may feel like the only way to put an end to his suffering.

The problem is, how does anyone really know that death is nothing? If there is no certainty that death is nothing, then death becomes an unknown, which makes it a risky and potentially dangerous option. Unknown *risks and danger*, hmmm…. Maybe this means that death, itself, is an adventure, which indicates that somewhere in the equation *the exciting* and *the remarkable* are also possible, and this is where new **life** is found.

So the subject of this film isn't just death; it's also about the possibility of renewing life, and both Riggs and Murtaugh are going to have to choose between them. Wherever there is a duality of opposing forces, be aware that you are most likely dealing with thematic material that addresses the need for *union*. This is the union of opposing parts of the self that requires the energy of the other half to make life whole and functional and bring it back into *balance*. We often hit a crisis in our lives when we pour an imbalance of energy into one area and sacrifice or starve another. For example, a person overworks to provide a big, fancy home for his or her family, but by denying them the very time and attention needed to *be* a family, the goal is lost.

As I stated earlier, when exploring theme, use any reference sources that may stimulate your understanding of the material. In my case, because I have a background in myth, I often look to these classic stories for inspiration. When I was considering the issues of life and death, balance, and the union of opposites, I thought about the myth of Castor and Pollux from Greek and Roman mythology. In this story, these brothers are inseparable until the day Castor is killed in battle. Inconsolable in his grief, Pollux beseeches Jupiter to allow him to give his own life so that his brother may be revived. Touched by the sincerity of Pollux's devotion, Jupiter allows them both to live. But there is a stipulation: Each must pass one day on Earth and the next in Heaven, in opposition to each other. Thus they form a perfect tension of the whole, like the rise and fall of a single breath. They are separate, but interdependent forces that are united as one.

It occurred to me that perhaps this is what Martin's grief is really about. He needs to be made whole again and his grief represents the unbearable emptiness of his missing half. He is seeking wholeness, union, connection. But why is this task so difficult for a strong, brave warrior like Martin? Certainly the death of his wife was terrible, but most of us will face the death of a loved one in our lifetime without becoming as completely bereft of hope as Martin.

Considering the theme of the story in this context, it's important to ask: What part of himself did Martin bury with his wife that the gods must resurrect if he is to survive? Her presence in this world obviously gave him something that he now feels is completely out of his own grasp.

In Carol Pearson's book *The Hero Within* (which I highly recommend), she reveals some powerful insights about the transcendent journey of the warrior archetype:

Warriors first develop confidence by proving their superiority to others, because they have taken more control over their own lives than most and make things happen while others seem to wait passively for things to happen to them. One of the gifts, then, when control fails, is the dawning recognition that fundamentally we are not all that different from one another. We are all in the same boat, and we are all, ultimately, inter-dependent: We need other people; we need the earth; we need God.[4]

Perhaps Martin's wife filled that need. She gave him something that slaying all the dragons in the world could never deliver: a sense of connection; the knowledge that he was not alone. He could finally rest in her arms. He didn't have to be the solitary, isolated warrior anymore. He found his home, his center, his renewable source of energy—and then it was taken away.

This may mean that the grief Martin suffers is really about the loss of this connection, and he is searching for the resurrection of that bond. But Jupiter did something very interesting when he restored Castor; he allowed the twins to be connected to each other in the same world and exist in each other's orbit, but they had to remain separate. In other words, the union of these opposites didn't make them one, but it did make them whole.

To resurrect his sense of wholeness, Martin needs to make a connection again. This is an important clue to the thematic structure of this story—and it also explains why having a co-protagonist is such an excellent choice for this film. (However, don't be concerned at this point in the development of the theme if most of your attention is focused on one of the co-protagonists over the other. If one of the characters seems dominant, it's probably because he or she carries the most thematic information, and that's what you're trying to understand. In the next chapter we'll begin to delineate with more specificity the role of each of the co-protagonists, especially as it relates to the theme.)

The subject of the theme of *Lethal Weapon* is not just death, but **life and death,** because they express the duality of the conflict, which is

---

[4] Carol S. Pearson, *The Hero Within: Six Archetypes We Live By* (San Francisco: Harper-San Francisco, 1986, 1989), 96.

what the co-protagonists are challenged to bring into balance. Ultimately, because this is a story of renewal, the thematic value developed
around the subject of *life and death* is that death will choose us soon
enough, and in the meantime we must **choose life.**

The next level of developing this theme is to decide how this value
will be internalized and externalized. Internally, it's clear that in order
to choose life Martin Riggs must connect, or reconnect, to others. He
needs others in order to find his own wholeness. Isolated, he won't survive; connected, he will flourish. As a warrior, however, he can only
achieve this level of understanding if the challenge of the plot, *to stop
the dangerous drug cartel*, offers him the opportunity to learn to **value
life** instead of obliterating it.

This is how the thematic structure is beginning to take shape:

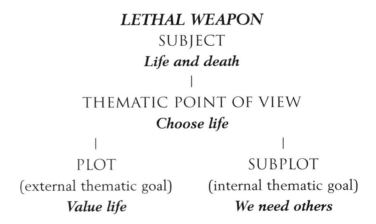

LETHAL WEAPON
SUBJECT
Life and death
|
THEMATIC POINT OF VIEW
Choose life

PLOT	SUBPLOT
(external thematic goal)	(internal thematic goal)
Value life	**We need others**

3) ORDINARY PEOPLE

Before beginning a thematic analysis of a character-driven film like
Ordinary People, let me offer a few words of caution: Don't confuse story
analysis with psychoanalysis. Most of us don't have psychoanalytic skills,
and that's not our job. Writers need to stay with what they know, which
is looking into the human condition with an honest heart. If your background happens to include a certain working knowledge of modern
psychology, philosophy, sociology, or mythology, that's terrific. It's a

part of you and therefore it's an excellent resource for the purpose of personal reflection. This background may confirm, explain, echo, or deepen what you know. In fact, don't hesitate to do a little digging in these areas; just don't go overboard, as it will merely become a mental distraction. On the other hand, it really doesn't matter if your views on life are underdeveloped or unsophisticated: **The value of your thematic message lies in the sincerity and the honesty with which you are willing to expose your own humanity to the rest of us.**

As I began working with the theme of *Ordinary People*, the first thing that appeared obvious was that the subject of the theme of this story is *family*. So this is where I dove in and began to contemplate the meaning of that word. For the most part my personal feelings on the subject of family were positive, which made me think about the phrase *family values*. I couldn't help but wonder exactly whose family we're valuing and why. When I see pictures of KKK families at church socials, eating apple pie and teaching their kids to *"heil Hitler"* while burning crosses, I have the uncomfortable feeling that these people believe they epitomize the good in "family values." This probably means that most of us also believe that our own moderate-to-highly dysfunctional families are portraits of virtue as well. And how could we know otherwise? Our own families are the primary frame of reference most of us have, and even if our home environment looks more like a battle zone than a comfort zone, it must be good and virtuous or why else would we live this way?

Sorting out what's true and valuable in his family is more difficult for Conrad, the suicidal son in *Ordinary People*, than it is for most people, because his family looks better than most. They're rich, hardworking, polite, attractive, orderly, and cordial. Mom serves french toast for breakfast on a normal school day and they get pressed, linen napkins with dinner every night. Best of all, they don't waste their time on any of that messy emotional stuff. Intimacy for them means maintaining control over their feelings at all times so that others won't feel uncomfortable. There seems to be no strife, no struggle, no discord. This isn't just an ordinary family, it's an *ideal* family. So, what's wrong with this picture?

To determine what's out of balance in a conflict, always look at which direction the energy is flowing. In this story, a huge imbalance of the energy is flowing away from the individual to support the ideal of a perfect family.

Once again, this took me back to my mythological roots and I thought about how the great myths tend to warn against identifying with an ideal. In Ovid's story of Narcissus, the young boy is so smitten when he sees his beautiful reflection in a pond that he loses track of everything else and dies of hunger trying to grab hold of his perfect image that vanishes every time he touches the water. In other words, his ideal didn't really exist except as an illusion, and he wasted away worshipping it. All his energy went out to this illusion, and nothing came back to nourish him. In Conrad's family, everyone pays homage to the image of the ideal family. All their energy is directed toward sustaining the illusion of happiness, leaving their souls starving for something of substance.

In her book *The Drama of the Gifted Child*, Alice Miller explains the consequences of fixating on a perfect image that doesn't really exist.

Narcissus wanted to be nothing but the beautiful youth; he totally denied his true self. In trying to be at one with the beautiful picture, he gave himself up—to death.... This death is the logical consequence of the fixation on the false self.... His passion for his false self makes impossible not only love for others but also, despite all appearances, love for the one person who is fully entrusted to his care: himself.[5]

Tragically, because the needs of the family in *Ordinary People* are so far out of balance to the needs of the individual, the imbalance not only threatens the life of the only remaining son, but it also threatens the existence of the family unit. The theme of family, therefore, centers on the

---

[5] Alice Miller, *The Drama of the Gifted Child: The Search for the True Self* (New York: Basic Books, 1994), 86.

question: Does the family serve the needs of the individual, or does the individual sacrifice his needs to serve the illusion of an ideal family?

Stated this way, it's hardly a choice. But in our own lives the sacrifice of our true self to religion, country, and family is often deemed heroic. Accommodation to the true self is usually characterized as selfish and arrogant.

This particular theme of how we value ourselves within the family structure is extremely powerful. Even families that are on the higher end of the emotionally responsive food chain tend to view individual members, to some degree, as supporting players. Therefore, the primary function of the individual is to help hold the family illusion in balance. Whether a person is the star of the family, the rebel, the caretaker, or the scapegoat, there is often an unspoken yet very strongly held belief that if anyone steps out of his or her role into his or her own true identity, the family will collapse. Of course, what is really threatened is the collapse of the illusion, but that is precisely why any attempts at authenticity in a family may be met with hostility, both overt and covert.

This elevates the quest for one's true, authentic identity to the stature of heroic. Look at the mountain of shame, guilt, fear, and self-loathing that an intrepid soul, such as Conrad, must navigate. And yet if he doesn't make the journey, what else is there for him but the illusion of a life, not an authentic one?

Finding the theme of a story often entails peeling back layers of meaning until you begin to see a reflection of your own life: your choices, your sacrifices, your illusions, and your pain. When it starts to hurt, when you get angry, sad, or depressed, then you know you've hit real thematic pay dirt. In fact, if it doesn't touch your emotions, you aren't there yet. This isn't something you can intellectualize, because *if it's not touching your emotions, you can bet it won't touch the audience either.* It takes a lot of processing to identify a theme, and there are no shortcuts. Getting just this far may take days, frustrating days, when you know you're onto something but articulating it remains just outside of your grasp.

So, what is really at stake for the family in *Ordinary People*? On the surface, Conrad attempted suicide because he holds himself in contempt for his brother's death. But it feels like the tragedy in this family occurred long before the fair-haired son drowned. Somewhere along the way, choices were made, and perhaps handed down for generations, that encouraged this family to hide from personal identity and place all value on the institution of family rather than on the individuals who comprise it. Where then does an individual like Conrad get his value? The truth seems to be that there is none to be had, which Mom aptly demonstrates by her willingness to sacrifice her only living child on the altar of her illusion of perfection.

The subject of the theme of *Ordinary People* is **family.** What this film has to say about family is defined by what is missing in the relationship between Conrad and his parents: They must learn **to value each other.** But this can only happen if the plot forces the Jarretts to begin to place a **value on the needs of the individual.** This will necessitate an internal transformation wherein they learn to place a **value on their own needs.** The marriage between Beth and Calvin can no longer stand as a mere façade, and if Conrad is to be pulled back from the suicidal brink, he will have to learn to care for himself, or he will never be able to stand up to life's misfortunes and disappointments.

The thematic structure for *Ordinary People* is beginning to take shape:

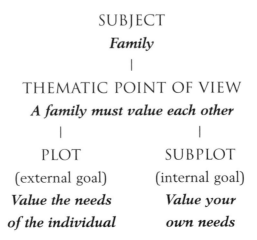

SUBJECT
Family
|
THEMATIC POINT OF VIEW
A family must value each other
| |
PLOT   SUBPLOT
(external goal)   (internal goal)
Value the needs   *Value your*
of the individual   *own needs*

Write What You Don't Know

The process of finding your story's theme takes time and a lot of thought and emotional processing. But this is the most essential work a writer will do and it demands complete immersion into the process.

An important part of this process is to let your thematic ideas flow. The theme of a story is something that reveals itself in layers, which means that every discovery and self-revelation is but an opening into the stream of greater consciousness. Therefore, you may process your theme to a certain point and move forward with the development of your story, only to later realize that there's more to it than you initially understood. This is not only okay; if you allow yourself to move with the flow, your writing will remain fresh and you will remain inspired.

Whereas we can only write what we know to be true in terms of the thematic values that have personal meaning to us, I've come to recognize that we are also called to *write what we don't know*. In other words, the thematic ideas that may inspire and instigate the writing process are usually values of which a writer is already somewhat aware. The creative need to explore those values already integrated into our lives is really rather minimal. But because internal development is an ongoing process, it's far more likely that the conscious impulse that is calling your attention to start the writing process is only the doorway to something deeper inside you that is trying to find expression.

If your theme is not chiseled in stone, it will have the elasticity to expand and grow, just as you do. The greatest thing that can happen to you in the writing process is to experience your own illumination, and this will come if you allow for change. Achieving this sort of flexibility often entails **penciling in your thematic ideas to the best of your ability and just moving on, trusting that the more you write, the more insight you will gain.** Writing is always at its best when it pushes past what we *think* and begins to tap into what we *feel*. In fact, writers who find themselves standing on shifting sands are much more likely to hit something fresh and exciting than those who only move forward when every step is paved in concrete.

As promised, what has been forged here with the theme is a powerful tool that will help move your writing process from trial and error to intention and purpose. In fact, the more you learn to work with theme, the more you will be able to communicate with style, subtlety, and eloquence the full power of your ideas and your creative vision. Upcoming chapters will utilize theme to develop deeper characters, stronger and more complex plotlines, layers of deepened subtext, and powerful, symbolic imagery that will leave an indelible imprint on the quality of your writing.

CHAPTER FIVE

THE FATAL FLAW
Bringing Characters to Life

Everything grows old,
all beauty fades,
all heat cools,
all brightness dims,
and every truth becomes stale and trite.
For all these things have taken on shape,
and all shapes are worn thin by the working of time;
they age, sicken, crumble to dust—
unless they change.

~ C.G. JUNG

Sacred Trust

Is all our pain and sorrow an absurd cosmic joke, or does it have meaning and value? Are the events in our lives ever an indication of absolutely nothing, or is the smallest activity part of a cumulative effect, defining who and what we are? Do we even exist outside of our experiences, or does that very notion betray the meaning of the word *existence*?

Somewhere encoded in every one of our stories is a conscious or unconscious response to these kinds of questions. Every portrayal of the human experience tells us something significant about ourselves. When it's done consciously, with purpose and intention, we get *Macbeth*, *The Godfather*, and *Schindler's List*. When it's given little conscious attention, we get *Dumb and Dumberer* (literally!).

Because there are no absolute answers to these kinds of questions, it's not necessarily the answers we're searching for. Instead, it is the *process* of the search itself that leads writers to higher ground. Here, broader vistas are opened, exposing greater insight and understanding of ourselves and our relationship to the world around us.

This is the sacred trust that is bestowed upon storytellers—to lead humanity to a higher place by holding up a candle so that the path ahead is illuminated and made a little less treacherous. **If we simply acknowledge in our stories that the events in our life do impact us, we connect on the most fundamental level to everyone else.** We confirm that the wide range of human emotions—including pain, loneliness, sorrow, disappointment, as well as passion, joy, love, and hope—are not only felt by us, but by all of humanity.

Just as there always comes a season when a snake must shed its skin in order to grow, our best stories likewise reveal that we too must shed and leave behind any part of ourselves that is obsolete and no longer benefiting our development. In fact, it is this very cycle of change that expresses the drama of our existence. There is a time when the skin we are in is comfortable, pliable, essential. But there always comes a season when we have filled it to capacity, when the boundary of our reality will expand no more and must be broken open so that a greater part of ourselves can grow in its place.

Because life depends on the ability to shed or leave behind the obsolete and grow into something new, having complete resistance to this process is *fatal*. **When growth stops, only decay and death will follow.** But death comes in many guises. Trying to avoid life's difficulties by numbing ourselves with food, drugs, or alcohol can lead to a real, physical death. However, there are other types of death that destroy us even if our physical bodies are not yet interred. Fear of facing life can kill hopes, dreams, and ambitions. Resistance to growth will destroy love, short-circuit creativity, and annihilate happiness. Manipulation of change leads only to moral decay and death of the inner spirit. If immaturity, cowardice, pride, intolerance, indifference, and deceit go unchecked they will kill everything in their path—most importantly relationships, opportunities, and possibilities.

System Breakdown

Jean Valjean, the tortured hero of Victor Hugo's enduring classic *Les Misérables* (which has been adapted for film and TV over eighteen times worldwide), is brought to his knees by the anguishing realization that he has become a man of no worth. Hugo powerfully describes the tormented depths to which his protagonist has fallen:

> *His cries died away into the mist, without even awaking an echo....* *[H]is knees suddenly bent under him, as if an invisible power suddenly overwhelmed him with the weight of his bad conscience; he fell exhausted...and cried out, "I'm such a miserable man!"* [1]

Having spent the past nineteen years of his life in prison, suffering unendurable hard labor, Jean Valjean has succumbed to such wretchedness that he is bereft of any honor or human compassion. In an effort to retrieve his lost soul from the abyss of eternal darkness, a kindly bishop opens his door and his heart to the ex-con, but Valjean repays his generosity by absconding with the cleric's silver. Even when he is caught and the godly man refuses to press charges, telling the police instead that the silver was a gift, Valjean is unmoved. He has become so hardened by the vile circumstances of his life that in response to this grand gesture of kindness he heads back to the highway, where he robs a young boy of a mere coin. It is the shock of this incomprehensibly wicked deed that finally awakens Valjean to the realization that the misery he now endures is of his own making.

Jean Valjean is one of the great protagonists in Western literature, yet when we first encounter him in the beginning of *Les Misérables*,

---

[1] Victor Hugo, *Les Misérables: Complete and Unabridged* (New York: Signet Classic, 1987), 110.

he is a despicable wretch who seems beneath human contempt. But just as the priest sees value in him, remarkably, so do we. In fact, the more the narrative reveals of his hideous, dismal, squandered existence, the more we find ourselves rooting for his survival and his redemption. Few, if any, of us will experience anything remotely similar to Valjean's horror-filled life, yet somehow we can't help but identify with his pain and emptiness.

We don't see a reflection of our humanity in perfection; we see it in imperfection. This means that if there's hope for Valjean, there's hope for us as well. And this is ultimately what makes a story compelling—not the scenery, the action sequences, the car chases, or the double-crossing plotlines. It is survival on the deepest human level. We identify with what is happening to Valjean because, in some way, it happens to all of us. Through relationships, careers, lifestyles, and so on, we all have invested in systems of survival that have gone bankrupt. And it is at this crisis point that the choice of staying in the old, lifeless vacuum of the past or moving into the new energy of change is most acute. This is the essence of the internal conflict that our stories must capture.

The experience of *system breakdown* has been with us since the moment of conception. The womb itself is our first survival system and it is programmed to self-destruct after just nine months. From there we are jettisoned into a whole new world where our survival relies on a system of complete dependency. But every day of our young lives we acquire skills and deepen our awareness and understanding of the world, so that we are able to someday move away from complete dependency on our parents toward a more independent lifestyle. And whether or not we feel ready for it, there comes a time when we are required to stand on our own. *The system of dependency that was once necessary for survival has broken down and outlived its usefulness.*

But as with all transitions, the move toward independence is a lot more complex in reality than it is in theory. Independence is usually associated with responsibility, dependability, duty, and so on. But what truly makes a person independent is not just the acceptance of his or her obligations, but the acceptance of his or her true nature, which is much harder to come by. So, delusional shortcuts are taken that in fact lead to *dead* ends.

Charlie Allnut (Bogart) in *The African Queen* found his dead end in the bottom of a bottle. But it's important also to examine the character of Rose (Hepburn) in the same film: Is her life any less terminal? Rose is a dried-up spinster who has committed herself to the aforementioned virtues that are supposed to epitomize maturity: responsibility, dependability, duty. Yet where is the feminine, passionate, imaginative part of Rose? Those vital aspects of her nature are buried to the point of near suffocation beneath layers of false virtue. And where did that system of survival get her? She is alone with broken dreams in the middle of the sweltering, war-torn jungle about to face her own extinction.

Consider Jake LaMotta in *Raging Bull:* The same rage that was once applauded and gave him his career and feelings of power and confidence eventually became the means of his self-destruction. His survival system created a false, or at least incomplete, sense of who he was, and so it was doomed to collapse. It always does. **Truth supports life; that which is false will destroy it.**

In *Dead Poets Society* John Keating tries to teach his young students that there is no place to hide from life except in death. We can't live inside our father's skin; we must find the courage to seek our own lives. This holds true whether the father is the quintessence of evil, such as Luke Skywalker's father, Darth Vader, in *Star Wars*, or a paragon of goodness, such as George Bailey's father in *It's a Wonderful Life.*

At the deepest level, our stories warn that the greatest human tragedy is a life that is lived disconnected from its own true nature. The deeper the connection to one's true self, the deeper the connection to others, to nature, and to the divine. Every step that leads toward growth opens up this pathway. Every step taken in retreat moves us further from the light of self-knowledge, self-understanding, and, of course, self-love. Thus it is the quest to *know* ourselves that forms the grand journey of our lives. When writers touch even a small part of this level of self-reflection, they reach into the soul of everyone.

When we are first introduced to Rocky Balboa in *Rocky*, it's immediately evident that his system of survival is falling apart. Even though he could hang around a few more years, brawling with the dregs of humanity, every fight brings him one step closer to his own demise because he's fighting the wrong battles. He isn't fighting to reveal his true nature or to defend it; he's fighting to avoid it. And the vultures are circling—the street hustlers and petty gangsters. They are poised and ready to pick whatever flesh of humanity is left on his bones. But there is a way out. Self-acceptance is always an option, and life offers Rocky exactly what is needed to make that choice, if he's willing to take on the challenge. This is what the fight of his life is really about.

In *Pulp Fiction*, Jules (Samuel L. Jackson) sees this writing on the wall (or more precisely a bullet in the wall). His two-dimensional world, where only the "tyranny of evil men" and their victims dwell, is in a constant state of siege and he suddenly realizes that it is only a dead man's game. There is no level field of battle; it is all rigged in one direction, because even if you are on the tyrant's team there is always someone with a bigger gun. Everyone is someone else's victim, as his partner Vincent (John Travolta) ironically discovers too late when he is shot to death. But Jules realizes that there is another option—a path where the game cannot be rigged, because it is the path of *truth*. This is the option he chooses before it is too late. It is, as he describes it, the path of the "righteous man."

What is consistent in these and countless other great stories is that the power of the drama comes from the internal struggle to either grow or perish. **A survival system that has outlived its usefulness will begin to diminish, not enhance, a person's true value, and it will carry the person only so far before it collapses under its own weight.** Once it runs out of energy, a new, higher level of self-awareness must be achieved for survival. To cling to the old way of being, where the energy is becoming exhausted, is certain death.

In *When Harry Met Sally*, the title characters are first introduced to each other when they are in their early twenties, and both are quite strident in their commitment to their limited view of life. Sally auda-ciously proclaims that most women would rather be in a passionless marriage as the first lady of Czechoslovakia than spend their lives in Casablanca with a man who runs a bar. Harry impassively attributes Sally's parochial notion of love to her never having had great sex. This is a reasonable observation for a hormonally challenged youth, who rebuffs the invitation to friendship with the classic commitment-phobic rejoinder that men and women can never be friends because sex always gets in their way.

Six years later, neither of them can remember making such inane remarks, but neither is yet ready to open the door to true intimacy. They still cling to false images of life and love. So, those irascible gods give them exactly what they wish for. Sally gets her Adonis, complete with stock portfolio and fringe benefits. Harry is bestowed with his very own Venus—chiseled in stone.

Another five years pass and their illusions finally begin to crumble. What is discovered amid the shards and rubble of their broken fantasies are sparkling little fragments of their own deeper natures, at last exposed. Stripped of illusion and finally vulnerable, they both are now open to a friendship that will lead to the intimacy and interconnectedness they've been seeking.

Like dependency, independence is also a survival system that will not sustain and fulfill a person throughout a lifetime. Whereas achieving autonomy does allow us to stand on our own and establish an identity separate from others, it can also set us apart to the point where we become isolated and alone. As we continue to develop, the structure that supports independence will ultimately erode as well so that a more balanced *interdependent* connection to each other, to nature, and to life itself can be formed.

There is no way to grow into any new stage of life without giving up the outer vestiges of who we once were. The child must leave behind carefree days and idle playthings in order to enter the realm of adult-hood. The young adult is required to cast off ego-driven self-indulgences to become a more selfless participant in the world of career, marriage, and family. But these used-up pieces of our old self are seldom surrendered without a struggle, and this is precisely the nature of the internal conflict that is told and retold in all of our stories.

The transformation of character in most great stories deals with the reclamation of Self. Loneliness, emptiness, despair, anger, rage, and apathy are our nursemaids; they care for our souls and are ever present when we abandon our true nature to the illusion of an idealized self. Were it not for their vigilant presence in the form of discontentment, depression, and self-destructive behavior, we might be forever lost. Therefore, if we want to capture the full essence of a character in our stories, it is essential to paint this pain and turmoil into his or her portrait.

Detective Frank Keller, in *Sea of Love,* is a shipwrecked soul who is clinging to life on the last waterlogged plank of his exhausted, one-dimensional identity. Ironically, the dark, murky waters that engulf him and forebode his doom are what he needs to dive into to find his salvation. Frank has sailed through most of his life on the good ship "Yo soy muy macho," valiant in his quest to slay the monsters that inhabit the deep. He doesn't know how else to be. Through tempest and typhoon he has clung to the mast, believing that he must be strong, brave, and, above all, true. But to whom is he true? Courage and strength are mighty weapons, but if they are only employed outwardly they will render that which lies within us unprotected, vulnerable, and defenseless. The abandonment that Frank feels is real, but it is not the abandonment by others that has left him in so much pain. It is he who has abandoned himself, leaving the unwanted and unclaimed parts of his true nature to swim with the monsters in the deep.

Even though *Sea of Love* is a police thriller, it is Frank's inner struggle for a connection to new life that really defines the drama. In the beginning of the story he is depressed, disillusioned, and angry. He's drinking too much and fighting too often. It's clear that he can't go on like this much longer. In fact, in an early scene we catch a glimpse of his father, a liquor-sodden, emaciated sack of bones, who foreshadows the sense of internal doom that awaits Frank if something doesn't change.

As the events of the conflict unfold, Frank is challenged to let go of the last remnants of a false or incomplete life that are holding him afloat. He needs to immerse himself in the real thing; it's time to sink and not just swim or tread water. Naturally, to plunge himself into that unknown part of his being that he has always denied could harm or kill him.

But it doesn't kill Frank. In fact, it feels wonderful, alive, and thrilling. In his investigation to find a serial killer, a potential suspect (Ellen Barkin) arouses emotions and passions in Frank that have been dormant for way too long. With every encounter she energizes his depleted soul. So he dives deeper and deeper, abandoning the rational side of his nature as he immerses himself completely into his passion. But abandonment is still abandonment, and Frank soon learns that to abandon completely the rational side of his nature can be just as lethal as abandoning his emotional, passionate self. Frank's true nature, our true nature, lies in a balance between the two. Ultimately, he must descend to claim his other half and merge into one; otherwise, he will be destroyed.

In the book *The Hero with a Thousand Faces*, Joseph Campbell writes, "One by one the resistances are broken. [The hero] must put aside his pride, his virtue, beauty, and life and bow or submit to the absolutely intolerable. Then he finds that he and his opposite are not of differing species, but of one flesh."[2] As life's pains and disappointments dismantle our illusions, we are constantly being given the opportunity to go deeper and become submerged in the baptismal waters that sanctify and give meaning to our existence.

Sea of Love is a smart, intense, and intoxicating thriller. But what would the story have been like if Frank's inner turbulence had been neglected by the writer? To negate the relationship between who we are and what we experience severely limits the audience's ability to identify and make personal meaning from the story.

A good illustration of this is seen in the film *Ransom*, which happens to also have been written by *Sea of Love* screenwriter, Richard Price

---

[2] Joseph Campbell, *The Hero with a Thousand Faces* (New York: MFJ Books, 1949), 108.

(and Alexander Ignon). This is a tale that is intended to show us how a man who did a corrupt thing brought the disease of that malevolent deed home and infected his family. It is a very powerful thematic idea, but one which never fully develops because the protagonist has no internal conflict. His external experiences impact his life in only the most superficial way.

Mel Gibson plays a wealthy industrialist, Tom Mullen, whose young son is kidnapped and held for $2 million ransom. The plot turns with Tom's sudden realization that no matter what he pays, the ruthless kidnappers will never return his son alive. So Tom decides to turn the tables and put the ransom on the kidnappers' heads. There is no place they can run or hide, he tells them, because he will pay the same $2 million to anyone who turns them in.

This is a terrific setup for a good suspense yarn, but we never become engaged enough to really *care*. As discussed in the first chapter, caring comes only through attaching the audience to the interior experiences of the protagonist, and in this story there just isn't much going on inside. Even though Tom and his wife are appropriately distraught over their son's kidnapping, this is really just a generic reaction that lies on the surface of their characterization. If being distraught is the extent of a character's sensory range, the audience's emotions will likewise be pretty superficial.

There is a lot of character potential in this script that is simply undeveloped. For example, it is made clear that Tom is a crooked businessman, but what does that really mean? He is described as a man who takes shortcuts; if he doesn't like the outcome, he exploits people and events to get what he wants. What this should reveal about his character is that it's rather low, that he's manipulative, deceptive, and unethical. This could not be a courageous man because it takes pure courage to face life on life's terms. Fear of life is what motivates people to lie and deceive. This is the description of a coward. But Tom isn't just any kind of coward, he's a coward with tremendous power, and that makes him a bully, someone who is too afraid to take a risk and trust the outcome, so he fixes the game. And it doesn't matter if someone else gets hurt in the process.

But what if that someone is his son? I'm sure this is not the game Tom signed up for. However, if he wants to play by coward's rules, then the weak are always fair game. What then becomes inevitable is that Tom is a victim of his own actions. This *should* be the connection between who he is and what he experiences. No one exists in a void, which is how the characterization of Tom actually appears in the film. Instead of the complexity just described, Tom is portrayed instead as an ideal. He's a loving, devoted husband and a terrific, supportive father—who also just happens to do dishonest things on the side. But that doesn't interfere with domestic bliss and, were it not for these really evil kidnappers who invade his ideal world, life would be forever blissful.

In other words, Tom's survival system, where the ends justify the means, is indestructible as long as *really* bad guys don't come along. What a deal! He gets to survive by deceit but exist as a righteous man. I bet Tom can't wait to share this life lesson with his son. Of course, teaching his child to be deceitful isn't a very good thing. But that doesn't matter—Tom will always be righteous because that's how he *acts*. And to be his wife, now there's a bargain. He might be a deceitful bully out of the home, but when he's in her lovin' arms he's always good and true. One thing has nothing to do with the other.

Or does it? This is hardly the way our own lives play out and it's the reason we can't connect with this type of story; there's no way in. There's no point where the audience can identify with the protagonist because he doesn't exist, except in make-believe. This is not to say that a corrupt man cannot be a nice guy at home; at least he can try. He can certainly have a pleasant outward demeanor. But if we know ourselves through our experiences, then what Tom *knows* about life is that it is something he must relentlessly control and manipulate so that he gets the results he wants.

To create a realistic character, it's essential to be consistent with this paradigm. Life might be very congenial at home, on the surface, but the audience must also sense that behind the façade there is something very uncomfortable. This is the *dis-ease* of the corrupted or false self with which Tom has infected his family. His need to control everything is not like a pair of gloves that he can take off when he enters the house to protect the people he loves from contamination.

If the storyline had truly reflected a strong thematic intention, then Tom's experience with the kidnappers would have afforded him the opportunity to look at himself in the mirror. The kidnapper clearly tells him that he chose Tom because he knows he is corrupt and pays to avoid life's difficulties. How does the kidnapper "know" this when he looks into Tom's eyes? Does he perhaps see his own corrupt reflection in Tom?

And, where does Tom's sudden epiphany that the kidnappers will never release his son alive come from? He's so certain about this that he bets his son's life that he can get the kidnappers to back down. This must mean that Tom has some inner awareness that ultimately the kidnappers are cowards. But, because Tom is such an idealized good guy it's impossible to relate this sudden awareness to Tom's own self-knowledge. It just comes to him from out of the blue, which is a pretty shaky place, especially when his son's life hangs in the balance.

Might it not have been much more realistic and far more dramatically interesting if Tom's sudden understanding had come from an abrupt awareness that if the kidnapper knows him, then perhaps he knows the kidnapper as well, that they are the same? And if they are the same, then the kidnapper's weakness is his weakness too. To face his weakness, his own cowardice, is a first and valiant step of *real* courage. And *then* to not pay the ransom is an act of true heroism.

How we face our experiences determines who we are. And there is simply no greater purpose for telling our stories.

The Fatal Flaw

Growth is the by-product of a cycle that occurs in nature; that which flowers and fruits will also eventually wither and go to seed. The seed, of course, contains the potential for renewal, but does not guarantee it, nor does the seed instantly *spring* to new life. There is a necessary dormancy where the possibility of death holds life in suspended anima-tion. As Thomas Moore explains in his book *Care of the Soul*, "We become persons through dangerous experiences of darkness; we can survive these difficult initiations. Any real initiation is always a move-ment from death to new life."[3] The irony, of course, is that in any moment when we face death we likewise feel most alive.

In the cycles of our lives, these near-death moments are rich with heightened dramatic possibilities that the writer wants to capitalize upon. These are the moments in the human drama where the stakes are the highest, where our choices matter the most: *What's it going to be, life or death?* For a story to be dramatically interesting and thematically important the protagonist must be at the point of great internal com-bustibility, where the conflict in his or her outer life demands inner transformation if survival is to be achieved.

This brings up the most essential demand for a well-dramatized script: **In order to create a story that expresses transformation, a need for that transformation must be established.** It is within this context that I can best define the **fatal flaw of character.**

First, it's important to recap or highlight the fundamental premise on which the fatal flaw is based:

- Because change is essential for growth, it is a mandatory require-ment for life.
- If something isn't growing and developing, it can only be headed toward decay and death.
- *There is no condition of stasis in nature.* Nothing reaches a perma-nent position where neither growth nor diminishment is in play.

As essential as change is to renew life, most of us resist it and cling rigidly to old survival systems because they are familiar and "seem"

---

[3] Thomas Moore, *Care of the Soul: A Guide for Cultivating Depth and Sacredness in Everyday Life* (New York: HarperCollins Publishers, 1994), 47.

safer. In reality, even if an old, obsolete survival system makes us feel alone, isolated, fearful, uninspired, unappreciated, and unloved, we will reason that it's easier to cope with what we know than with what we haven't yet experienced. As a result, most of us will fight to sustain destructive relationships, unchallenging jobs, unproductive work, harmful addictions, unhealthy environments, and immature behavior long after there is any sign of life or value in them.

This unyielding commitment to old, exhausted survival systems that have outlived their usefulness, and resistance to the rejuvenating energy of new, evolving levels of existence and consciousness is what I refer to as the *fatal flaw of character.*

The FATAL FLAW is a struggle within a character to maintain a survival system long after it has outlived its usefulness.

In *It's a Wonderful Life*, George Bailey has committed himself to a survival system that operates under the assumption that if he takes care of everyone else, somehow, magically, his own needs will be met as well. There was a time in George's life when developing his ability to care about the needs of others helped George grow into a more loving and less self-serving human being. Powerful feelings of self-worth accompanied these actions. He felt good about himself because he was getting as much as he was giving. His life had a balance to it. But there came a point of diminishing returns when the value of what was coming in was no longer equal to the value of what was going out. As more and more demands were made on George to put the needs of family and community above his own, his identity as a caretaker became fixed. Other aspects of George's nature were suppressed or ignored and the only things that grew in their place were anger and resentment. The system of putting everyone else's needs before his own was breaking down and George felt unhappy and unfulfilled, but he continued to heave all his energy outward until the day when there was absolutely nothing left. That was the day he decided to jump off a bridge.

The flaw in George's limited perception of his own identity was about to prove fatal. Therefore, the real drama of the story centered on his ability to expand this self-perception by reclaiming his greater value before it was too late.

Identifying and utilizing the fatal flaw is one of the most powerful tools a writer can develop. It distinguishes an aspect of character that not only determines behavior, but also establishes the internal conflict that will ultimately drive the story. George's *fatal flaw*, his inability to fulfill his own needs, is expressed in his behavior by portraying him as someone who takes care of everyone else's needs at the expense of his own. The interior conflict that results in suicidal desperation is, therefore, not a random choice made by the writer. It is a logical consequence of George's flawed perception that he is all used up.

A fatal flaw does not always relate directly to a physical death. It may foreshadow a more metaphorical death, a killing of dreams, desires, passion, identity, or any other aspect of the self that would open up to a greater, more expansive view of the character's *whole* nature. In *Sea of Love*, Frank Keller may not physically die if he remains disconnected from the deeper, passionate side of his nature, but in the inebriated, desolate image of his father the audience is able to catch a glimpse of the living death that awaits Frank if he doesn't grow and evolve.

Most importantly, **a fatal flaw is not a judgmental verdict that a writer places on a character, nor should it ever be a moral judgment.** For example, if a sixteen-year-old has sex or gets drunk, it doesn't mean he or she is fatally doomed. The fatal effect occurs when life stops, when growth and change are held back. Therefore, always look to the winter of a character's cycle—*"the winter of our discontent"*[4]—and ask what has become exhausted in terms of self-perception. A sixteen-year-old who is completely dependent on his or her parents to make all decisions may be in far more jeopardy of not maturing than the teen who casually experiments with sex, drugs, and rock and roll. This is not

---

[4] William Shakespeare, *King Richard III* (I, i, 1).

to say that a teen who exclusively uses artificial stimulus in place of developing real self-esteem isn't in jeopardy as well, but it depends on the degree to which any system of survival is out of balance to everything else.

Identifying the fatal flaw instantly clarifies for the writer what the internal journey of the character will be. This is no small thing, because once the writer is clear about what the protagonist needs in terms of internal growth it will clarify the external conflict as well. **The physical challenges in the plot serve the function of pushing the protagonist to grow past old boundaries that define who he or she is so that the person can potentially become someone greater by the end of the story.**

Every action Michael Dorsey (Dustin Hoffman) takes in *Tootsie* brings him one step closer to an internal day of reckoning. This film could easily have been a one-joke romp about an actor impersonating a woman to get a job. But that's only the froth on the surface. The real movement in the story comes from the inside out. Where will Michael Dorsey be five or ten years down the road if he doesn't change? At the beginning of the film he's already reached a point where no one will hire him and he can't maintain a relationship. He's totally ego-driven, self-important, and self-absorbed. These are definitely survival systems that have outlived their usefulness. Remaining at this level of development will not only undermine his growth, but will also severely diminish his ability to connect to others. He is only moving toward fear and isolation. It doesn't matter how talented an actor he may be—nothing will grow in infertile soil.

The plot, therefore, has little to do with Michael Dorsey simply parading around in a dress, but is instead a compelling series of events that give him an opportunity to face himself and make changes. Intentional plot choices serve to strip Michael of the outer veneer that has allowed him to bully his way through life, forcing him to expose his more feminine, nurturing, expansive self, one that *can* make a deeper and more selfless connection to others.

Finding the Fatal Flaw

If the fatal flaw is determined by mere guesswork, or by trial and error until something *feels* right, the entire substructure of the script will be based on a random, arbitrary choice. The results, of course, will be random as well. To define the fatal flaw organically, so that it rises to meet the writer's intentions, **it must be drawn from the theme.**

Because the fatal flaw reveals an aspect of character that can potentially destroy the opportunity for growth, it is always created around a value that opposes the theme and the internal goal for the protagonist. Therefore, we can say that:

1. **The fatal flaw represents the opposite value of the theme.**
2. **The fatal flaw is determined by inverting (finding the opposite value of) the internal goal of the theme.**

For example, in *Dead Poets Society,* the theme of *seize the day* sets up as an internal goal for the protagonists the need to *be true to their own natures.* Their fatal flaws, therefore, must be something in their character that betrays or is false toward their true nature.

Defining the fatal flaw of character greatly enhances the writer's understanding of what is driving a story. In the breakdown of *Dead Poets Society,* we can see that the addition of the fatal flaw instantly turns all the other work we've done with the theme into *tangible* character development. We don't yet have the details of how the co-protagonists will

> ### *Dead Poets Society*
>
> SUBJECT
> *Manhood*
> |
> THEMATIC POINT OF VIEW
> *Seize the day —*
> *TAKE control of your life*
> |
> SUBPLOT
> (internal goal)
> *Become true to your nature*
> |
> FATAL FLAW
> *Being false to your nature*

behave, but knowing that they are false to their nature gives a writer an enormous amount of information to work with.

There would be no conflict to resolve in *Dead Poets Society* if becoming true to their nature was something the boys were already good at. Therefore, when we first meet them in the setup of the film, it must be apparent that they are struggling *against* being true to their nature.

Once the fatal flaw is defined, it begins to provoke essential questions for the writer to ponder. Why would someone struggle against being true to their nature? What does being false to one's true nature actually mean? And is it really possible to be false to one's nature?

Again, there are no specifically correct answers to these questions, but the technique of finding the fatal flaw demands that writers investigate their own perceptions of the theme. Most importantly, it channels the writer's thinking toward issues that will ultimately play out the dramatic conflict that is implicit in the theme.

To see this more clearly, let's put some skin on the bones of these characters who are **being false to their nature.** Because an idea like this can be interpreted in so many different ways, being false to one's nature certainly doesn't mean one specific thing. It can mean that a person is living a lie, hiding from himself or herself, hiding from others, living in fear, not being authentic, denying his or her own needs, and so on. The choices are vast and they need only to reflect the writer's vision of the theme. This is why ten people can write a story about coming of age, utilizing the theme of being true to one's nature, and each writer would have a very different story to tell.

Utilizing theme to determine the fatal flaw eliminates having to poke around in the dark, trying to define a character's behavior and motivation randomly. **If behavior and motivation don't fall strictly in line with a writer's thematic intention, they run a very high risk of becoming distracting and meaningless.** On the other hand, in a film like *Dead Poets Society* it's easy to see how the protagonists' behavior relates directly to being false to their nature. From the first frame of this movie forward there is an inauthentic, pretentious, and controlled atmosphere that surrounds the students, who themselves seem constrained and guarded. This behavior is highlighted even further when the boys find a moment to themselves and they instantly become more relaxed and self-confident, out of sight of authority figures. This focus on the contrast in their behavior clearly signals to the audience exactly where the source of their problems lies. The boys do not behave naturally out in the open, only in private where they feel safe. It makes them come across as *deceptive* and certainly *insecure*. One of the students even has difficulty acting naturally among his peers. He seems not only to be *withdrawn* but completely out of touch with what feels natural to him. Further, as the story develops, the effect of not expressing his true nature *destabilizes* one of the boys to the point of complete self-destruction.

In this script, *deceptive, insecure, withdrawn,* and *unstable* are all strong choices for creating characters who demonstrate what it looks like to be false to one's nature. Here is what the thematic scheme of *Dead Poets Society* looks like once we add the character traits that were determined through the fatal flaw of character:

SUBJECT
Manhood

|

THEMATIC POINT OF VIEW
Carpe diem — Seize the day

|

SUBPLOT
(internal goal)
Be true to your nature

|

FATAL FLAW
Be false to your nature

|

CHARACTER TRAITS
Deceptive
Insecure
Unstable
Withdrawn

While there are many more details and complexities to be filled in, what this breakdown shows a writer is that there is a direct and authentic way to arrive at story choices that will support the writer's vision and keep it focused on what he or she values.

Turning Theme into Character

When a film lacks a fatal flaw of character that is connected to the thematic spine of a story, the development of character traits for the protagonist often serves other agendas, such as making a character likeable, memorable, or politically correct. These types of choices seldom connect well or deeply with a writer's thematic objectives and will render a story shallow and ineffective, even if it is well intentioned with strong thematic underpinnings.

An excellent example of a story that lacked the thematic development of the fatal flaw is *Don Juan DeMarco*, starring Marlon Brando and Johnny Depp. I use this particular example specifically because it was *not* a bad film. In fact, it is one of those enchanting, romantic tales that you want to love, but it never quite hits the spot. Even though this movie does attempt to tell a story of transformation, it doesn't establish a protagonist with a serious enough problem that needs changing. The agenda for this film seems to focus on the need to make Brando's character likeable, and it succeeds at that. He plays Dr. Mickler, a retiring psychiatrist who is the smartest, kindest, wisest, funniest, and most well adjusted of all his co-workers. He also appears to be happily married to a beautiful woman (Faye Dunaway), with whom he has good communication and a somewhat passionate relationship. While this is all very nice, where can the doctor grow from here? Does he just get smarter, kinder, wiser, and funnier? And if so, who cares?

Judging by the final scene of the film, which shows the doctor dancing on an exotic beach with his wife, I was left with the impression that his experiences in the story were meant to bring about a reawakening of passion in the doctor and a renewal of love for his wife. The problem, however, is that we never saw the doctor as unloving, incapable of loving, or even having forgotten how to love.

In the setup of this story Dr. Mickler takes on the case of a young, suicidally inclined patient (Depp) who has delusions that he is the historic romantic figure Don Juan, the world's greatest lover. Even though Mickler has only a week left before his retirement, he becomes fascinated and challenged by this young man, who regales him with fantastic tales of passion, romance, swordfights, and honor. This stimulates the great doctor to look into his own life and rediscover his lost passions.

The problem is that Dr. Mickler really has no lost passions, and so the story never hits its stride. In fact, after one of his first sessions with Don Juan, the doctor goes directly home and has great sex with his wife, but even that scene is undermined by the insinuation that their sexual relationship isn't really in trouble anyway. It's implied that they usually have good sex; in this scene they have better sex. Emotionally, this causes the rest of the script to pretty much flatline.

Thematically, this really isn't a story about sex; it's about the need to have passion for life. Even though Don Juan's dazzling tales are implausible, we want them to be true because they're so full of exuberance and energy. It's important, therefore, to consider how a theme about the need for passion to fulfill one's life might be better internalized and revealed in the actions of the protagonist. If the doctor is to find his passion as a result of his experiences in the story, in what emotional condition must we find him when the story begins? Remember, he can't find something he never lost or isn't in need of. If we are to send him in search of his passion, we want his character to begin the story as far to the opposite end of the passion spectrum as possible.

With this single clue to character development, a writer can begin to define Dr. Mickler by simply interpreting what it means to be passionless. A good place to start designing a character is to put together a list of words that are evoked by the concept of being passionless.

Dry	Quiet	Apathetic
Empty	Indifferent	Unpleasant
Humorless	Cold	Mean-spirited
Grumpy	Angry	Selfish

Because the fatal flaw did not evolve through indiscriminate guess-work, but as the result of a natural logic that ties the emotional condition of the protagonist to the conflict of the plot, any or all of these character descriptions could work (and probably many others). Defining the fatal flaw is an organic starting point that sets the character off in the right direction. Instinct or intuition might draw a writer to the same conclusion, but it might just as easily open up other agendas.

Without a technique to *consciously* evaluate choices, writers can't know what is motivating them. As a story consultant, I receive many scripts that have characters designed around a writer's sense of wish fulfillment rather than reality. This often means that characters behave as alter egos, going where the writer is afraid to go in real life, which makes the characters idealized, stilted, and two-dimensional.

I once worked on a script with an extraordinary plot idea, but the first draft had such enormous problems with character development that the story was quite ineffective. The protagonist was a young man who had a cruel, domineering father, and in a pivotal scene he marched in and boldly told his dad to go to hell. Because this scene, in particular, had a very false-sounding ring to it, I attempted to get the writer to step into the shoes of the protagonist to try to bring his emotional reality to life. As we worked together, I asked him if he had any personal experiences that were similar to the father/son relationship depicted in the story. It took a minute before he responded, but surprise suddenly registered on his face. He confessed that up to that moment he had not consciously connected with the obvious. He did indeed have a terrible rapport with his own father, who was an intimidating tyrant. I then asked if this was how he would speak to his own father under the same circumstances and he visibly shuddered. We then improvised what this confrontation might actually have been like. It was uncomfortable, painful, and *real*. I not only cared about the young man in the story, I began to care about the callous father as well—and I certainly cared more about my client.

An interesting paradox occurred here: **When the writer instinctively created a strong, invulnerable character to step in and fight his battles for him, the story itself lay impotent. However, when the writer got**

honest and connected his own ineffectual feelings with what the protagonist was experiencing, his story gained strength and power.

Backstory

Creating a backstory is an excellent and productive activity that
helps breathe life into characters by giving them a history before the
story even begins. But just making up a random biography is hardly
worth the trouble. Instead, utilize the fatal flaw as the entry point
into your protagonist's past. The most important question that needs
to be answered is: How did his or her experiences lead to this internal moment of reckoning?

I used to live on a street where there was an old man who gave the
neighborhood children a very difficult time when they played in front
of his house. He was also cranky about pets, delivery people, and lawn
mowers. For years, I would walk my dogs well out of his range so that
I didn't have to encounter his wrath. One day a neighbor mentioned
that he'd been this way ever since his only child died in a car accident
many years earlier. This didn't change my perception that he was difficult and cantankerous, but I did find myself occasionally offering a friendly
wave and a smile when I passed him on the street.

**By creating a backstory that gives a history to the fatal flaw, a writer
is able to connect with the character's humanity.** When writers make this
connection for themselves, they are likewise making it for the audience.
If Dr. Mickler is redefined as someone who is passionless, and he behaves
with irritability, detachment, and unresponsiveness, wouldn't knowing
that he lost a child in a car accident make you feel more compassion
toward him as well?

Through thematic intention there are innumerable ways to develop
a backstory. For example, if the writer's thematic perspective of *Don
Juan DeMarco* is that no matter how old a person is, without a passion
for life there is no viable life, then the backstory might focus on passion
and aging. Dr. Mickler is a man who is traversing one of the great
passages in his life as he heads into retirement. He is moving from the

peak of his usefulness and effectiveness on this earth toward his decline and ultimate physical demise. How can his survival systems not be in a state of serious disturbance at this time? As adolescents experience conflict moving from dependence to independence, there must be forces of equally profound discord facing people entering the final chapters of their life. Their knowledge, wisdom, and abilities are at an apex, yet their energy, vitality, and physical capabilities are beginning to wane as their life force slips away, out of their control.

Dr. Mickler's defenses against aging and death had to have started many years prior. Perhaps his drive to be a good doctor intermixed with early feelings that if he was good he would always be needed, and if he was always needed he would always be around. However, as he aged that simple system of survival began to prove false. The reality of his life is that no matter how good he is, he will not always be around. But that doesn't mean he willingly accepts this reality; only fantasy characters do that. The truth that resonates inside most of us is that we hold on devoutly to what we are until we are forced to change. As life keeps hurling Dr. Mickler forward toward death, against his will, a very natural reaction would be for him to respond with anger, frustration, and fear of the unknown. His instincts would tell him to make it stop, which could easily translate into behavior that attempts to make everything stop. This, unfortunately, might include feeling, communicating, and even loving, which would naturally lead to isolation, inflexibility, and inattentiveness. Of course, this might make the doctor less charming when we first meet him in the film. But if he's real we will identify with his humanity. This is the key to emotionally attaching the audience to the outcome of the story.

It is also the key to attaching the writer to the story. When the back-story is developed through the theme and the fatal flaw of character, it is honest and meaningful. So it should be no surprise at all to find that the source of the protagonist's fear, anxiety, and self-doubt may be directly related to the writer's own emotional condition. When I am working with a client on a screenplay, it is almost inevitable that at this point in the story analysis he or she will say to me, "I never realized it before, but this script *is* about me."

Turning Theme into Plot

Even though defining the fatal flaw will give a writer tremendous insight into creating the protagonist, a full portrait of this character will not emerge until one more vital element of the story is put into place—the CONTEXT. Remember: Great stories tell us *how a character grows and changes* (fatal flaw), *within the* **context** *of the events* (plot) *that are unfolding.* How could a writer know where to begin to design the character of Dr. Mickler if all that is known about him is that he is passionless? It's an interesting character flaw, but it's rather meaningless if it exists in a void. However, notice that all kinds of intriguing possibilities begin to surface when the passionless psychiatrist is put into the context of having to work with a delusional patient who is willing to die for his passion.

Obviously, to find the context a writer needs to look no further than the conflict of the plot. But as with the development of the protagonist, there are a lot of agendas that can motivate a writer in the creation of a plot, and this is what needs to be sorted out. The only agenda that really matters is the one that serves the theme. Many action films, for example, cripple an otherwise excellent premise because the agenda gets focused on the size and frequency of the explosions, rather than on meeting the internal needs of the protagonist. When writers (and producers and directors) learn to trust their story and follow where the metaphor of the theme leads, they will find that action films will have even greater explosiveness, love stories will have even more passion, and thrillers will be even more thrilling.

A great example of an authentically driven plot is found in the Academy Award–winning film *Unforgiven*, written by David Webb Peoples. In the setup of this story the protagonist, William Munny (Clint Eastwood), seeks to avenge the savage butchery of a young prostitute. But that's only what the plot superficially reveals to us; its metaphor runs so much deeper. Munny is a reformed gunslinger who himself is no stranger to savagery. But, for the love of a good woman, he's hung up his holster and now does penance with a hoe on a dusty, isolated farm. Salvation, however, is not so easily acquired. Evil has stained his soul and will only be vanquished when he accepts the totality of his whole nature—the light along with the dark. In other words, it's not enough to admit we've been bad or done wrong; we must likewise seek and acknowledge our worthiness and our value. Otherwise, the wrong we've perpetrated will always dominate our identity. It will loom out there as a vengeful god to whom we must constantly pay homage. But no offering will ever be enough to appease this god and we will deteriorate into nothingness, heaping any morsel of joy and happiness we experience upon the sacrificial bonfire.

Munny's fatal flaw is that he can't forgive himself, so it's clear that what he must achieve for redemption is to reclaim his self-worth. No sinner can be redeemed until he comes to honor God's greatest work—himself. This is an eternal story that can be told and retold a thousand different ways. It certainly is the driving force behind a literary classic such as *Les Misérables*, but it's also been a popular theme throughout the history of modern cinema. Films such as Alfred Hitchcock's thriller *Notorious*, Alan Pakula's tragedy *Sophie's Choice*, Bernardo Bertolucci's passionate drama *Last Tango in Paris*, and Clint Eastwood's other Oscar winner, *Million Dollar Baby*, all deal with this kind of redemption. However, none of these stories resembles each other. They all found their *context* in differing external metaphors.

On the surface, the external metaphor for *Unforgiven* is the taming of the Wild West. This is the place where those who are armed, dangerous, self-serving, unscrupulous, and evil will be brought to justice. In most incarnations, this well-trod western landscape is used as a backdrop to exploit the simplistic and moralistic battle between good and evil. However, there is something intrinsically unsettling about any altruistic perspective, because here again it promotes idealized behavior as a standard that excludes rather than includes most of us. It certainly excludes Munny. In fact, it is the pomposity of this view that has rendered his life valueless because it presumes that there isn't enough good in the world to undo his evil deeds. So he and his offspring and their off-spring will continue to till infertile soil, meekly inhabiting the earth. That's his punishment; so be it. And it makes us feel virtuous just knowing that he and his kind are doing penance. But what the *context* of this parable brilliantly demonstrates is that, according to this paradigm, all sinners (and that includes the lot of us) are in effect hoeing this same dusty hole. As long as we refuse to acknowledge Munny's humanity in its wholeness, which gives his light as much value as his darker side, then the wholeness of our own being is not achievable either. In other words, in order to value ourselves *we must value others.*

So it is within, so it is without—this is what lies at the heart of a story's metaphor. ***The internal goal and external goal of the theme support each other.*** **By inverting the external goal of the theme, the writer can define the protagonist's environment. The environment in a story contains the obstacles that work in *opposition* to or are *antago-nistic* toward the protagonist's achieving the goal of the plot.** When the external thematic goal of *Unforgiven* is reversed from **valuing others** to **devaluing others**, it gives clear and specific information about how to determine the nature of the antagonistic forces in this story: They devalue everyone.

To see how this works, let's take a look at how the conflict of the plot is set into motion in the opening of this film. The story begins when a prostitute is severely cut up by a couple of rowdy, drunken customers. Not only does this indicate that they don't value her, but then local law enforcement diminishes her value even further by allotting restitution for this crime to the brothel owner, not to the prostitute herself. She and the other prostitutes are so outraged by this injustice that they seek out the services of a hired gunman to kill the men who committed the horrific offense, assigning them no redemptive value either. This keenly illustrates the perspective that once the devaluation process begins it has a snowballing effect, providing the story with a compelling momen-tum that likewise begs the all-important thematic question: Where will it end? This is indeed hell. When a single one of us is deemed valueless, it creates an inevitable legacy of valuelessness, which is the *context* in which Munny's character must function.

From this perspective, look at how excellent the choice is to utilize the western as the context for this story. This genre and its modern-day counterpart, the action adventure, commonly capitalize on the popular yet self-defeating myth that good *conquers* evil. *Unforgiven* utilizes this shallow perspective to create a dramatic irony that illustrates a much more profound principle: When good sets out to *destroy* evil it becomes what it conquers. However, when good *embraces* its own darker side it becomes whole and therefore potent.

The best illustration of this thematic dichotomy can be seen in the depiction of the story's antagonist, Little Bill Daggett (Gene Hackman), who on the surface appears to be dedicated, purposeful, stalwart, and highly moral. In fact, he has all the outward characteristics of the prototypical western hero—he's the good, honorable guy who cleaned up the town. Daggett may have done just that, but virtue unchecked begins to believe its own press. In *fighting* for "right," he's become wrong. He's become what he conquered. Instead of leading the town to its fullest and greatest potential, he has preserved its heritage as an outpost for fear and the degradation of the human spirit.

In essence, Daggett is the darkest shadow of the protagonist's character. He is what Munny must ultimately confront: that part of himself that will not forgive his sins so that he may become whole. In this allegory, it's painfully apparent where the true evil lies: *Judge not that ye may be judged*, and thereby destroyed.

When applying this same process to *Dead Poets Society*, we get a slightly different take on a similarly drawn antagonist. In the last chapter it was shown that in order to *seize the day* and honor their *true nature* (internally), the boys in *Dead Poets Society* needed an external context that *valued their individual nature*. What they got, however, was just the opposite. The context that provided the plot with its conflict and dramatic tension put the boys in a world (i.e., society, school, family) that ***devalued*** *the individual.* In other words, by inverting the external goal of the theme, the conflict of the story becomes obvious. The boys are seeking their identity in an environment that is covertly trying to suppress it. Not only is their individuality not appreciated, it is treated with contempt. The atmosphere of the school, therefore, is *harsh, judgmental, unaccepting,* and *disrespectful* toward the students who are trying to be true to who they are.

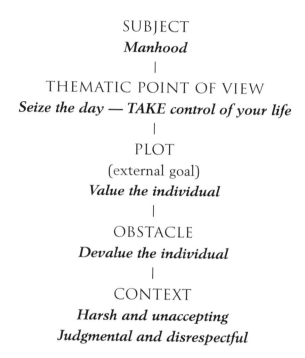

SUBJECT
Manhood
|
THEMATIC POINT OF VIEW
Seize the day — TAKE control of your life
|
PLOT
(external goal)
Value the individual
|
OBSTACLE
Devalue the individual
|
CONTEXT
Harsh and unaccepting
Judgmental and disrespectful

Defining the primary conflict of the film this way does not directly give the writer all the details of the plot or a full description of the antagonist, but it does define the single most essential ingredient necessary to create these elements: ***focused, conscious intention.***

When developing any story, it's highly likely that a great deal of relevant plot information will naturally and intuitively evolve. In a story like *Dead Poets Society*, the idea of a prep school full of impressionable boys who have to struggle against a conservative establishment in order to define their own identity might easily have rolled out of the writer's imagination at the intuitive stage. But to get to the layers of depth and introspection that this film reveals, it is necessary for most writers to have some kind of process that will help them excavate below the surface of what they have intuited. Without consciously understanding, for example, that the primary obstacles in this plot are connected to the devaluation of the individual, the writer is left to play a very hit-or-miss game. On the other hand, processing theme into character and context not only opens up a vast expanse of creative possibilities for the story, but it also potentially opens up the writer's awareness of this conflict in his or her own environment as well.

As an exercise, you may want to re-watch the first twenty minutes of *Dead Poets Society*. Notice how the filmmaker communicates the depth of the internal and external conflict in this story through the use of tone and symbolism before any of the plot is revealed. From the opening shot, you see that the dialogue and images conspire to make you feel the ease with which these boys and their families are willingly to sacrifice aspects of their authentic nature to the seductive promise of security, wealth, and status.

On the Other Hand...

Of course, there are exceptions to this technique of inverting the theme to define what stands in opposition to the protagonist's achieving the goal. Bearing in mind that the reason for inverting the theme is to define what is antagonistic in the protagonist's environment, in some stories this very notion may run contrary to the value the writer is trying to express. For example, in *Groundhog Day* the point of the tale is that the external world is fine just the way it is; it's the attitude of the protagonist that must change. Therefore, while the internal thematic goal must be inverted to create a fatal flaw of character, the story's external thematic goal is expressed directly. The town of Punxsutawney, Pennsylvania, and its annual Groundhog Day celebration may be a bit corny and sentimental, but it has something that the jaded, cynical protagonist doesn't have and desperately needs: a heart. Therefore, the town's refusal to let him go until he finds one is what creates the drama.

In *Forrest Gump* the situation is reversed. The theme of the story illustrates that we are all perfect in our imperfection. Therefore, the fatal flaw belongs solely in the outer world, where Forrest is dismissed as value-less because of his mental shortcomings. This doesn't mean that Forrest can get by without an arc of character, but it is a subtle arc that brings him from innocence to independence. Without this transformation, he could not care for himself in the real world. As dramatists, however, it's important for us to note that the secondary characters of Jenny and Lieutenant Dan do have strong fatal flaws that are attached to the internal thematic goal. They are two extremely damaged people who only come to find their wholeness in their imperfection. Consider how flat the story would have been without these two characters.

Understanding the basic principle that *theme is expressed through the actions of the characters* allows writers the complete range of human experiences in which to create a story. In most cases the protagonist will bear the transformational burden of being pushed to achieve a greater awareness of self-identity and of his or her relationship to the rest of the world. But as *Forrest Gump* aptly illustrates, sometimes it is the protagonist who sets into motion a chain of events that transforms his or her environment. **As long as there is some kind of internal movement in the story that expresses the reality that our actions do impact us, and that it is our experiences that shape our character, the thematic value of the story will shine through.**

Case Studies
1) *ROMANCING THE STONE*

The romantic comedy is one of cinema's most popular forms, yet very few actually work. Most fall victim to terminal cuteness, due to the overuse of worn-out clichés based on shallow perceptions of love. This occurs so often, in fact, that many of us have come to dismiss the entire genre as insignificant, which is too bad because romance, intimacy, and love are vital aspects of our lives. By its very nature, romance tends to bring out the awkwardness in most of us, so it's not a stretch to put the mating ritual into a humorous form.

The most dangerous pitfall that romantic comedies tumble into is the random design of character traits that have no thematic relevance whatsoever. For example, in *My Best Friend's Wedding*, Jules Potter (Julia Roberts) is a manically controlling, obsessive woman who only seems to want what she can't have. On the surface, this may sound like the stuff of which fatal flaws are made, but because there's almost no connection between this unappealing behavior and any clear thematic goal, the character's actions are for the most part unredeemable. Jules begins the story as a petty, spoiled, self-obsessed woman, and she ends the story pretty much the same. Even though her behavior throughout ninety percent of the film is quite deplorable, she is depicted as adorable and all is forgiven with a wink and a nod.

There is also no real love interest in this "romantic" comedy because the object of Jules' obsession is someone she really doesn't want. Likewise, the adorable best friend, to whom she clings throughout the story, is sexually unavailable because he's gay. So, since all of this amounts to no love lost or gained, what's the point of the story? If the writer wanted to write a film about valuing platonic love, then that's where the fatal flaw of the character should have been aimed. Instead, because Jules values her platonic friend from the beginning of the story, dancing in his arms in the climax doesn't carry any symbolic weight. The ending was therefore meaningless—the protagonist had gained no insight into the value of love, and neither did we.

Romancing the Stone, on the other hand, gives the audience a clear thematic point of view regarding love. By turning the thematic intention—*love is an adventure*—into tangible character and plot conflict, Joan Wilder's experiences become something to which audiences can identify and internalize in terms of their own life experiences.

Joan begins the story as a woman who desperately wants to find her true love. But unless he turns out to be the postman or the pizza delivery boy, there's no way he can scale the unrealistic heights of her cloistered little world, where she spins passionate yarns into golden romance classics. In all her feminine fantasies, men are, above all, faithful, devoted, and loyal, which in real-life terms would pretty much narrow her field of suitors to Labrador retrievers and basset hounds. This doesn't mean that men can't be faithful, devoted, and loyal; it just means that to limit her connection to them by preferring only those who are guaranteed not to cause her pain is to limit her connection to true love almost completely.

For all of us, the quest for true love is not a secure, neat, safe experience, but it is *an adventure*, where the exciting and remarkable intermingle with risk and danger. In the last chapter we determined that because of the risk and danger, Joan needs to find the courage to *follow her heart*. To do so, she must learn to *trust the adventure*.

By simply inverting the internal goal—*follow your heart*—it becomes clear that Joan's fatal flaw is leading her in the opposite direction: away from her heart. This means that instead of being open to possibilities, her heart is closed—or at least it is in hiding. As a writer, think about what you can do with this little piece of character information: *Joan hides from her heart.* Let's compare this character description as backstory to an entire list of random character choices:

RANDOM	INTENTIONAL
1. Born in Minnesota	1. She hides from her heart
2. 5'3" tall	
3. 120 lbs.	
4. Attended Sarah Lawrence	
5. Dropped out of college	
6. Married high school sweetheart	
7. Got a divorce after one year	
8. Wanted to be an Olympic swimmer	
9. Her father was a compulsive gambler	
10. Favorite color is lavender	

From which column can you create a fully dimensional character? From which description do you feel a universal connection? More importantly, from which description do you personally connect to the character yourself? I like lavender, but I've never been to Minnesota and I haven't weighed 120 pounds since I was twelve. But, I do hide from my heart—more often than I'd like to admit.

Focusing on the fatal flaw is where the real artistry of creation can begin. What does it mean to *hide from one's heart?* Volumes of poetry have been inspired by far less. With this single piece of information, a writer can begin to paint with moving images the portrait of a woman whose pain and fear have caused her to retreat from the most vital source of life—her own heart.

The choice to make Joan a romance writer, for example, is great. It's the perfect place for her to hide in plain sight because it gives her the *illusion* that she is immersed in love. It's only her soul that aches for the real thing. Therefore, we know that whatever occurs in the plot must give Joan the opportunity to grow toward what is real by abandoning the world of illusion.

While there are a vast number of choices a writer could make to depict Joan's fatal flaw of character, the field is narrowed sharply when the conflict of the plot is factored in. The overarching *context* in which this story is held is that it is an adventure. Remember that the most important value of a metaphor is that it reflects in the outer world what is going on inside the protagonist—*so without, so within.* This reveals that what Joan is facing in the outer world is what she most needs to conquer inside of her. The best plot, therefore, would be one that reflects back to Joan that her idealized fantasy of love is just that: a fantasy. To achieve this she must confront her illusions, which is just what occurs when the romance/adventure writer herself is forced to go on a romantic adventure of her own. The conflict is centered on breaking down Joan's illusions, which means that the adventure must become real: real danger, real risk, real excitement. And the reward is real as well—real, *true* love.

If we were to use the fatal flaw to examine the backstory on a character like Joan, we might easily find a point where her fictional life intersects with our real one. Why does this woman avoid real love and intimacy? How did she get this way? What hurt her so deeply that she felt the need to hide that part of her that most needs to be exposed? Maybe her father (or your father) was a compulsive gambler. Maybe she (or you) did want to be an Olympic swimmer and maybe her (or your) high school sweetheart did leave her (or you) wounded and disillusioned…. There's something very real about a character that begins to evolve in this manner because her essence is real and identifiable, not idealized. She's someone who hides from her heart, and we know her, because to some degree we've all done what she's doing. The avoidance of our own heart has caused us, too, to put up defenses, play it safe, avoid closeness, and circumvent the real adventure of life.

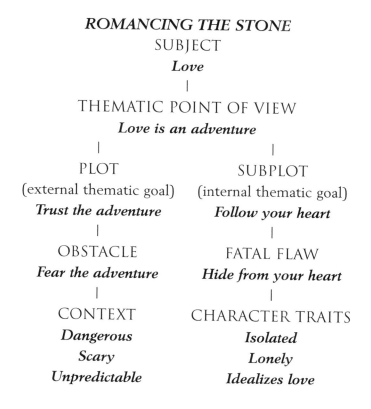

ROMANCING THE STONE
SUBJECT
Love
|
THEMATIC POINT OF VIEW
Love is an adventure

PLOT	SUBPLOT
(external thematic goal)	(internal thematic goal)
Trust the adventure	**Follow your heart**
OBSTACLE	FATAL FLAW
Fear the adventure	**Hide from your heart**
CONTEXT	CHARACTER TRAITS
Dangerous	**Isolated**
Scary	**Lonely**
Unpredictable	**Idealizes love**

An interesting thing occurs in this script that is worth noting. The antagonists who kidnap Joan's sister and lure her to Colombia are not terribly threatening. In fact, the thug played by Danny DeVito is extremely funny. Because this is a comedy, the film needs the humor, but the story also needs real danger in order for the adventure metaphor to work. So, instead of sacrificing the humor, the writer added an alternate set of villains, who are deadly serious. They shoot real bullets and are playing for keeps. It's very important to be true to your metaphor and if it calls for danger and peril, then give it everything you've got.

2) LETHAL WEAPON

In the last chapter, the theme of *Lethal Weapon* was defined as the need to *choose life*. On the surface of the story that certainly is Martin Riggs' dilemma. Many scripts that attempt to utilize this theme get as far as the concept of life vs. death and then they develop the drama around a suicidal tendency or death wish. This is fairly obvious character behavior to attach to the need to choose life. But if that's all there is, it's rather superficial, and in most cases the story never really deals with the interior issues that have brought the protagonist to this profound crossroad.

Lethal Weapon, on the other hand, does dig deeper without ever having to sacrifice any of the film's high-intensity action. This is because the protagonist's internal struggle is systemic; it's part of the whole story. In fact, it tends to be the predominant driving force behind most of the action.

The internal goal for Riggs is, in order to choose life, he needs to learn that he's not alone in the world, that *he needs others*. When the story begins, however, he is in the opposite place. He's the resilient warrior who has learned only to rely on himself for survival: *He needs no one*. This lack of connection to others is the real source of pain that has put Riggs in his life-and-death struggle. The one time he opened himself to another person, she died—she abandoned him—so vulnerability and connectedness are definitely not to be trusted.

Ironically, of course, the inability to make a connection to others is what is destroying him. Aloneness, though necessary to create a sense of self, is not an end but a means to an end. The destination is connection—

which is where life is found. Permanent aloneness leads to isolation, *detachment*, alienation, and that of course leads to many kinds of death. Martin's suicidal inclination, therefore, is not a random act or simply a dramatic contrivance; it is the natural, logical manifestation of a heroic ideal based on a survival system that has outlived its usefulness—a fatal flaw of character.

The next piece of logic that is intrinsic to the thematic development of this story is that if *connection* is the goal, then the protagonist needs someone or something to whom he can connect. While the most obvious solution would be to replace what he's lost by giving him a new love interest, the writer made a more interesting and even profound choice: *To need others* means *all others*, and therefore the source of connection for Riggs comes through friendship, not romantic love.

Understanding Riggs' character in this way clarifies Murtaugh's character as well. Because the protagonist is split in two, Riggs is half of a whole. This means that Murtaugh is the other half, which makes him Riggs' opposite. Therefore, if Riggs is portrayed as someone who has lost his connection to life through too much *detachment*, then Murtaugh must be someone whose connection to life is in peril because of too much *attachment*.

Both detachment and attachment are attributes of connection, but if they are tipped too far in either direction they create a loss of emotional and spiritual equilibrium. The more seriously askew they are, the more the character is expressing one side of his nature with a conspicuous disregard for the "other." So, while Riggs is throwing life away, Murtaugh is holding on too tight. For both characters, their only hope for salvation is to achieve balance, which they can do by learning to give and receive from each other.

The union that these two co-protagonists seek in order to redeem their fatal flaw still needs a **context** that forces them to take action. Our theme work with this story revealed that they must learn to **value life** in order to choose it. By inverting this external thematic goal, the context becomes instantly clear: They must confront antagonists who *devalue life.*

Consider for a moment how much more mileage a writer can get from the thematic idea of *valuing life* as compared to once again using that worn-out, old notion of good vs. evil, or right vs. wrong. As in *Unforgiven*, there is so much more emotional depth to explore when working with a theme that has real human dimension rather than one that is based on mindless, overwrought clichés.

In *Lethal Weapon*, notice how the concept of *devaluing life* serves as the backbone for the structure of this plot. The film opens with a very drugged-out, beautiful young woman, casually taking a nosedive over the balcony of a high-rise. Not only does she devalue her own life, but we come to learn that the real cause of her untimely demise is her adoring father's misadventures into the life-wrecking drug trade. The co-antagonists, Joshua and the General, are a pair of soulless malcontents who represent the very bleakness of death itself. While there is a lot of humor in this film, this detestable duo is about as funny as cardiac arrest. They perfectly illustrate the darkest shadow of what is internally ailing our co-protagonists. Their extreme *attachment* to the material world has left them completely *detached* from all the rest of human life. We know that the outcome of the plot will be their defeat, not because good always conquerors evil, but because they are already dead. They have failed to make the choice that is being offered to the protagonists: *choose life.*

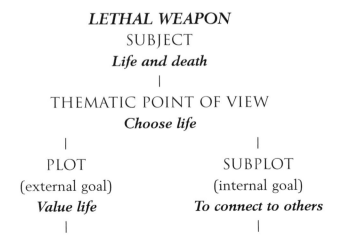

LETHAL WEAPON
SUBJECT
Life and death
|
THEMATIC POINT OF VIEW
Choose life

PLOT	SUBPLOT
(external goal)	(internal goal)
Value life	***To connect to others***

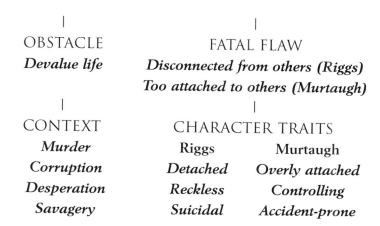

OBSTACLE	FATAL FLAW
Devalue life	*Disconnected from others (Riggs)*
	Too attached to others (Murtaugh)

CONTEXT	CHARACTER TRAITS

CONTEXT	Riggs	Murtaugh
Murder	*Detached*	*Overly attached*
Corruption	*Reckless*	*Controlling*
Desperation	*Suicidal*	*Accident-prone*
Savagery		

3) ORDINARY PEOPLE

Ordinary People is an excellent illustration of the importance of developing characters at a point in their lives when their survival systems are breaking down. Were we to have entered the story of Conrad and his family five years prior to the death of his brother, it might have been as dramatically interesting as watching paint dry. In reality, the family unit was no sounder then than it was after the brother died, but their system of valuing the image of the family over the interests of the individuals was highly functional.

The fatal flaw only becomes activated when characters reach a point where the behavior, attitudes, and conduct that once worked are no longer acceptable or workable. It's difficult if not impossible to motivate a character to grow and change if his or her system of survival has not yet broken down. Who among us willingly moves out of a comfort zone of contentment or even complacency? We all know people who are in marriages or jobs that aren't fulfilling, but they aren't terrible either. So people stay and wait for it to get better. But better can't happen unless growth is taking place.

Dramatically speaking, it is the tension of hanging on to the old as we are being pulled into the swift current of change that makes our stories alive and relevant. Because this family has no capacity to swim with the shifting tides, they are being dragged into the undertow right along with the drowned son. This is what happens when we become fixed on an ideal; there is no allowance for movement. It's no surprise then that their survival system crashed when the son drowned. Something that terrible wasn't supposed to happen—at least not to them. They had invested everything into an ideology that guaranteed prominence, prosperity, and social acceptability in exchange for hard work, upstanding behavior, good citizenship, and a positive, happy demeanor. This implied contract said nothing about calamity, heartbreak, and misfortune.

In all fairness, most families would have a terrible time dealing with an occurrence as devastating as losing a son, but the difference with this family is that there is no Plan B. They can't just throw into doubt everything they ever believed in. This is why the mother is deeply conflicted. The old belief system is central to her sense of identity. It's the only way she knows how to live. This is tragic, not evil or malevolent, and it's why Beth is almost a sympathetic if not pathetic character.

Working with thematic goals in a story like this is particularly important, because although it's relatively easy to see what's wrong with this family, it's far more difficult to understand what they need in terms of their survival. While the theme expresses a generalized perspective that *families need to value each other* in order to be whole and functional, at best this points to the problem, but it doesn't give the writer much to work with in terms of the solution. On the other hand, the external and internal goals of the theme point directly to what is needed to heal this family.

In order to learn to *value each other*, they must come to appreciate not only each other's individuality, but also their own. They have to expand their identity past the roles that only support the family structure. In addition, they need to recognize their own unique value as well as accept the family itself as something unique and special—even if it doesn't conform to some arbitrary cultural standard. In the end, in fact, that's exactly what happens. The family, with or without Mom, is redefined by bonds of intimacy, recognition, and acceptance—not social acceptability or "traditional values."

By allowing the thematic goals to be the guide, a writer will find that setting up the conflict is obvious and logical, because the story must begin in opposition to those goals. If coming to *value the individual* is to be relevant, then the family must demonstrate a profound inability to appreciate that value in the beginning of the story—and that is precisely what occurs. There is a compelling tension in the opening of this film that is drawn from the simple reality that these people are struggling with all their might to get things back to "normal." Even though it is Mom who epitomizes and consciously vocalizes this need, the other family members do not resist. In truth, they are very willing accomplices. The possibility that it is their sense of "normal" that may be destroying them is not even a consideration in their minds. But the audience is able to pick up on the depth of this conflict because the filmmaker uses the subtlety of images, body posture, and subtext in the dialogue to consciously reveal how the wound in this family won't heal because it's festering from the inside out.

In fact, this is what pushes them to act in opposition to the internal thematic goal. Instead of *valuing their own needs,* none of them has any conscious notion of what those needs could even be. They struggle to play their roles as adequately as possible, but nothing they do seems to be "good enough" to compensate for the death of the family's shining light—including the attempt by Conrad to sacrifice his own life.

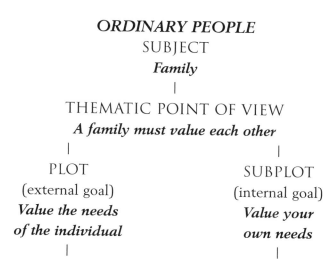

ORDINARY PEOPLE
SUBJECT
Family

|

THEMATIC POINT OF VIEW
A family must value each other

| |

PLOT	SUBPLOT
(external goal)	(internal goal)
Value the needs	**Value your**
of the individual	**own needs**

|

OBSTACLE
Devalue the needs
of the individual

|

ENVIRONMENT
Demands conformity

|

FATAL FLAW
Devalue your
own needs

|

CHARACTER TRAITS
Inflexible and controlling (Mom)
Inauthentic, self-doubting,
and anxious (Dad)
Unaware, depressed,
and suicidal (Conrad)

PART TWO

BUILDING THE ARC OF CHARACTER

Whosoever wishes to know about the world
must learn about it in its particular details.
Knowledge is not intelligence.
In searching for the truth be ready for the unexpected.
Change alone is unchanging.
The same road goes both up and down.
The beginning of a circle is also its end.
Not I, but the world says it: all is one.
And yet everything comes in season.

~ *HERAKLIETOS OF EPHESOS*

CHAPTER SIX

INSIDE STRUCTURE
Swimming in the Deep End

True ease in writing comes from art, not chance,
as those move easiest who have learned to dance.

~ ALEXANDER POPE

Structure—That Dirty Little Word

Story structure is the part of the writing process we all love to hate. It's too rigid, too predictable, too confining, and way too *un*-artistic. Yet without structure our stories just won't hold together. Actually, there isn't much in this world that can hold together without it. Form and structure are an essential part of nature; the very bodies we inhabit, the molecules of air we breathe, all plant and animal life exist in a functional form based on sound evolutionary development. So why would a film script be exempt from this principle?

If you think about it, *all* art is contained in some kind of form. Paint doesn't just hang in the air; it needs a canvas. Musical notes played merely at random are only a cacophony of sounds. Architects don't dump a pile of wood on the ground and call it a house; they have builders organize the lumber in a manner that gives definition to their creative vision. But don't be disheartened; **as the process of writing ceases to be a mystery, you can look past the boundaries it creates and find opportunities for unique self-expression.**

Perhaps more than any other literary endeavor, screenwriting is a creative form that is dependent on its ability to speak to an extremely broad and diversified audience. To reach such a wide group of people, the creative impulse or inspiration that ignites the screenwriter *must*, at some point, be translated into a recognizable form. That form has a customary (though not necessarily rigid) structure.

When studying the screenplay form, it becomes clear that there are certain recurring characteristics that are consistent in nearly all great films. Breaking these elements down and identifying their functions offers the writer tremendous insight and clarity into what gives a cinematic story its unique shape and appearance. But this doesn't mean that a writer must be limited to using structure only in ways that are tried and true. To the contrary, great artists—which, of course, includes great filmmakers—are able to take existing knowledge and stretch it to new limits. The more a writer understands the dynamics of how story structure works, the better use he or she can make of it.

Certainly, there have been writers who've created cinematic masterpieces without so much as a passing conscious thought to form and structure. However, that kind of a spontaneous system for achieving excellence is extremely difficult to duplicate every time. If your creative impulses are flowing freely toward perfection, then by all means get out of the way and let them pour forth. But if that flow dies down to a trickle, don't assume it's because you're all dried up. When the process of connecting words to express images, ideas, and emotions becomes excruciatingly difficult or confusing, it can merely be a signal that you must dig even deeper into those dark, internal places where self-discovery and self-truths are often hidden or buried. Especially under these circumstances, understanding the form and structure of a story is an excellent tool to help you trench your way back through the mire and complexity into the mainstream of the great story that is struggling to emerge.

One of the primary reasons some screenwriters spurn the idea of structure is that it is often taught or explained as a set of arbitrary rules and requirements that feel antithetical to the creative process. Artistically, writers don't want to assemble a script in the same manner that a mechanic would build a carburetor: each piece die-cast to fit perfectly into an assembly-line replica of all the others. Following arbitrary guidelines or following guidelines arbitrarily can lead to very stilted, unimaginative, benign writing. Art can never be a calculated risk. As soon as you enter the safety zone of merely filling in a form, you severely diminish the possibility of tapping into those interior regions where sacred originality and profound insights dwell.

The Dynamic Duo

True story structure is organic, not arbitrary or manufactured. It is the natural form a story wants to take. The origin of that natural form evolves from a basic law of nature that says:

THINGS CHANGE
The result of change is *movement…*
The result of movement is *progress…*
The result of progress is a *new order…*
The result of a new order is *new life…*

RESISTANCE to this natural process of change impedes the movement toward renewed life. Yielding to change *RELEASES* the flow back into new life. For human beings it is a natural process to constantly pass in and out of conditions of *resistance* and *release*. These two dynamics form a tension that we see everywhere in nature: waves crest on the ocean, birds flap their wings, hearts beat, and pulses throb. The pattern of *resistance* and *release* generates the pounding drumbeat of life.

Resistance and release also defines the nature of conflict and resolution. **A conflict is a conflict precisely because there is resistance to the solution.**

Resistance doesn't necessarily mean that an answer or solution isn't desired or worked toward; it just means that the information, perspective, or perception surrounding an existing dilemma isn't sufficient to solve or resolve it at the time. The harder an issue is to solve, the greater the conflict; the greater the conflict, the harder it is to get to the solution. This causes resistance to increase and tension to escalate.

But *resistance* can't intensify indefinitely. At some point, like an over-extended rubber band, the tension will reach a breaking point and *release* will follow. No squabble, argument, dispute, or war in history has ever gone completely unresolved. Some sort of reconciliation, compromise, peace treaty, overthrow, invasion, beheading, or surrender occurred that released the conflict toward a resolution and established a new order. It wasn't necessarily a better order, and no one necessarily won or lost. In fact, you can bet that the new order brought about a new set of conflicts, and the pattern of *resistance and release* was set back into motion.

This is also true in human relationships. Take adolescence, for example: Every milestone in a young person's development marks a hard-fought battle for independence. Parents generally don't loosen their grip on a child's boundaries until there is solid evidence of increased maturity. Likewise, it's impossible to imagine a successful marriage that hasn't had to endure relentless overt and covert battles over power and control.

If a story is to ring true in terms of conveying the human experience, then this pattern of *resistance and release* is perhaps the most basic element of an organic story structure. It represents the rudimentary view of conflict and conflict resolution that begins to set up the structural pattern.

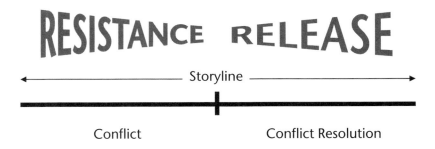

Notice that the *storyline* that runs the length of the *resistance and release* pattern has been bisected. This is to indicate that these are two halves of the same whole. Of course, the word *half* is a relative term, because no story should be held hostage to such a fixed ideal. However, conceptually it does help to see this principle in terms of two complete halves, because in that ratio they help to hold the story in balance. In other words, if you set your story conflict into motion and begin to resolve it by page 30, what are you going to write about to fill in the other eighty pages left in the screenplay? Conversely, if you keep layering conflict on top of conflict, with no movement toward resolution until you are three-quarters of the way into the script, the climax and resolution are going to feel forced and underdeveloped.

As the structural model becomes more and more detailed in the following chapters, you will find that holding this pattern of *resistance and release* in some sort of balance will help you establish and maintain a stronger and more powerful dramatic tension in your script.

A Bend in the Road

In terms of story development, this principle of *resistance and release* causes the story to naturally rise and fall, in effect forming an *arc* with its movement. As the conflict escalates, it climbs to an apex, where something causes it to shift and then descend into the resolution.

Story does not exist in a static environment; as in all aspects of life, it is ever-changing and progressing. The arc represents this movement in the human experience, which is non-random because it is directed toward a *goal*. In story, again as in life, that goal is the attempt to resolve a conflict by overcoming obstacles.

Think about something as simple as setting off for work in the morning and not being able to find your car keys. At first you may casually look in all the usual places, but as the minutes tick away your situation becomes more and more desperate. Your actions don't get calmer; they become more frenetic. "Where are those darn keys!" you explode at your kids, as if the five-year-old snuck out in the middle of the night for a joy ride. Pillow cushions get tossed, drawers slammed, pockets turned inside out, but none of these actions are going to necessarily bring you your desired results. You are in the first half of the arc, where *resistance* to the goal is escalating.

From here there are several possible scenarios: 1) You calm yourself down, retrace your actions from the night before, and remember that you entered the house with an armload of dry cleaning, which is where you find your keys, ensnared in a tangle of hangers; 2) you finally give up and call a locksmith, who comes to make you a new key; 3) you trip over your five-year-old's toy, twist your ankle, and call your boss to say you're in too much pain to come to work; 4) you don't trip over your child's toy, but you call your boss with the same *lame* excuse and decide to worry about the keys and your job tomorrow morning.

Notice the scenario that isn't even considered—you keep looking for your keys forever, never finding them, never going to work again, never leaving the house to buy groceries; you just spend the rest of your life relentlessly searching for your keys. That would be absurd. **All conflict has a breaking point, where our resistance to the solution is shifted toward a resolution, even if it's not the original resolution we had in mind.** This shift represents the apex of the arc. As a story moves up the arc, the need to resolve the conflict grows in intensity, but at some point something occurs that breaks the tension and brings a solution into consciousness. This begins to release the story toward a resolution, putting it on the downhill side of the arc.

Essentially, the arc works with gravitational pull. As with climbing a mountain, or ascending in a roller coaster, the higher one goes, the more energy it takes, causing resistance to escalate. At the apex of the arc, tension is released and this creates a descent that will escalate in speed and velocity. According to Newton's basic law of physics: the higher the ascent, the steeper the fall; the steeper the fall, the greater the momentum. This can make getting to the resolution not only precarious, but downright dangerous and unpredictable.

Dramatic? I would say so, which is why Newton, whether he knew it or not, has also given us one of the basic laws of organic story structure:

All drama begins with an escalation of tension and is resolved as the tension deescalates. Don't underestimate the power of working with this simple principle. Your protagonist can't resolve a conflict that hasn't been established and developed; what would he or she be resolving? This doesn't mean that a writer can't play with the story in terms of starting at the end, or arranging the linear story elements completely out of order. It does mean, however, that no matter what device is used, the conflict will still rise and fall. For example, if the writer wants the audience to witness the climax in the opening scene, as in *Memento*, then the climax must be used, in effect, to introduce the conflict. If the story is told out of sequential order, as in *Pulp Fiction*, then the new order will still hold this rise and fall of the conflict. If it doesn't, the audience simply won't be able to track the story, and/or they will feel so confused that they will never become engaged enough to care about the outcome.

The Pattern of Life

The limitation of this simple arc pattern is that it is free-floating, in that it begins and ends abruptly because it is not connected to anything. If story is a reflection of our lives in motion, then no conflict that we encounter can be free-floating or disconnected from everything else. **All conflict is part of a developmental continuum that comes from somewhere in our past and takes us to someplace new, opening the**

door to our future. Therefore, there must be a trail that leads into and out of this arc that represents where we've been, where we are, and where we're going.

For example, after you find your keys you leave for work, but because you were running late, you neglect to check your gas tank and you run out of gas on the freeway. Now, only because you solved the first problem do you get to the second dilemma, and even after you resolve the gas crisis you still have to face your employer, who's not interested in excuses because this is the fifth time you've been late in the past two weeks.

Instead of being a singular arc, the loss of the keys is now part of a series of arcs, representing past, present, and future conflicts that need to be resolved:

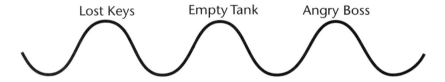

Lost Keys   Empty Tank   Angry Boss

Notice how the arcs are connected by a continuous rise and fall; the ending to one problem opens the pathway to encountering and resolving the next. Of course, the stories that we write aren't usually about things as mundane or trivial as losing keys and running out of gas. Those tend to be some of the behavioral details that are embedded into the greater arcs of our stories, where the protagonist loses his job because he's continually late and irresponsible, which is the by-product of alcoholic behavior that has been aggravated by a recent divorce. Irresponsibility, alcoholism, and divorce are all factors that had a history of conflict and resolution prior to the moment the new story began. Drinking, for example, may have been the solution to an unhappy childhood, and for awhile it might have actually worked at numbing the pain caused from abusive parents. But that same numbness may also have become the catalyst for irresponsibility and the inability to maintain an intimate marital relationship.

Difficult Childhood   Failing Marriage   Troubled Career

Notice that any one of these arcs would yield a complete story within itself. They also could become individual incidents that could produce a story in an even greater context, which might look at the overarching question of whether or not this character can get sober. His troubled childhood, the loss of his marriage, and the damage to his career may represent the intensification of the conflict that finally forces him to take a very serious look at his life.

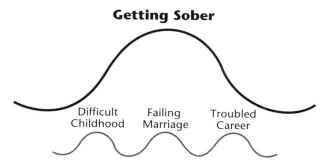

Getting Sober

Difficult   Failing   Troubled
Childhood   Marriage   Career

The Sphere of Influence

One of the most interesting aspects of this rise and fall pattern formed by the arcs is that if any one of the arcs were turned inward on itself, it would form a *circle*. The circle is a very ancient symbol of wholeness.

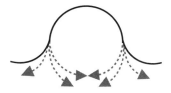

But this particular circle is in reality a never-ending cycle of expansive growth and development, which means that the arc pattern never actually closes in on itself completely. Instead of becoming a finite circle, it essentially develops into a continuous circling pattern that forms a *spiral* created from arc after arc folding in on itself.

In her book *Signs and Symbols*, Clare Gibson explains that, "In common with the circle, the spiral shares the symbolism of continuity and cyclical movement, but it also signifies involution and evolution: While it contains elements of the old order, it branches out into new spheres and thus represents change and development."[1] The symbolism of the arc, therefore, reiterates the most predominant, recurring theme of this book: *Story structure is a reflection of the natural movement of the life process because…*

IT REPRESENTS CHANGE AND GROWTH

From Here to Quaternity

The change and development that brings about the constant renewal of life is dependent on the attempt to reconcile or bring into balance opposing forces within us all: Masculine seeks feminine, shadow seeks light, chaos seeks clarity, and ignorance seeks wisdom. In order for any and all of these conflicting opposites to find a balance that resolves the tension between them, what is *unconscious (unknown)* at the beginning of the story must become *conscious (known)* by the end. This will bring what was *dying (the fatal flaw of character)* into a new stage of *life (transformation)*. The union of these two sets of interrelated opposites forms a powerful quaternity, which is a four-fold symmetry that symbolizes wholeness.

---

[1] Clare Gibson, *Signs & Symbols: An Illustrated Guide to Their Meaning and Origins* (New York: Barnes and Noble, 1996), 81.

Consciousness and **unconsciousness,** **life** and **death** are the two primary sets of opposites that are *always* at play in the human experience, which is why they are also *always* at play in the human story. In our personal dramas, each individual sex (male and female) is constantly struggling to *know* the other; different parts of our nature (e.g., intellect, aptitude, self-image, etc.) are always striving to *connect* with their opposites. In the larger social and cultural drama, these tensions are often manifested between the haves and the have-nots, the powerful and the weak, the old and the young, the righteous and the corrupt, and so on.

From this perspective, films such as *Schindler's List* and *Casablanca* aren't only about opportunistic men caught in the crossfire of history who must make selfless choices to help others survive. In an even greater sense they are stories about people (just like us), caught between the desire to stand alone and the need to be connected to others. The dynamic tension between this type of conscious and unconscious split is part of all of our lives, and it constantly demands that we make choices. In *Schindler's List* and *Casablanca*, the underlying question is: Who do we serve, our *Self* or *Others*?

The snare here is that, again, there is no right answer. Where there is tension (conflict, disharmony) there is an imbalance in the *force* between the opposing energies. One side is getting too much attention and the other side is getting too little.

SELF vs. OTHERS

In the case of these two films, both Oskar Schindler and Rick Blaine are so consumed with their own selfish needs that they have lost contact with the needs of others. This leaves them isolated and alone, even though they are surrounded by many people. They both consider themselves to be strong, independent men who need nothing and no one. However, what we see of them in the beginning of their stories is that they are suffering greatly from this isolation. Their lives aren't fulfilled and content, but desolate and meaningless. They do need a connection to others, but that need is completely *unconscious* or *unknown* and, if it remains so, it will clearly destroy (metaphorically kill) them.

This doesn't mean that the need for *others* is greater or more important than the needs of the *Self*; it just means that these two aspects of who we are are seeking to find a balance within us. For example, in our earlier exploration of *Dead Poets Society* and *Ordinary People*, we saw that the boys in these two stories diminished the value of their own needs out of a sense of obligation and duty to their families and their communities (*others*). This also brought about strife, struggle, and conflict, which if left unresolved (*unconscious, unknown*) would ultimately destroy their emerging sense of *Self* identity. So here the weight of the imbalance was reversed:

SELF vs. OTHERS

At its core, the structure of a story is framed around the conflict that ensues as a result of this sort of gross imbalance. Remember, **conflict is always a matter of imbalance.** Think about how imbalance creates strife, stress, rivalry, dissension, incompatibility, and just about any other expression of conflict that you can imagine. So writers must ask themselves: How does this imbalance apply to my own life and to my stories?

Getting Back in Shape

To get a greater sense of how these opposing tensions are expressed in story structure, we need to reopen the circle and put it back into the linear wave pattern that forms the arc. This enables us to better track the movement of the protagonist. When we reopen the circle, we will leave the quadrants in place, thus the storyline is now divided into four (relatively) equal parts.

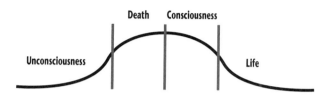

It does seem, however, that the concepts of *life* and *death*, *consciousness* and *unconsciousness*, may be a bit grand and too cumbersome for many types of stories. Therefore, I found it helpful to modify these terms and give them an expression that is easier to work with. *Consciousness* is really just an indication that something is **known**, and its opposite refers to what is **unknown.** *Life*, in story language, usually means that something is moving toward a **renewal** of energy, and its opposite is a movement away from or an **exhaustion** of energy. When these concepts are integrated into the arc, they can tell writers quite a lot about how the protagonist will move through a story.

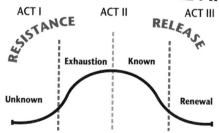

For example, the protagonist will always enter the story in a condition of great *unknowing*. There must be some aspect of the conflict that he or she doesn't know how to solve or resolve, or there would be no story to tell.

When we first meet Oskar Schindler and Rick Blaine, for instance, they are both living under the cynical delusion (in their respective films) that as long as they get their extravagant share of the spoils of war, they've got everything they need. They are completely oblivious to how empty their lives have become. Throughout the first halves of *Schindler's List* and *Casablanca*, both of these protagonists demonstrate great *resistance* to any effort to make real human contact. However, the greater their resistance to change, in the first half of the arc, the more *exhausted* and non-functioning their old attitudes and behaviors become. In the second half of these films, Oskar and Rick become aware of their emptiness and begin to figure out how to resolve their internal and external conflicts. It is from this new place of *knowing* that they are pushed to fight for a *renewal* of life in the climax. What was unconsciousness (unknown) becomes conscious (known); what was obsolete dies (becomes exhausted and runs out of energy) and has the potential to invigorate (renew) their spirits, bringing both their internal and external conflicts into a new sense of balance.

As Simple As ABC

Setting up conflict at the beginning of a story establishes the plotlines that will guide the story throughout. There are three primary plotlines in a story: a plot and two subplots. It can often feel as if there are more than these three, but, as you will see, all storylines are usually an aspect of either the plot or one of the principal subplots.

In the film industry, **the plot is referred to as the "A" STORY.** Chapter Two covered in great detail how the plot is developed. If you recall:

Heightened *CONFLICT* creates *JEOPARDY*.
JEOPARDY creates a need for *RESOLUTION*.
Getting to the *RESOLUTION* establishes a *GOAL*.
The struggle to achieve the *GOAL* generates dramatic *TENSION*.

In Chapter Two we also discussed that a lot more is going on in a script than just the external line of action or plot. If a story is true to our own human experience, then for every *external* action there is an *internal* reaction. This internal reaction represents the inner drive of the protagonist, and it is what MOTIVATES his or her external actions, creating a *cause and effect* or *symbiotic* relationship between the two.

Here's how it works:

1. Something happens in the *outer,* physical world that creates an **external conflict,** which produces a response based on the *inner* needs of the protagonist.
2. Those inner needs cause an **internal reaction.**
3. This internal reaction stimulates a character to take physical action, eliciting an **external response.**
4. The external response creates an **internal shift** in how the protagonist sees him- or herself and the rest of the world.
5. As a result of this internal shift, the protagonist is capable of resolving the **external conflict.**

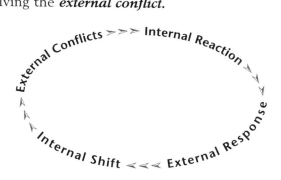

To some degree *all* stories observe this principle of internal reaction to external conflict. Even in the worst films, characters will still have some sort of emotional reaction to the stimulus in their environment. Danger engenders fear, a pretty girl inspires lust, loss evokes sorrow, and so on. But those emotional responses will pretty much dangle around on the edges of a story unless they are made part of the substance of the story itself.

To weave the internal conflict of the character into the fabric of the story it must be given form, weight, and dimension in much the same manner as it is given form and shape in the external conflict. This means that when the INNER CONFLICT rises to a level that is great enough to demand RESOLUTION, it establishes a GOAL that inspires ACTION. This forms a STRUCTURE that is contained in an internal plotline of its own. **This is the nature of a subplot.**

> NOTE: *Many theories on writing consider a subplot to be a storyline that is merely secondary or complementary to the plot. Its primary function, therefore, is to complicate or add dimension to the external line of action. While to some degree it is true that a subplot does complicate and add dimension to the story, I find this definition to undervalue the function of subplots, and it likewise gives the writer very little information or understanding of how to design and develop them.*

For our purposes, do not think of subplotting as secondary or subordinate to the plot. Here, *sub* does not mean "less than," it means "foundational"—as in *sub*-floor or *sub*-strata. A subplot is the *sub*stantial underpinning of a story that not only motivates the activity but also gives the action its true meaning and value. This bears repeating:

A subplot motivates activity and gives meaning and value to the action of the plot.

As mentioned, there are two primary subplots in a well-developed story. Chapter Five covered at length the development of the fatal flaw of character, which is where the internal conflict is developed. This subplot is called the **"B" STORY.**

The "B" story reveals what the protagonist needs to achieve *internally* in order to help resolve the external goal of the plot. But there's a fundamental problem here: How does a writer "show" internal conflict? In a novel or poem, there can at least be a wordy discourse on what a person is thinking and feeling. But film focuses on our actions, not our thoughts. So the question screenwriters and playwrights must constantly ask themselves is: How do characters express their inner emotions in their external behavior?

In this regard, let's take another look at the film classic *Casablanca*. Few would quarrel with the depiction of movie critic Robert Ebert, who describes Rick Blaine as a "disappointed, wounded, resentful hero," who has a "veneer of neutrality and indifference."[2] But how do we actually *know* this about him? The plot only reveals that Rick's old lover Ilsa shows up one day and asks him to help her and her husband escape Nazi occupation. There's not much justification for brooding and bitterness in that little request. A simple "yes" or "no" would do. But it's not quite that easy because Rick and Ilsa have a past, an unresolved past: *a disappointing, wounding, and resentful past.*... As the story unfolds we learn that Rick, a man for whom love and intimacy have never come easily, once gave his heart completely to Ilsa and the result was that she abandoned him—at least that's how he remembers it. So he covers his pain and heartache with a *veneer of neutrality and indifference*, never intending to let his heart become vulnerable again. Then, one day, "of all the gin joints in all the towns in all the world," she walks into his and the ice that surrounds his heart begins to thaw.

In the "A" story *(external conflict)*, something very big is at stake: Rick is asked to help Victor Laszlo—one of the leaders of the Allied Resistance—to escape from the malevolent grip of his Nazi pursuers. But because of the "B" story *(internal conflict)*, Rick cynically refuses to get involved. Thus, Rick's sense of isolation and apathy puts him in *opposition* to achieving the goal of the plot. This establishes the dramatic tension that needs to be resolved: To help Victor escape the Nazis, Rick must get over the disappointment and resentment of his past in order to care enough to want to help Victor.

What becomes clear is that the "A" story is dependent upon the "B" story for resolution. In other words, if Rick's internal issues don't get resolved, he will not help Victor escape. So the primary concern a writer must wrestle with is: How does Rick resolve his inner conflict?

As a writer, always rely upon what you experience in your own life to answer a question like this. How do you resolve your own inner

---

[2] RogerEbert.com. *Casablanca* review. September 15, 1996.

conflicts? Can inner transformation ever be a passive act? Does self-determination and willpower alone truly resolve inner torment? It's not that self-determination and willpower aren't effective tools, but they can't be used in a vacuum. Behind all inner commitment to change there must be *actions* that will validate whether or not that change has occurred. This means that *internal change is demonstrated in **relationship** to something in the outer world.*

A person's inner conflict isn't resolved just because he or she says so. If a marriage is on the rocks because of a husband's infidelity, it can't be fixed simply by an apology and a claim that he'll never do it again. He might be telling the absolute truth at the moment, but only time and consistency in *relationship* to his spouse will demonstrate whether or not anything has really changed within him and within her as well.

RELATIONSHIP, therefore, is another necessary aspect of the transformational arc. **The relationship conflict forms a second primary subplot, called the "C" STORY.** In *Casablanca*, Rick doesn't help Laszlo escape because he awoke one morning and decided it would be a nice thing to do. Rick helps Laszlo escape because he has *a change of heart*. That change occurred in ***relationship*** to how his love for Ilsa transformed him when the conflict between them was resolved. The internal relationship plotline is separate but not detached from the rest of the plotlines. It is one of the essential strands finely woven into the texture of the whole story. This distinct yet supporting quality is what makes the relationship storyline a subplot entity unto itself.

It's important to note that there can be some confusion regarding the relationship subplot, because sometimes a relationship can also define what is driving the plot or the external conflict itself. But these two types of relationship storylines are not the same at all. These are the distinctions:

- In the "A" story, a relationship conflict is driven by *external obstacles* that block the people in that relationship from achieving their external goal.

- In the "C" story, a relationship conflict primarily focuses on the protagonist's internal conflict and it serves to internally challenge him or her to change and grow in *relationship* to someone or something.

In other words, the "A" story can be about a couple getting married—which makes the goal of the plot revolve around whether or not they will physically get to the altar. However, the issues that they face internally in order to open their hearts to love and acceptance of each other are aspects of the "C" story.

For example, in *An Affair to Remember,* the plot or "A" story (*external action)* is driven by a love affair between a man and a woman who meet onboard a ship and fall in love and are planning to get married—only not to each other. They each have prior marriage commitments, so the conflict of the plot revolves around whether or not they can overcome these entanglements and other physical obstacles (she becomes disabled at one point) in order to unite and live happily ever after—with each other.

In this example, there is no killer to catch or big game to win in the "A" story. The central question of the whole plot revolves around whether or not Nickie (Cary Grant) and Terry (Deborah Kerr) can overcome other marriage commitments, and even physical handicaps, in order to get together in the end. But in truth, these external problems are not what pose the biggest threat to their union. Both of these people have sold out. In the beginning of the story, we learn that Nickie is set to marry a woman because she's rich and beautiful. Terry is similarly betrothed to a rich man who wants to make her into the ideal wife and society hostess. Furthermore, these marriages of convenience have caused them both to turn their backs on their own artistic endeavors (Nickie is an artist and Terry is a singer).

So, the central question of the "**A**" **story** (plot) is **will this couple (*physically*) get together?** But, the primary obstacle to their union lies in the "B" story (internal subplot), which shows us through their fatal flaw that **they both have lost faith in themselves** (in their artistic ability and in their capacity to love). But it's in the "**C" story** (relationship subplot) where the challenge for them to **learn to trust true love** is actually played out. If they can achieve this trust by regaining a belief in themselves again, they will not only resolve the "B" and "C" stories, but this will also cause them to form a union with each other, which resolves the "A" story as well.

If a relationship storyline is part of the plot, it explores the physicality of how a relationship is formed—boy meets girl, boy loses girl, girl lets boy catch her, etc. But, **as a subplot, a relationship storyline examines the internal value that the protagonist needs to acquire in order to succeed at achieving the relationship in the plot.**

Don't confuse a relationship plot with a relationship subplot. Plot-driven relationship stories as seen in *An Affair to Remember* and *When Harry Met Sally* are actually quite rare. Even when the love story feels as though it's the most prominent part of the film, more often than not the plot itself has very little to do with love. In *Sea of Love*, the goal of the plot or "A" story is to catch a serial killer. In *Shakespeare in Love*, the driving conflict of the plot or "A" story is to produce a play. In *The African Queen*, the primary objective is to escape the Germans and blow up one of their ships along the way. As in real life, love isn't usually our primary goal; it tends to be what happens to us while we're doing other things.

Relationship subplots aren't just about romantic love; they can be about the protagonist's need for relationship with *anyone* and any*thing*. The relationship that Oskar Schindler grappled with was between himself and the rest of humanity. In *Amadeus*, Salieri's fight was between his conscience and the divine. In *Moby Dick*, the clash with nature became the metaphorical battleground for the protagonist's struggle to accept and come to value his own nature. In Toni Morrison's novel *Beloved*, her protagonist, Sethe, wrestles with her own soul in the ghostly form of the daughter she murdered in an act of desperation to keep her "safe" from the hands of slavers.

One final and very important note to keep in mind when you are in the process of defining your plotlines: *Never lose connection with the theme.*

In a strong story it is always the thematic **value** that the protagonist is striving to achieve. Therefore:

1. The external events in the "A" story represent the opportunity in the *outer world* for the protagonist to grow and evolve toward that thematic value.

2. The internal conflict (fatal flaw of character) in the "B" story represents what is *lacking inside* that is forcing the protagonist to grow toward that thematic value.

3. The relationship conflict of the "C" story shows the impact that the lack of this value is having on the protagonist's *ability to connect* with someone or something.

If, for example, we were to say that the theme of *Casablanca* is simply that **we need each other,** then:

1. The external events in the "A" story must be set up as an opportunity for Rick to be needed. Hence, he is asked to save Victor Laszlo from the Nazis.

2. In the setup of the "B" story, the theme is expressed by showing us what Rick personally lacks in terms of having this need for others. He believes he needs nothing and no one, and his manner is portrayed as surly, brusque, ill-tempered, non-communicative, and impersonal.

3. In the "C" story, Rick's lack of valuing others leaves him isolated and alone, even in a crowd. This chasm between himself and others is widened even further when Ilsa appears on the scene and asks for his help. He not only spurns her because of the way he believes she once rejected him, but seeing her again drives him even further into himself. This makes the goal of the plot—to get Laszlo out of Casablanca—feel even more unattainable.

The Wholly Triad

As mentioned, there are many different approaches to understanding plot and subplot. But if a story is to be meaningful, it must express the writer's values and thematic point of view—an agenda that demands collaboration from every aspect of the story. **Plot and subplots, therefore, are interdependent parts of the same whole. They have an individual nature, but they need each other in order to become fully expressed.**

When the "A", "B," and "C" plotlines are clear and well balanced, they tell a powerful and compelling story.

- The "A" story shows us the problem in the *outer* world that can only be solved if:
- There is a shift of consciousness in the protagonist in the "B" story, which represents the *inner* world.
- That shift of consciousness primarily occurs in *relationship* to someone or something in the "C" story.
- And it is then through the relationship that the problem in the "A" story is resolved.

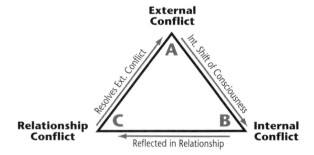

In *Casablanca*, the conflict of the "A" story—**Laszlo needs Rick's help to escape the Nazis**—can only be achieved if the conflict of the "B" story—**Rick connects with others**—is resolved through the conflict of the "C" story—**Rick learns to love unconditionally.** Rick learns to love unconditionally through his reunion with Ilsa in the "C" story, and this change deepens his connection to others, which motivates him to help Laszlo escape.

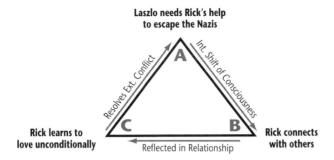

In *It's a Wonderful Life*, the conflict of the "A" story—**George must stop Potter from taking over the town**—can only be achieved if the conflict of the "B" story—**George learns to let go**—is resolved through the conflict of the "C" story—**George lets others care for him.** When Potter forces things to get so bad in Bedford Falls that George feels the only way out is to let go completely and jump off a bridge, he is rescued by an angel who shows him how important his relationships are with everyone in the town. Through this action George comes to realize that everything he ever really wanted he already has, including friends who will care for him as much as he cares for them. As long as George was holding on so tightly to his belief that he had to take care of everyone and everything, Potter was able to maintain a stranglehold on the town and its inhabitants. When George let go, the townspeople proved that they could uphold their end of the burden as well, and the effect of this union was to force Potter out of commission permanently and to allow George to get on with his life.

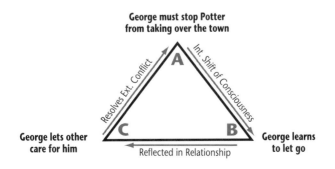

As a writer, one of the most effective ways you can begin to self-analyze your script is to ask yourself this simple question: **In order to resolve the external conflict, what will the protagonist achieve internally at the end of the story that he or she is not capable of achieving at the beginning?** If the answer is nothing, or very little, then you can be pretty certain that there isn't much internal subplotting going on. This means that your protagonist has come equipped in the beginning of the conflict with everything he or she needs to fight the final battle in the climax. And if this is true, then it doesn't really matter how much action and activity takes place; not much of a journey has occurred. In effect, the story doesn't really "go" anywhere.

A film I found disappointing for just this reason was Roman Polanski's *The Pianist*. According to his Director's Notes, Polanski was attracted to this autobiographical material about the holocaust because its author, Wladyslaw Szpilman, portrayed his own experience during this period with "surprising objectivity, which is almost cool and scientific."[3] While it may be a powerful and even compelling character trait for a protagonist to suffer through this sort of horror and misery with emotional detachment, the story itself cannot be told from that perspective or it will leave the audience detached as well. This is not to say that images of Nazi violence and inhumanity in this film aren't deeply disturbing, but they alone aren't enough to connect us to the emotional depth of the protagonist.

The plotline, or "A" story, in *The Pianist*, tracks Szpilman's survival during World War II. With the help of friends and courageous strangers, Szpilman is hidden away in various apartment rooms throughout Warsaw for the duration of the war. During most of the film, the audience watches Szpilman as he looks out his apartment windows and watches the Nazis slaughter nearly every Jew in the ghetto. There is no real development of any internal issue that impacts his ability to survive, so there is no fatal flaw, or "B" story, in this film. Further, even though we

[3] *The Pianist*. Roman Polanski. Director's notes. http://www.thepianist-themovie.com/pianist.htm

see people for whom Szpilman demonstrates great feeling and caring, there is no substantial relationship conflict that Szpilman needs to resolve in order to cope with or gain inner strength from his experiences. Therefore, there is also no "C" story. In the end, the Nazis are defeated and Szpilman becomes free to resume his illustrious concert career. This is something he was quite capable of doing (internally) since the film began. So, for all the horror Szpilman witnessed, there isn't much in the way this story is told that shows that he became any greater or lesser for his experiences. Again, this doesn't imply that in real life Szpilman was not profoundly changed by the hardships he had to endure, but the film never takes us into that internal reality.

Today one of the most popular genres in which there is a prevalent and glaring lack of a strong "B" and "C" subplot is the romantic comedy. Because the internal arc of character and the relationship conflict give meaning and value to a story, a romantic tale told without conscious attention to these plotlines will convey almost no thematic information about what it means to love. If we return to the example of *My Best Friend's Wedding*, discussed in Chapter Five, what we see at the end of the film is that Jules "surrenders" the man she *doesn't* love to the woman who already has his heart. Not only does this tell us absolutely nothing about the nature of love, but, if you think about it, it doesn't even make sense. How can you surrender something you don't have to somebody who already has it?

In an early draft of a script, a writer may be inspired by complex plot contrivances that produce surprising twists, unpredictable turns, funny situations, and intriguing dilemmas. While it's extremely important for all of these avenues to be fully explored, it's also a very dangerous trap for a writer to believe that cleverness and complexity alone will ultimately substitute for value and meaning. As the writing process evolves, it is important to identify what impact all the action, mystery, suspense, humor, and romance will actually have upon the lives of your characters. This is not something you want to wait to summarize in the end; rather, it is essential that you develop it at the beginning of the story in the form of emotions such as pain, emptiness, sadness, desire, and need.

If you succeed at establishing this emotional content, there is a very strong possibility that you will have succeeded at establishing or setting up the internal conflict in the story as well.

Case Studies

1) ROMANCING THE STONE

I especially like using *Romancing the Stone* as an example because the structure is so solid and straightforward. Straightforward, however, doesn't mean formulaic or unimaginative. This film is a wonderful model of how inner character development can turn something simple and nearly clichéd into a meaningful and memorable story.

In Chapter Four we explored how the theme of *Romancing the Stone* was developed around the metaphor that *love is an adventure*. Adventure, if you recall, has a dual nature; while it can lead us toward something that is thrilling and remarkable, it also takes us into unknown territory that feels dangerous and unpredictable. Finding the courage to trust the adventure, therefore, is the essential requirement of the intrepid soul who is searching for love. This thematic information now becomes very useful in order to **non-randomly** set up the three primary storylines in this film. Let's take a look at the thematic breakdown we constructed in the last chapter to see how it helps define the "A," "B," and "C" storylines.

The theme of this film offers a lot of information for designing the plot. If the film is going to express the value that Joan must learn to **trust** *the adventure of love*, then the only way she is going to come to appreciate this value is if she *experiences* a real adventure for herself. Because a real adventure will include real danger and peril, the stakes can be very high and not easily attained. This also indicates that the antagonists will represent the dark side of the adventure—and must truly be dangerous. Therefore, designing a plot that makes the antagonists kidnappers who threaten the life of Joan's sister is an excellent setup for the plot of this storyline.

"A" STORY	JOAN MUST SAVE HER SISTER
(PLOT)	FROM RUTHLESS KIDNAPPERS

On the right side of the illustration of the thematic structure, you can see that Joan's goal in the subplot is to learn to follow her heart. This very directly defines what she must achieve in the "C" story (relationship subplot). But if this goal is going to be a challenge for her, **then it must be something that she is not capable of achieving when the story begins.** Indeed, Joan's fatal flaw is that she is a coward when it comes to facing the unknown and trusting in the adventure that leads to love.

THEMATIC STRUCTURE
SUBJECT
Love

|

THEMATIC POINT OF VIEW
Love is an adventure

PLOT ("A")	SUBPLOT ("B" & "C")
(external thematic goal)	(internal thematic goal)
Trust the adventure	*Follow your heart*
OBSTACLE	FATAL FLAW
Fear the adventure	*Hide from your heart*
CONTEXT	CHARACTER TRAITS
Dangerous	*Isolated*
Scary	*Lonely*
Unpredictable	*Idealizes love*

"B" STORY	JOAN FINDS THE COURAGE TO
(INTERNAL SUBPLOT)	FACE THE UNKNOWN
"C" STORY	JOAN LEARNS TO FOLLOW
(RELATIONSHIP SUBPLOT)	HER HEART

It's important to test your "A," "B," and "C" plotlines to see if they support each other in making the story whole. In *Romancing the Stone*, Joan will be able to save her sister from the ruthless kidnappers *only* if she finds the courage to face the adventure of the unknown. Joan can only acquire this courage by learning to follow her heart, which will also help her save her sister. And, of course, the by-product of learning to follow her heart is that it will lead Joan to love.

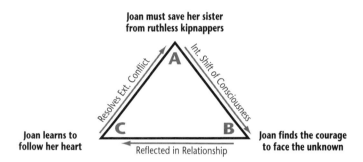

2) *Lethal Weapon*

The original *Lethal Weapon* works as well as it does primarily because it has such a strong character arc. Both co-protagonists must grow and evolve if they are going to solve the goal of the plot:

"A" STORY	RIGGS AND MURTAUGH MUST STOP
(PLOT)	THE DANGEROUS DRUG CARTEL

But unlike most of the heroes in modern action films, Riggs and Murtaugh **do not** come fully equipped to stop the dangerous drug cartel when the story begins. Even though they are up to the task in terms of being brave, smart, and tough, they are also both set on a course of self-destruction. If nothing changes, it's unlikely either of them will live long enough to defeat the enemy.

Both men are vulnerable because they have abandoned their trust in the life process: *Riggs has lost too much*, and *Murtaugh has too much to lose*. The thematic breakdown illustrates that as a result of this distrust,

Riggs is intent on throwing his life away and Murtaugh is holding on to his life too tightly. To bring both of their lives back into *balance*, they must **learn to trust life.** But trust is not an ideal that can be achieved by mere contemplation. It is achieved through effort in **relationship** to something or someone that challenges the very thing that is feared. In this story, the biggest source of distrust for both men is each other. Riggs believes that Murtaugh is dangerous because he's too timid for a cop, and Murtaugh is afraid to be anywhere near Riggs because he's too reckless. In reality, they are both right. But they're stuck with each other and in order to solve the goal of the plot they have to unite as a team, which means **learning to trust each other.**

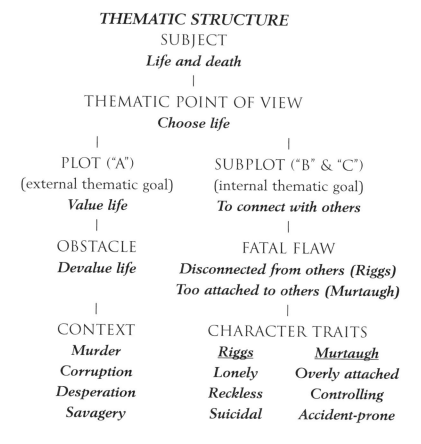

THEMATIC STRUCTURE
SUBJECT
Life and death
|

THEMATIC POINT OF VIEW
Choose life

PLOT ("A")	SUBPLOT ("B" & "C")
(external thematic goal)	(internal thematic goal)
Value life	**To connect with others**
|	|
OBSTACLE	FATAL FLAW
Devalue life	*Disconnected from others (Riggs)*
	Too attached to others (Murtaugh)
|	|
CONTEXT	CHARACTER TRAITS
Murder	*Riggs* *Murtaugh*
Corruption	*Lonely* *Overly attached*
Desperation	*Reckless* *Controlling*
Savagery	*Suicidal* *Accident-prone*

"B" STORY
(INTERNAL SUBPLOT)

RIGGS AND MURTAUGH
LEARN TO TRUST LIFE

"C" STORY
(RELATIONSHIP SUBPLOT)

RIGGS AND MURTAUGH MUST
CONNECT AND FORM A TEAM

Notice how well the plotline and subplotlines triangulate to support one another in this story. Riggs and Murtaugh will **stop the deadly drug cartel** *only* if they **learn to trust life again** and stop being too reckless or too timid. They achieve these goals by learning to **trust and connect with each other,** and thereby gain the support they need to change. Ultimately, it is through the strength of their teamwork that they stop the cartel and resolve the goal of the plot.

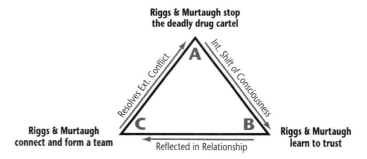

3) ORDINARY PEOPLE

Anyone who is writing a character-driven story would be well advised to review *Ordinary People* and observe how strong the external plotline is. There's a tendency in character-driven films to emphasize what people are thinking and feeling, not what they're doing. Thoughts and feelings are not only difficult to communicate in a film, but they also don't convey the full scope of how we humans deal with our inner issues. Just as external actions cause internal reactions, it can also be said that our internal reality is always based on external circumstances. We don't get depressed, agitated, afraid, worried, or even joyful and ecstatic for no reason. There is a cause-and-effect relationship between external stimuli and an internal response.

For the family in *Ordinary People*, there is nothing they would like more than to keep a tight lid on their emotions. Therefore, in order for their thoughts and feelings to become big enough that they can actually be seen and understood, something quite significant has to *happen* to them. In fact, even when something as bad as the death of their first-born son occurs, they have such powerful coping mechanisms in place that most of the pain and heartbreak they feel is suppressed. Therefore, if a writer wants to expose their feelings and emotions, the family will have to be pushed, by external events, past the breaking point—and this is precisely where this movie begins.

THEMATIC STRUCTURE
SUBJECT
Family

|

THEMATIC POINT OF VIEW
A family must value each other

PLOT ("A")	SUBPLOT ("B" & "C")
(external thematic goal)	(internal thematic goal)
Value the needs	*Value your*
of the individual	*own needs*
OBSTACLE	FATAL FLAW
Devalue the needs	*Devalue your*
of the individual	*own needs*
CONTEXT	CHARACTER TRAITS
Demands conformity	*Inauthentic and controlling (Mom)*
Inauthentic	*Self-doubting and anxious (Dad)*
Desperate	*Depressed and suicidal (Conrad)*

From the thematic breakdown, we can see that the greatest emotion this family is suppressing is a feeling of personal value. They would probably deny this if confronted, but if you observe them it is easy to see that there is no outlet for them to express how they're feeling or what they need. Everything stays neatly on the level of cordiality. In fact, if Conrad were to have been interviewed on the night he attempted suicide, he would probably have said he was doing it because he didn't want to trouble anybody anymore. But this act of sublime selflessness has just the opposite appearance to the family. Whereas his brother's accident couldn't be helped, Conrad does have control over his actions. Allowing his emotions to be displayed so conspicuously, therefore, is a huge and intolerable breach in the family code of honor. It's so big that it draws attention to this unspoken, *unconscious* code, and gets Dad thinking (and feeling) that maybe it's not such a good code after all.

The accidental drowning and the suicide attempt are the events that set this story into motion, and, interestingly, they take place before the film even begins. They are, nonetheless, a big part of the setup. Without them, or something just as overwhelming, it is unlikely that this family would ever budge from their delusional state of happiness. But because of the brother's drowning, Conrad has become overtly self-destructive. His attempted suicide is an action meant to rectify things and make the pain go away, so everybody can be "happy" again. Of course, it doesn't work, but that is exactly what happens when a character is on the *resistance* side of the arc of transformation. If this problem were easy to resolve, it wouldn't really be a problem. As a result of Conrad's actions, the real issues in this family begin to surface, both physically and emotionally. Had Conrad's suicide attempt succeeded, there wouldn't be much of a family left, but if he becomes emotionally stable and puts suicidal thoughts aside, he will challenge the very foundation upon which this family is built. Therefore, in a very physically demonstrative way, the plot of this story is defined as the struggle of this family to survive.

"A" STORY	THE FAMILY STRUGGLES TO
(PLOT)	REMAIN A FAMILY

Note how perfectly all of the family members serve the multiple function of being part of the family, both collectively and individually. To adequately fulfill the function of co-protagonists, each family member must have the same internal and external goals. They each must have a strong desire to remain a family, even if it's for different reasons and even if they have a different perception of what it means to be a family. Mom's idea of saving the family entails getting things back to the way they were before—back to "normal." Both dad and son, on the other hand, have come to realize that things need to change. All of those messy emotions that have been so neatly tucked away are exploding inside Conrad, and if they don't get the attention and validation they need, he won't survive and neither will the family. For the family to truly survive, they must learn to face themselves honestly, meaning they must begin to place a value on their own needs, perceptions, feelings, and emotions. This internal shift will subsequently lead them to value those same things in each other.

"B" STORY	THE FAMILY MEMBERS MUST GET
(INTERNAL SUBPLOT)	HONEST ABOUT THEMSELVES
"C" STORY	THE FAMILY MEMBERS MUST
(RELATIONSHIP SUBPLOT)	LEARN TO VALUE EACH OTHER

Here, again, if we triangulate the "A," "B," and "C" plotlines, it brings the essence of the story into clarity and focus. For **the family to survive,** each person must **get honest about him- or herself.** This will help them understand and value their own needs, feelings, and emotions. Learning to understand themselves will help develop their ability to understand and **value each other.** If they can learn to value each other, they will form a *real* family that is capable of surviving anything.

Putting It All Together

The *organic* structure of a story is beginning to take shape. The quadrants express a natural form of dramatic tension that delineates the story into what we commonly refer to as the THREE-ACT STRUCTURE. But, how do four quadrants equal three acts?

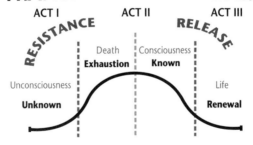

Notice in the diagram that the second act is divided into two halves, thus it is (relatively) twice as long as the first and third acts. In fact, it may be for just this reason that some experts in this field use a four-act model when defining screenplay structure. However, it really doesn't matter what you call it. It's more important that you *feel* the tension of these opposing quadrants as they pull against each other, for it is they, not some arbitrary act break or page count, that will define the movement of a story.

On the other hand, act breaks and page counts are extremely relevant in terms of giving the writer guideposts and boundaries within which to organize and make maximum use of structural elements. In the upcoming chapters we'll examine these elements as they are traditionally defined within the context of the *Three-Act Structure*, but we'll also explore them for their deeper human values.

The transformational arc is not just the arc of any one character; it is the arc of the *human* character. This means that *all* movement within a story must be a mirror of our own movement in life. How we rise to a challenge by making choices and accepting change ("A" story), how we are capable of self-destruction and re-creation ("B" story), and how we relate to each other ("C" story) are what bring storytelling to life.

CHAPTER SEVEN

ACT I
Fade In…

People wish to be settled:
only as far as they are unsettled is there any hope for them.

~ RALPH WALDO EMERSON

Where to Start?!

Contrary to what may seem obvious, a story doesn't begin at the beginning; it begins in opposition to the ending. The ending is where the story clarifies its value and purpose. Therefore, the story must begin at a point where achieving the value and purpose are necessary and relevant.

The tale of *Little Red Riding Hood* doesn't begin the day she learned to knit an afghan or tie her own shoes; it begins on an ordinary spring day when she is told to go into the forest by herself to visit her sick, old grandmother. Sending a young girl out alone into the untamed wilderness is a pretty strong indicator that something unpredictable, if not downright perilous, is about to occur. We don't yet know what fate will befall her at the end of the story, but we do have a sense of foreboding because young, innocent girls and dark, scary woods are at opposite ends of our comfort spectrum. Even before the introduction of the Big Bad Wolf we already feel a compelling sense of dramatic tension.

On a much more sophisticated level, that same sort of apprehension also pulls us into Martin Scorsese's award-winning film *Goodfellas*, written by Nicholas Pileggi and Scorsese. In an opening scene, young

Henry Hill, a wide-eyed adolescent, peers out the window of his apartment onto the wild, untamed *mean streets* of Brooklyn and ponders his future:

> HENRY (V.O.)
> As far back as I can remember, I always
> wanted to be a gangster. To me, being a
> gangster was better than being President
> of the United States. Even before I first
> wandered into the cabstand for an after-
> school job, I knew I wanted to be part of
> them. It was there that I knew that I
> belonged.

A naive, young boy aspiring to join the ranks of such dubious role models as Fat Andy, Frankie the Wop, Freddy No Nose, and Pete the Killer is certainly as dangerous a proposition as Little Red Riding Hood going into the dark, forbidding woods alone. Both kids are poised on the edge of the great underworld abyss, and neither can tell a Big Bad Wolf from a cocker spaniel.

> HENRY (V.O.)
> They weren't like anyone else. They did
> whatever they wanted. They'd double-park
> in front of the hydrant and nobody ever
> gave them a ticket. In the summer when
> they played cards all night, nobody ever
> called the cops.

Little Red even goes so far as to give the smooth-talking wolf her grandmother's address and assure him that the little old lady is sitting home all alone. At this point in both stories, the opposition of the young, naive child to the dangerous, devouring world *out there* indicates that above all else what's really at stake is the child's survival.

Understanding the issues in opposition to each other is the key to setting up a good story. The first half of this book focuses on developing your thematic intention, because without some understanding of the values being expressed in your script it can be extremely difficult to identify the forces that oppose the outcome or goal of the story. This lack of understanding can easily make the setup of the first act unclear and undirected.

The exclusive purpose of the first act is to set conflict into motion. Every image, every movement of character, every nuance of dialogue must serve the function of establishing conflict. Re-watch just the first five minutes of *Goodfellas* and observe a master storyteller at work. While it's an emotionally powerful choice to enter this story through the fanciful imagination of a twelve-year-old who idolizes neighborhood thugs, this film takes a step back and begins instead with a terrifying preamble that manages to convert Henry's childhood whimsy into tragic irony. Before getting to the dreamy-eyed boy, the audience must first meet the fear-driven man that Henry is on the verge of becoming. We see him in the opening scene as a glorified lackey, driving a couple of two-bit hoods out into the middle of nowhere so they can dispose of a body, locked in their trunk. Unfortunately, the body isn't quite as dead as they had hoped and, when it begins to thrash about, the gangsters pop open the trunk and mercilessly club and shoot the poor slob to death as Henry watches in amazement (or perhaps awe).

On every level—intellectual, emotional, instinctual—the audience is challenged by these juxtaposed images of brutality and innocence. But if this is the underlying conflict between two opposing values, then it hardly seems like a fair fight. After all, who would willingly give up the safe, warm womb for such horror and misery? Actually, the real question is *who gets a choice?* The world can be a harsh, unfair place and, as even Little Red Riding Hood discovers, everyone gets gobbled up at some point. We *know*, therefore, that Henry is going down; the real conflict that he faces is whether or not he can rise again. Does he have the fortitude of Little Red Riding Hood and her biblical predecessor Jonah, who managed to extract themselves from the belly of the beast before it was too late? Or will his own flesh become part of the flesh of the beast itself?

For a writer to give life to this kind of work, it isn't necessary to know the end of the story before beginning to write, but only to know the point of view that the ending will express. Whether or not Henry takes the high or low road is relatively inconsequential, meaning that it's a matter of creative choice. *Pulp Fiction, Unforgiven, Malcolm X, Leaving Las Vegas,* and *Citizen Kane* are just a few of the modern stories that do battle with similar opposing forces. Even though none of these stories looks, feels, or sounds alike, all of them show us a view and give us a perspective on what it means to be swallowed up by shadowy, underworld forces. Some characters break out, some are consumed, and some, such as Henry Hill, tragically will never learn to tell the difference.

At the end of *Goodfellas,* after selling out everybody and everything he ever cared about to save his own hide, Henry is stowed safely away in the witness protection program. Yet he still complains:

```
EXT: STREET IN MIDWESTERN ANDY HARDY TOWN - DAY

TRACK down the street.

                    HENRY (V.O.)
        And that's the hardest part. Today
        everything is different. There's no action.

CAMERA TRACKS past white picket fence.

                    HENRY (V.O. cont'd)
        I have to wait around like everyone else. You
        can't even get decent food. Right after I got
        here I ordered some spaghetti with marinara
        sauce and I got egg noodles and ketchup.
```

```
CAMERA APPROACHES house and tracks IN TO DOOR OF HOUSE
as it opens.


A MAN, still in pajamas, leans out to get the milk and
newspaper. He looks up. It's HENRY.

                    HENRY (V.O. cont'd)
                    (talking to camera)
          I'm an average nobody. I get to live the
          rest of my life like a schnook.
```

Anatomy of a First Act

Once the "A," "B," and "C" storylines in a script have been identified, as described in the last chapter, the process of setting up the conflict in the first act becomes much clearer. The plot and subplots each portray what's at stake for the protagonist in terms of: A) the external problem, B) the internal conflict, and C) the relationship conflict. Most importantly, the first act will show how and why all three of these storylines are interrelated.

To demonstrate this, let's play with a simple cop caper. If the "A" story revolves around a cop solving a murder, then the audience needs to see or at least learn about the murder in the setup. In addition, they must also be made aware of any external obstacles that are blocking the cop from instantly solving the case. These obstacles will consist of things *outside* of the cop's control, such as a devious killer who uses multiple disguises, or a delay in discovering the body that causes the trail to grow cold.

To set up the "B" story, the audience needs to be shown that there are personal problems or internal issues creating obstacles to solving the murder as well. For instance, the cop might arrive at the crime scene drunk or hungover, which makes him unable to properly assess the evidence. Or perhaps he is so aggressive that he abuses a suspect's constitutional rights, which forces the court to release the killer back onto the streets, where he immediately strikes again.

While these internal scenarios are interesting, if they stand alone the protagonist will merely come across as either a worthless drunk or a heartless bully. It's important, therefore, to show a *relationship* between this behavior and what is causing him to drink excessively and/or act out aggressively. If this information isn't present, the audience won't *care* whether or not he can resolve his drinking and hostility problems. For example, in the setup of the first act it could be shown that his wife just left him or that his boss just passed him over for an important promotion. It is then through his relationship with his wife or his boss that the conflict of the "C" story comes into focus, which adds depth and dimension to the "A" and "B" storylines.

In the first set of examples for the "A" story, all of the obstacles are external. Who the killer is and how long it takes before a body is discovered are aspects of the environment in the outer world. But the fact that the cop is drunk or overly aggressive relates directly to what is going on inside of him. Both sets of circumstances impact the outcome of the story; both are important and both need to be resolved. But also notice that it's highly unlikely that the first problem—*to stop the killer*—will be solved unless the cop can bring his drinking and/or his aggression under control. How the cop can potentially do this is worked out in the "C" story (relationship subplot), which is where he finds the opportunity to resolve the internal issues that created those conflicts.

When setting up your plotlines, be aware that there are generally four possible scenarios for the outcome of this three-dimensional story. It's vital that you clearly point the story in one of these directions in the setup, so that the audience has some sense of where the story is taking them.

SCENARIO 1

The cop catches the killer ("A" story) because he is able to stop drinking and/or being abusive ("B" story). He overcomes these self-destructive qualities by resolving the issues that caused the relationship conflict ("C" story).

*This demonstrates a **heroic arc of character** because it shows us that once the cop deals with his inner demons and brings them under control, he is then capable of dealing with the demons in the external world.*

SCENARIO 2

The cop doesn't catch the killer ("A" story) because he is unable to stop drinking and/or being abusive ("B" story), which also indicates that he was unable to resolve the relationship conflict ("C" story).

*This scenario is **tragic** because it shows us that if our internal demons aren't dealt with, the external demons will prevail.*

SCENARIO 3

The cop catches the killer ("A" story) even though he fails to stop drinking and/or being abusive ("B" story), which indicates that he likewise failed at resolving the relationship conflict ("C" story).

*This is also **tragic** because it indicates that the cop achieved a hollow victory. He only looks heroic on the outside, but on the inside he is at risk of becoming the demon himself.*

SCENARIO 4

The cop doesn't catch the killer ("A" story) even though he does stop drinking and/or being abusive ("B" story), which he achieves through resolving the relationship conflict ("C" story).

*This scenario can be **heroic** if it shows us that catching the killer wasn't really the right thing for him to do in the end. Maybe, for example, he realizes that the killer himself was a victim of a much greater wrong or that the system is so broken that catching the killer puts the cop on the wrong side of doing what is right.*

There is also a more cynical conclusion that can be reached with this type of story: that no matter how much we try in life, we ultimately have no control over the actions of others and over outside circumstances. (While this can bear some very thoughtful and interesting philosophical fruit, be careful when you enter this complex realm because there can be a fine line between exploring the seeming pointlessness of random events in life and having the story itself come across as pointless and insignificant.)

Notice that in all of these scenarios the "C" story, or relationship conflict, is the lynchpin for resolving everything else. It is primarily in the "C" story that we see the internal issues of the "B" story worked out, and from that new source of strength and courage the protagonist is then able to resolve the "A" story. This is why in a good film we are most often drawn to the relationship storyline over everything else. When you think of plot-driven films such as *Casablanca, The Godfather, Taxi Driver, Fatal Attraction, Thelma and Louise,* and *Notorious,* what lingers in your memory are the relationships that evolved much more than the strongly detailed plots that did, in fact, move the action forward.

Image Is Everything

If the three plotlines are well established, chances are good that the first act will be strong and well defined. However, conflict that is strong and well defined doesn't necessarily imply that the actual writing is powerful and compelling. This quality is far more illusive to achieve and will depend greatly on the writer's innate ability to communicate the layers of internal and external conflict with subtlety, subtext, wit, nuance, and insight.

There are no simple rules or guidelines a writer can follow to tap into these qualities. However, there is one very powerful source of inspiration that a writer must utilize if he or she wants to avoid mediocre, predictable, unimaginative storytelling...

Follow the Image!

Because film is a visual medium, conflict and theme can best be expressed through images. What you *see* in great films is that images have more of an impact on drawing the audience into the conflict than any other story element. Individually the action, dialogue, and setting only tell us a part of what is going on. But when they work in collaboration with one another to imply an image, they give the film a deeper sense of wholeness. Images penetrate the surface of the story to tell us what is *really* going on inside.

By "image" I do not mean that a screenwriter should pen lengthy, detailed, poetic descriptions of the environment of the story. Scripts are meant to be read quickly and easily and should never be bogged down with overwrought narrative passages. A screenplay is the foundation of an artistic vision that is expressed in moving pictures. Those moving pictures can be used to merely show us the one-dimensional movement of a character in a scene, or they can collectively conspire to form an image that will take the audience into the emotional, psychological, and spiritual depths of the story.

In the opening scene of *Rocky*, for example, the audience is *not* told directly through dialogue that he's a down-and-out fighter who needs a big, important match to breathe new life into the shambles he's made of his career. But within five minutes of the opening credits, this conflict is made clear through very powerful imagery, relaying more than just the bleakness of Rocky's boxing future, but also the loneliness, disappointment, sadness, and confusion that are completely destroying him. To express this desolate reality, the filmmaker bombards us with images of human waste—or what amounts to the waste of a human life. Beginning with the dark, shabby, callous atmosphere of the fight arena, we immediately sense that we are in a shadowy underworld place. Its inhabitants, who are likewise wretched, grubby, bottom-feeding creatures, convey feelings of desperation and hopelessness. Therefore, as we become engaged in the fight between Rocky and his opponent, the imagery makes us *feel* that the stakes are very, very high. This is not because Rocky is winning or losing the two-bit fight, but because the images that envelop the fight scene convey a foreboding sense of doom. This leaves the audience feeling that something much greater is at stake.

In contrast to this ill-fated atmosphere, there is also a singular image of hope shining through all the despair. Presiding over this temple of reckoning is a giant, embracing mural of Christ with his arms outstretched on the cross. It doesn't feel as though the symbolism here is meant to be particularly religious, but to imply that there is no depth to which the human soul can descend that it cannot be redeemed, that on the other side of doom is always the potential for resurrection.

Ultimately, the plot of this story revolves around Rocky's ability to do the impossible: defeat the heavyweight champion of the world. However, what we see in the first act is that less emphasis is paid to the big prize fight than to what Rocky is actually fighting for. This sort of attention to the development of inner character conflict over plot detail in the first act is quite common in a lot of great action-driven films. *The Godfather, Chinatown, Fatal Attraction, Thelma and Louise, Braveheart, Dances with Wolves, Platoon, Goodfellas,* and *Unforgiven* all built their stories on the nuances of inner character conflict in the first act. This allowed audiences to personally identify with the plight of the protagonist, so that as the balance shifted toward the external conflict (the big fight) in the second and third acts we were emotionally, not just intellectually, invested in the outcome.

An excellent exercise that will help you to better articulate this sort of subtle imaging in your own writing is to conjure scenes for yourself that describe the mundane activity of your protagonist. What is the weather like? How does he or she get out of bed in the morning? What's for breakfast? What is the energy level? What does the ambience of the scene convey about his or her mood or situation in life? If he or she is feeling depressed, anxious, lonely, or afraid, how can you create an atmosphere that reflects those inner emotions? It doesn't matter whether any of this ever becomes part of the script. It's an effort to help you look past the details of the plot and see the humanity of the character. When practicing this exercise, include your knowledge of the theme and how it translates into the fatal flaw of character. Rocky's fatal flaw was that he had given up. The hell-like atmosphere of the fight arena in the opening scene, therefore, is the perfect image of the interior wasteland that his life has become as a result of his sin of self-abandonment.

Images are the most powerful way to convey the theme in both its positive and negative value. In *Dead Poets Society*, the theme expresses the need to honor our authentic nature. Sometimes, therefore, beautiful shots of nature (e.g., woods, lakes, trees) are used to set up scenes in which the boys feel robust and inspired about their possibilities in life. In contrast, the school itself is a shadowy, oppressive, stark environment where conformity, consistency, and routine are treated as its highest virtues. The film begins, in fact, with an annual opening day ceremony, where the boys recite their commitment to the four resolute pillars on which the institution stands: "tradition, honor, discipline, excellence." The compulsory, rigid, and banal nature of this formal ritual evokes a very uncomfortable sense of constraint and limitation. This image clearly signals to the audience that nothing very creative or original is meant to happen here. Thus the conflict over the boys' futures is subtly and yet profoundly conveyed.

To craft an image, keep in mind that you are constructing something that mirrors, reflects, or symbolizes its value. Working with image demands that you ask yourself: What does this mean to me? What am I really trying to say? An image is not a direct replication of an object or a situation, but a personal interpretation of what that object or situation means. This is why it is absolutely essential to have a personal perspective or bias toward what you are writing. Without it, your material will be lifeless and of no particular significance to anyone…especially yourself.

No Points for Ambiguity

It could be argued that the imagery in *Rocky* is as subtle as a ton of bricks. Perhaps that's true, or maybe it's just that the beauty of an image is in the eye of the beholder. One thing that can't be debated, however, is that the imagery in *Rocky* effectively draws us into the conflict of the story and, therefore, it's done its job. Within the first twenty pages of a film, if the audience doesn't understand what's at stake they won't be concerned about what's coming next. Vague, puzzling images, dialogue, and activity only serve to confuse and confound us; they don't connect us to the plight of the protagonist.

Many writers tend to confuse subtlety with ambiguity. Because no one wants to be accused of writing with a heavy hand, it may feel appropriate to draw the audience into the mystery of the situation by leaving the setup vague and non-specific. **This doesn't work!!**

Until the audience knows what's going on in a story, they won't *care* about the outcome. Utilize the first twenty pages of your script to clearly set up the conflict in all three storylines. Two common terms used to identify how the "A" story is set up are the **INCITING INCIDENT** and the **CALL TO ACTION.** The *inciting incident* doesn't have to directly relate to the protagonist. It can be a murder, a plane hijacking, or an errant meteor headed toward Earth that the protagonist knows nothing about. The inciting incident simply instigates the beginning of a chain of events that *must* eventually pull the protagonist into the story and call him or her to action. **The call to action is absolutely mandatory.** As emphasized, if the protagonist isn't called to resolve the conflict of the plot, then either he or she is not your protagonist, and/or the conflict is not related to the story that you are trying to tell about your protagonist. This doesn't mean that you have to create a protagonist who wants to be called into the action or one who is even aware of being called. It just means that willingly or unwillingly, consciously or unconsciously, somewhere in the first act the audience must be able to clearly track the protagonist's actions as he or she is being pulled into the central conflict of the story.

Star Wars, for example, opens with Princess Leia being captured and taken hostage by Imperial forces. Not only is Luke Skywalker unaware of this incident, he doesn't even know who Princess Leia is or that he is part of a legacy of Jedi knights who are the defenders against the

Imperial forces. It takes nearly fifteen more minutes of film time before Luke's destiny becomes directly intertwined with the princess's and he is called to rescue her and help save the world from the grip of the evil Empire. But notice that by this point in the first act, the setup of the "A" story is clear and the audience understands and can track the external conflict.

Setting up the "B" and "C" storylines can be a little more complex in terms of making the conflict equally clear so that the audience will become emotionally engaged. The inciting incident and the call to action that define the conflict in the "A" story may not be sufficient to define the conflict of the "B" and "C" storylines. When Rick learns of Laszlo's need to get out of Casablanca, he is rather indifferent toward helping him. "I don't stick out my nose for nobody" is his constant refrain, and even though he's a compelling character we don't yet have enough information to clarify what all his internal angst is about. Up to this point Rick is just cranky and contrary and we really don't care very much about him, just as he doesn't care very much about anyone else. However, all that changes when he sees Ilsa again, and we begin to understand the nature of his pain. Notice how clearly and emotionally this is conveyed when Ilsa asks Sam to play *their song*. Her melancholy and Sam's trepidation lay a powerful foundation for Rick's anguished reaction to hearing the unbearable melody again.

I refer to this emotionally charged sequence as a **DEFINING MOMENT** in the setup, because it brings clarity and focus to the internal dilemma of the protagonist. As you begin to develop a portrait of the protagonist in the first act, it's fine to use some amount of subtlety, but don't go too far without making sure that the internal conflict gets clearly spelled out, or the audience may not fully understand what is really at stake. This clarification will only feel clumsy or clunky if it isn't done with some amount of finesse and sensitivity.

In the following examples of a *defining moment*, notice how simple and yet straightforward the incidents are and how they bring the internal conflict directly into focus.

The first scene is from *Rocky*, written by Sylvester Stallone. This text begins about fifteen minutes into the film when Rocky confronts Mickey, the trainer, about how he's being treated at the gym.

                    ROCKY
    My problem is I been talkin' to ya man,
    Mike. I wanna know how come I been put
    outta my locker?
                    MICKEY
    Because Dipper needed it.

Rocky turns and looks at DIPPER sparring… Dipper is a young, muscular heavyweight with a mean expression.

                    MICKEY
                 (continuing)
    Dipper's a contender. You know what you
    are? — You're a tomata.
                    ROCKY
    …Tomata?
                    MICKEY
    Yeah, let's face it. I run a business
    around here -- not a goddamn soup kitchen.
    Did ya fight last night?
                    ROCKY
    Yeah —
                    MICKEY
    Did ya win?
                    ROCKY
    Yeah, I won. Kayo in the second.
                    MICKEY
    …Who'd ya fight?
                    ROCKY
    Spider Rico.

```
                        MICKEY
     He's a bum.

                        ROCKY
     You think everybody I fight is a bum.
                        MICKEY
     Well, ain't they? Ya got heart, but ya
     fight like a goddamn ape — The only thing
     special about you is ya never got ya nose
     busted — Well, leave it that way; nice and
     pretty and what's left of your mind.
```

For the first fifteen minutes of the story, we see Rocky halfheartedly win his fight, collect money for a bookie, and make a pass at a shy girl in a pet store. These scenes are rich with character detail that very effectively draw us into Rocky's marginal existence and make us care about what will happen to him. However, we don't understand the precise nature of the internal conflict ("B" story) until Mickey nails it for us by calling Rocky a "tomata" in this scene at the gym, and he tells him that he isn't interested in working with a fighter who doesn't have any real fight left in him. Just prior to this encounter with Mickey, Rocky discovers that he's been kicked out of his locker and that his belongings are hanging in a duffel bag on a rack that is euphemistically referred to by the other boxers as "skid row." We don't know yet that Rocky will be called to fight the current world heavyweight champion, but we do know that if Rocky doesn't learn to stand up and fight for himself, he's going down for the count.

In *American Beauty*, writer Alan Ball is even more direct about the nature of the internal conflict that emotionally sets his story on course. In an opening scene he uses the voice of the protagonist himself to explain his dilemma:

```
EXT. ROBIN HOOD TRAIL - EARLY MORNING

We're FLYING above suburban America, DESCENDING SLOWLY
toward a tree-lined street.
```

                    LESTER (V.O.)
     My name is Lester Burnham. This is my
     neighborhood. This is my street. This... is
     my life. I'm forty-two years old. In less
     than a year, I'll be dead.

INT. BURNHAM HOUSE - MASTER BEDROOM - CONTINUOUS

We're looking down at a king-sized BED from OVERHEAD:
LESTER BURNHAM lies sleeping amidst expensive bed
linens, face down, wearing PAJAMAS. An irritating ALARM
CLOCK RINGS. Lester gropes blindly to shut it off.

                    LESTER (V.O.)
     Of course, I don't know that yet.

He rolls over, looks up at us and sighs. He doesn't
seem too thrilled at the prospect of a new day.

                 LESTER (V.O. cont'd)
     And in a way, I'm dead already.

He sits up and puts on his slippers.

INT. BURNHAM HOUSE - MASTER BATH - MOMENTS LATER

Lester thrusts his face directly into a steaming hot
shower. ANGLE from outside the shower: Lester's naked
body is silhouetted through the fogged-up glass door.
It becomes apparent he is masturbating.

                    LESTER (V.O.)
                     (amused)
     Look at me, jerking off in the shower.

                    (then)
          This will be the high point of my day. It's
          all downhill from here.

Over the course of the next twenty minutes of this film we see the reality of Lester's life, and he's right; that was the high point. He is so marginalized in every aspect of his day-to-day existence that he may as well be dead, for all anybody seems to care. Most importantly, it is Lester, himself, who has ceased to care, indicating that the healing of inner wounds can only start from within.

Notice how strongly thematic the pronouncement of the central internal conflict is in these examples. Here again you can see how important it is to have some insight into the real nature of your story. Knowing something about the theme is invaluable for setting up the internal conflict and drawing your audience into the core of what is at stake for your characters. Within the first fifteen minutes of *Dead Poets Society*, John Keating cautions his fledgling students to *seize the day* (Carpe diem!), *and make their lives extraordinary.* Introducing the theme as the core of the central conflict doesn't get much clearer than this.

The Great Unknown

An important key to understanding what is occurring in the first act is to recognize that all of the plot elements have something to do with *what the protagonist doesn't know.* This isn't to imply that the protagonist will be completely ignorant of everything that is going on around him or her; it just means that there are aspects to resolving the conflict that are obscured, unidentified, undefined, or unknowable at the beginning of the story. (*Remember, a conflict is a conflict specifically because the protagonist doesn't know how to resolve it. The moment he or she figures it out, the problem no longer exists and the story is well on its way to the ending.*)

In the last chapter, the story was divided into two opposing halves: **Resistance** and **Release.** It was also separated into four opposing quadrants: **Unknown, Exhaustion, Known,** and **Renewal.** To get a deeper understanding and more fundamental view of what is going on in the first act, let's bring these elements back into play.

TRANSFORMATIONAL ARC

Words that are synonymous with *resistance* include: *struggle, defiance, challenge, denial,* and *refusal.* Resistance can also be an involuntary condition based on circumstances of *ignorance, innocence, dependence, servitude,* and *oppression.* In the first act, it's important to identify the system of resistance that is keeping the protagonist from getting to the goal of resolving the conflict. As always, *this must be related to the theme.*

In Chapter Five, I described how inverting the theme, or looking at its opposite value, tells the writer a great deal about the condition in which the story begins.

> **Externally:** The opposite value of the theme generally defines the *antagonist* or *antagonism* of the plot.
> **Internally:** The opposite value of the theme defines the *fatal flaw of character* and establishes the protagonist's need to resolve a *relationship* issue.

If the core thematic value in *Casablanca* is *the need to connect to others,* its opposite value defines what is occurring in the plot in the first act that is creating **resistance** toward achieving the goal of getting Victor Laszlo to safety. The inciting incident that initiates this story is the theft of some transit papers that could have spelled instant freedom for Laszlo. But those papers will be very hard to reclaim because in Casablanca the fear and desperation provoked by the war have created an atmosphere in which *every man is out for himself.* Notice how this attitude of selfishness is diametrically opposed to the need for connecting to and caring for others, which is what it will take to get the papers in Victor's hands and get him out of town. In fact, what it really takes in the end of this story is an act of complete selflessness—something that is in very short supply when we first meet Rick Blaine, the man to whom the papers are given at the beginning of the film.

Rick is the standard bearer for the "every man for himself" ideal. When he is asked to help Laszlo, his immediate response is to refuse to become involved. He has no sentimental or patriotic attachment to the war effort, and therefore he has no trouble **resisting** the *call to action.*

What Rick **doesn't know** in the beginning is that Laszlo is the husband of the woman who broke his heart. He also **doesn't know** how dangerous it's becoming in Casablanca—especially for someone who's holding on to the transit papers. More importantly, however, what Rick **doesn't know** is how much he really does need other people. He is **unconscious** of how motivated he is by the anger of being left behind in Paris, and how that anger is turning his life to ashes.

It's extremely important to set your character up in some condition of unconsciousness or unknowing in Act I. This can include unawareness, ignorance, obliviousness, and so on. **Unknowing helps establish the arc of character because transformational change is, in fact, the act of growing into new consciousness.**

In *Dead Poets Society*, the boys begin the story completely *unaware* that their creative and authentic impulses have any value. In *Rocky*, the aging fighter is *oblivious* to the magnitude of what he's losing by giving up on himself. In *Schindler's List*, Oskar has so thoroughly buried his head in the sand that he *cannot see* the tidal wave of human suffering that is about to engulf all of humanity—his own humanity, in particular.

Taking a Turn for the Worst

This notion of *unknowing* plays an especially important role in understanding what occurs at the end of the first act, which falls on or around page 25 in a film script. This act-ending sequence is commonly referred to as the ***first turning point.***

A TURNING POINT is an escalation of the conflict that turns the story in a new and unexpected direction, substantially raising the stakes for the protagonist.

At the first turning point in a story, something big and unforeseen must happen to change the course of action the protagonist is taking; otherwise, getting to the resolution is too easy and the conflict is virtually resolved. For example, in *Goodfellas*, at the first turning point Henry is caught selling stolen goods from the trunk of his car and believes he is in pretty serious trouble. But after a brief court hearing he anxiously faces his mob bosses, who surprise him with affectionate cheers: "You broke your cherry! You broke your cherry!"

This incident opens up a new era for Henry. The script fast forwards by a decade or so and we see Henry as a full-fledged hood, stealing everything he can get his hands on.

```
                    HENRY
     By the time I grew up, there was thirty
     billion a year in cargo moving through
     Idlewild Airport and, believe me, we tried
     to steal every bit of it.
```

While it's not unexpected for Henry to have turned out to be a hoodlum, it's quite jarring to see the shift from the "innocent" fringes of gang life to a place where dangerous underworld activity is considered "normal" and desirable.

                    HENRY
    For us to live any other way was nuts.
    To us, those goody-good people who worked
    shitty jobs for bum paychecks, who took the
    subway to work every day and worried about
    their bills, were dead. They were suckers.
    They had no balls. If we wanted something,
    we just took it. If anyone complained twice,
    they got hit so bad, believe me, they never
    complained again. It was just all routine.
    You didn't even think about it.

By this point in the story, the stakes are seriously escalating for Henry. What he isn't thinking about (is unconscious of) is that this "routine" of hitting anyone who doesn't conform to the whims of the mob includes everyone—and that means Henry himself. Whereas he thinks he's free to take whatever he wants and make up the rules as he goes along, he's actually more subservient than the poor suckers he believes he lords over. This point is driven home in a subsequent scene where Henry and the crew are enjoying a raucous night out when his psychopathic pal Tommy turns the laughter into a deadly confrontation. Henry has the good instincts to back down and make a joke of it, but the incident is so chilling that we know it could have gone the other way.

In the "A" story, the first turning point occurs as a result of a shift in the *external* action. In *Goodfellas*, this shift in the external action occurs when Henry's "cherry" is broken and he is initiated into the mob, launching him into a full-on career as a thief and bully. In *Rocky*, the external action shifts at the first turning point when Apollo Creed chooses Rocky as his opponent for the World Heavyweight title. In *When Harry Met Sally*, the two characters meet again at the first turning point just as the respective relationships with their ideal mates are falling apart.

It's relatively easy to find the first turning point in any existing well-written film. However, when working with your own original material, the turning point might be quite a bit harder to locate. There is no directory in which you can look up a great turning point (which means you certainly want to be wary of computer programs with turning point lists that promise instant turning point gratification). The turning point, like all significant story elements, is something that needs to find its way organically and naturally into your story. Again, this is why understanding your thematic intention is so vital to the development process. The theme *always* reveals the true nature of what your protagonist is struggling against, so look to your theme to define all of the obstacles that appear in his or her path.

The theme of *Goodfellas* seems to reflect on the idea that the quality of a man's character is determined by the quality of the life to which he's committed himself, and there are no shortcuts in life to reach this goal. So as the tragedy of this film is set up, it's imperative that we see Henry seduced into the world of shortcuts: easy money, easy women, and easy friends. Because this easy life runs counter to real-world experience, the film must establish a culture that is turned upside down: bad is good, wrong is right, and boys who get arrested for theft are applauded and celebrated.

The theme in *Rocky*, on the other hand, is not expressed through tragedy but through the heroic path to redemption. In the first act, Rocky has all but given up on himself, rendering his existence almost totally insignificant. It may be corny and cliché, but at our lowest point how many of us feel like shaking our fist heavenward and proclaiming, "If I only had a chance! I'd show 'em!" A *natural* choice for a turning point, therefore, is to give Rocky that chance, albeit a chance so huge it clearly dwarfs him—and therein lies the jeopardy.

In *When Harry Met Sally*, the theme also reveals how the first act will end. Up to this point in the story, both of the title characters go after and get exactly what they think is true love...but it isn't even close. Not only are they both left rejected and alone; more importantly, they are also left without any idea of what love is or where to find it. What they do find in its place, however, is someone with whom they can commiserate, some-one who cares, someone who understands—in other words, a friend. The implied jeopardy behind this turning point is that their love-inflicted wounds may not allow them to eventually move past the friendship into the committed intimacy of acknowledging their true love for each other. Hence, their friendship becomes a double-edged sword.

The use of strong imagery at the first turning point is essential for making this moment as powerful and dynamic as it can be. By magnifying and underscoring the theme, imagery has the ability to allow the audience to *feel*, not just understand, what is really at stake for the protagonist.

In the film *The Fugitive*, there is a very memorable first turning point with a cataclysmic crash scene. Visions of a colossal fire-spewing loco-motive bearing down on the mangled corpse of a bus that holds the wrongly accused doctor in its iron clutches is an image that is etched into most of our memories. But as much as we all love to watch a good train wreck, that's not the reason this scene works as well as it does. While there's no doubt that this is one of the great pyrotechnic achieve-ments in cinema, its real power is derived more from its imagery and symbolic resonance than from its explosiveness.

In the setup of the "A" story, Dr. Kimble (Harrison Ford) has been falsely accused and convicted of murdering his wife. Toward the end of the first act, he is unceremoniously manacled and forced to board a bus that will take him to a death row prison cell. Along the way, however, another prisoner attempts an escape that causes the bus to crash on a railroad track—just in time to meet up with an oncoming train. At the last second, Kimble is able to evade the clash of these two heavy metal titans and escape to freedom in all the chaos. That is, he is free to run from captivity, but as a result he becomes a very desperate and wanted fugitive. This point is considerably strengthened a few scenes later when a persistent U.S. Marshal (Tommy Lee Jones) enters the picture and vows to relentlessly hunt him down. Hence, in the "A" story, the stakes are driven sky high for Dr. Kimble.

But something else very significant happens at this point in the story. Kimble makes a critical decision that will greatly influence his fate.

At the moment of impact, one of the guards is seriously injured and needs immediate assistance if he is going to survive. As the train is bearing down on them, Kimble decides to risk his own life to get the guard to safety. While this leaves the guard alive to become a potential eyewitness and threat to Kimble's survival, the writer has used this as an opportunity to show the audience that Kimble is not a man who will sacrifice others to save himself. This single action significantly elevates the quality of the drama, because from this point forward we're not just cheering to save an innocent man, we're cheering for a man who is worth saving. As a result, the imagery that follows takes on even more meaning and power.

Once he is free of the wreckage Kimble tries to run to safety, but a derailed boxcar flies at him like a raging, devouring behemoth. There's an interesting passage in Job (40:19) that says of the behemoth: "He is the chief of the ways of God"—the implication perhaps being that without a destructive force there can be no renewal. This fire-breathing monster scorches the land, turning the terrain into a hellish inferno from which Dr. Kimble must struggle to emerge in order to reclaim his life. But because he has proven himself worthy, he will find that he is not alone. From out of the darkness emerges a large, firm hand that helps pull him to safety.

While in reality the hand belongs to one of the other escaping convicts, it seems meant to take on the appearance at first of divine intervention. Even when we realize who this man is, his presence looms so large that it seems to signify that he represents something even bigger and more symbolic. Indeed, he tells Kimble as he helps him out of his shackles that he doesn't care which direction he takes, he just doesn't want Kimble to follow him. Taken literally this is simply an admonition to keep away, but figuratively it sets the emotional tone for the entire second act. If Kimble is to make his way back into the world, he must find his own path. This will mean abandoning the false security of his old identity. All that follows begins to take on symbolic power as well, especially as Kimble strips out of his bright yellow prison garb with the telltale initials *IDOC* (Illinois Department of Corrections) emblazoned on the back and puts on the generic overalls of a common working man. He is no longer the proud, secure, renowned doctor, but an obscure, humbled, common man being forced to take on life in a new way and with renewed purpose.

I urge you to re-watch the first act of *The Fugitive* and observe how the use of symbolic imagery greatly enhances the dramatic tension at this point in the story. But also notice that in spite of the powerful imagery and symbolism, there is a clear lack of internal character development in the beginning of this story. Dr. Kimble really has no fatal flaw of character, which means that the terrible events happening to him are nothing more than terrible events. They have no metaphorical resonance until we get to the turning point. Then, fortunately, a subtle, yet pervasive thematic undercurrent begins to take over and the story becomes quite riveting.

However, because of the lack of strong internal development, Kimble's character can never really get out of first gear. He's always strong, smart, and indomitable, which makes him only a one-dimensional character. To fix a problem like this, a writer only needs to look at the symbolic urgency that emanates from the first turning point. The fact that Kimble is forced to take on the identity of a common man in order to survive would have been much more compelling if he had been the kind of guy in the beginning of the story who held himself above other men.

In contrast, Kimble's co-protagonist, U.S. Marshal Gerard, does hold the quality of the theme in his characterization, and notice how he virtually bursts off the screen every time he's in a scene. Both Tommy Lee Jones and Harrison Ford are terrific actors, so this has nothing to do with their abilities. No matter how great an actor is, he or she will always be limited by the depth to which the character is developed on the written page.

Gerard's character holds himself above other men in that he is so *fixed* in his belief that he is always right that he's become arrogant and prideful—which can be quite dangerous (in fact, he nearly kills one of his own men). This gives his character a very strong arc that brings him to a point at the end of the story where he helps resolve the conflict by taking an action that he was not capable of taking when the story began. Rather than continuing to hide behind his idealized view of *justice*, which has been impersonal and impenetrable, he makes the decision to use his own *judgment*, which makes him human and, therefore, vulnerable. Dr. Kimble experiences no such transformation because there was never anything to transform. He's just a guy who had really bad luck, and we are left with no sense that his future will be any greater or worse for the experience he's just survived.

A Rude Awakening

To understand what's happening in the internal realm at the first turning point, it's necessary to look more deeply into the impact the external experiences are having on the internal reality of the protagonist. Keep in mind that the "A" story is driven by external action and the "B" and "C" stories are driven by an internal reaction to that activity.

Because the purpose of a story is to move a protagonist toward resolving conflicts, the writer must design the plotlines so that the protagonist is constantly confronted with a greater and greater need or urgency for achieving those goals. Hence, the situation must constantly worsen or heighten. This will shake, if not completely unsettle, the foundation of the protagonist's inner world.

If a strong fatal flaw of character has been established in the setup, then the inner world of the protagonist will be in grave need of a shakeup anyway. Remember, the fatal flaw *feels* like a condition of being stuck or trapped at some point in life. In the first act, Luke Skywalker, Henry Hill, and Little Red Riding Hood feel trapped in adolescence. Harry, Sally, and Rick Blaine feel stuck in a world without love. George Bailey feels trapped by self-denial. Oskar Schindler feels trapped by meaningless self-indulgence. In reality, however, nothing in life is fixed; there is always movement. Sometimes that movement is so slow it's imperceptible, but sometimes it hits like an avalanche or an earthquake that rocks our internal sense of stability. That inner sensation of imbalance, uneasiness, or disorientation can feel like you are being jolted out of a deep sleep (unconsciousness), and this is exactly what the writer wants to establish at the first turning point in the "B" and "C" storylines. This is why I refer to the internal aspects of the first turning point as an AWAKENING, because it is, in fact, a wake-up call for the protagonist, though not generally a welcome one:

- Luke wants to grow up, but the reality that there is evil in the world is not what he expects or wants, especially when that evil kills his family and threatens the future of the Republic.
- Harry and Sally want love, but they don't want the pain, disappointment, and heartache that are part of the bargain.
- Rocky wants to be the big champ of the world, yet he's not even willing to stand up to that little inner voice that doubts and mocks his ability.

Inner jeopardy will do more to ignite dramatic tension than anything you can crash, burn, or blow up at the first turning point. It's not that explosions aren't emotionally thrilling, but if that's all there is the audience's emotional connection to the story will fade along with the fireworks. On the other hand, if a big bang at the first turning point is set off by an inner spark, I can guarantee that no one will leave their seat for popcorn anytime soon.

In *Thelma and Louise*, for example, the first turning point in the "A" story is developed around the attempted rape of Thelma, which leads Louise to shoot and kill the attacker. It's made clear, however, that it isn't just the act of aggression toward her friend that makes Louise pull the trigger. In fact, she remains very much under control when she puts a gun to the rapist's neck and gets him to back off of Thelma. But we sense that Louise, herself, has been down this road before, and *she's* just not able to take it anymore. Something inside her snaps at the man's arrogance and remorseless sense of entitlement over a woman's body. So she shoots him.

A short time later, Thelma tries to get Louise to tell the cops that the man was trying to rape her. Louise refuses, adamant that, because Thelma had been dancing and flirting with the guy earlier, no one will believe them—even though Thelma has bruises all over her face. This is so irrational that it greatly adds to the impression that there's a big internal conflict causing Louise to overreact. Although Louise's backstory is never clearly spelled out in the film, she is obviously behaving out of fear and suppressed rage. Throughout the first act, Louise is portrayed as a woman who has her emotions very tightly under control. But at the first turning point those feelings are *awakened* by the shock of confronting a sexual predator in the act of rape. Once jolted loose, her emotions take on an energy of their own and forever change the course of her life.

Obviously, not all turning points need to be fiery and cataclysmic. The overarching function is to set the story on a new course that will disrupt the status quo and add more urgency to the need for resolution. This new direction can be achieved in ways that seem tame on the surface but still carry a very big punch, especially when they are set off by a strong internal conflict.

In the action/thriller *Sea of Love*, a seemingly innocuous moment becomes a turning point that resonates so deeply from inner turmoil that it sets off a chain of events that nearly gets the protagonist killed. The story begins with a couple of murders that all point to the possibility that a serial killer is on the loose, targeting heterosexual men who respond to personal ads. This leads the police to believe that the killer is a woman, but they don't know who she is or where she'll strike next. Detective Frank Keller (Al Pacino) teams with Detective Sherman Tilley (John Goodman) from another precinct. They both seem to be after the same killer and Tilley is also baffled about how to catch her. The two men become instant friends and Sherman invites Frank to his daughter's wedding, a traditional, middle-class affair replete with disco band and taffeta-clad bridesmaids. Even though it's a bit corny, Keller is drawn in by the genuine feelings of warmth and affection that permeate the event. He especially seems to respond with wistful envy at all the love and laughter that surround his partner and his family—something he's already admitted he very much wants.

Sitting on the sidelines, enveloped in an atmosphere of melancholy, Keller retreats even further into himself, as if he's thinking about all he's lost or never really had. The lighting mimics his mood and dims while music plays and other people dance. Just as the song ends and the lights brighten, Keller bolts upright, invigorated by a sudden idea that has just popped into his head. Excitedly, he grabs Sherman and tells him he's figured out how to nab the killer: They need to put their own personal ad in the paper and lure the killer to them.

That's it. That's the turning point in the "A" story and nothing was detonated, blasted, or demolished. Another murder does occur a few scenes later, which helps Frank convince his boss to go along with his wild idea. The new murder also heightens the jeopardy because the killer is hitting with more frequency. But the story gets its real surge of urgency because Frank's idea to go undercover puts him directly in the killer's line of fire. If he is going to pose as a man looking for a date through the personal ads, he is setting himself up as a potential victim.

For most cops this wouldn't be that dangerous, but from what we've already seen of Frank, he's a lonely, desperate drunk who may not be capable of making the most rational decisions. Even his boss foresees problems and admonishes Frank to personally stay away from these women.

Without the internal development of Frank's character, this idea of posing as a date would not carry enough power to serve as a first turning point. However, because the plan evolved out Frank's sense of loneliness, it really feels as if something very great is at stake for him.

I also want to draw your attention to how the lighting effects and applause that naturally follow the dance number coincide with Frank coming up with his idea. Atmospheric accents like these can really help send a subliminal signal to the audience that this is an important moment in the story. When you are devising a turning point, use every means possible to call attention to what is happening. If a turning point does not increase the audience's emotional involvement, it will be very difficult to sustain their interest throughout the second act.

Here is a diagram of the transformational arc, showing the objectives that must be met (internally and externally) in the first act, in order to set the conflict into motion.

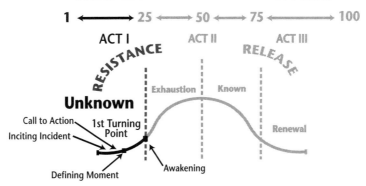

Case Studies

1) ROMANCING THE STONE

Defining the "A," "B," and "C" plotlines helps the writer focus and clarify the general direction in which the overall story is headed. But it is the setup of the individual conflicts of the plot and subplots in Act I that establishes the tone and, most importantly, generates a sense of urgency that drives the story. Urgency is a vital element that pulls an audience into a story and makes them care about what is happening on the screen.

In Act I of *Romancing the Stone*, several things occur in the "A" story to establish this sense of urgency.

"A" STORY (PLOT)	JOAN MUST SAVE HER SISTER FROM RUTHLESS KIDNAPPERS

On page 12 there is an *inciting incident* in which we see a panic-stricken young woman being abducted in broad daylight as she tries to flee her home. This follows an earlier scene where the superintendent of Joan's apartment building is murdered right in front of her door by a man with a thick Latin accent. Joan returns home a short time later to find that her apartment has been ransacked. Then, suddenly, the phone rings. Her terrified sister is calling to tell Joan that she's just been kidnapped and is being held in Cartagena, Colombia. Joan is instructed to check her mail, where she will find a treasure map that the kidnappers want in exchange for her sister. Overwhelmed, Joan whimpers, "I can't go to Cartagena..." But her sister's pleas for rescue override Joan's trepidations and she reluctantly succumbs to the *call to action*.

While all of this activity clearly defines the nature of the *external* conflict ("A" story) and sets into motion a wild and exciting adventure tale, this is not the only source of dramatic tension the story produces in the first act. In fact, this plot is not even set up until the film has been well underway for ten minutes or more. As a priority, the writer first sets up a more complex and compelling sense of *internal* urgency in the subplots, where she shows us Joan's deep desire to find true love ("C" story). However, she also exposes the limitations Joan has unconsciously placed on her ability to achieve that goal, which sets up the fatal flaw of character ("B" story).

The film opens with an overwrought romantic-action sequence set in the Wild West. A beautiful, yet scrappy, heroine fends off a dastardly desperado only to be descended upon by an even larger, meaner gang of thugs. All seems lost, when suddenly she sees the silhouette over the horizon of her beloved Jesse riding in to her rescue. With perfect aim Jesse easily wipes out all the varmints, never breaking a sweat. The grateful heroine runs to the arms of her champion, and they ride off into the sunset together.... "Forever...."

As the music swells to a climax, it is suddenly interrupted by the sound of sobbing and (thankfully) we realize that this is not the beginning of a cornball, western melodrama, but it's the end of a cornball, romantic novel. Its author, Joan Wilder (Kathleen Turner), blubbers over her typewriter, enraptured by the tale of "true love" she has just penned. Toasting this victory with Romeo, her cat, Joan dozes off and doesn't wake up from her euphoric stupor until the next morning when the phone rings.... But, ominously, nobody's there.

Rushing off to a meeting with her literary agent, Joan doesn't notice a dark, swarthy man lingering around her apartment. But as earlier noted, the superintendent of her building unfortunately confronts the guy and receives a knife in his belly for his troubles. Joan, meanwhile, lunches with her agent, Gloria, who tries desperately to get her young novelist interested in meeting some men at the bar.

```
                    GLORIA
     Hold everything; get a load of this
     character. Now, what about him?
                     JOAN
     Oh no. He's just not...
                    GLORIA
     Who? Jesse?
                     JOAN
     Maybe it's silly, but I know that there is
     somebody out there for me.
                    GLORIA
     Oh, yeah. Where?
                     JOAN
     Certainly not here. Gloria, why do we
     always have to have this same conversation?
```

While it's done with a humorous tone, what the script clearly establishes by the end of this scene is that Joan is a woman who is in love with love. Actually, she's in love with the ideal of love and has given him the name of Jesse. Jesse is not only the romantic leading man in all her novels, but he also symbolizes her own unshakeable fantasy of love.

This clearly signals the audience that Joan is searching for love, but it also implies that it's not very likely that she's going to find the "perfect" man if she keeps hiding away in her apartment. In fact, it's highly unlikely that she's going to find someone who fulfills all of her unrealistically high ideals anywhere.

Her agent sums it all up in a *defining moment*, when she says to Joan: "I hate to see you all alone waiting for somebody who's not going to show up." This sets the "B" and "C" storylines fully into motion. Whether the audience is aware of it or not, they are now invested in Joan's plight. They want her to find love. They see her as a charming gal who just needs to get out more and take a bit of a risk instead of pining away over a man who doesn't exist, except in her fantasies. But to do this, Joan is going to have to find some *courage:*

"B" STORY	JOAN FINDS THE COURAGE TO
(INTERNAL SUBPLOT)	FACE THE UNKNOWN

Joan is also going to have to bring her heart out of hiding and follow it wherever the adventure of love may lead.

"C" STORY	JOAN LEARNS TO FOLLOW
(RELATIONSHIP SUBPLOT)	HER HEART

For the metaphor to work, the plot, or "A" story, needs to be a real adventure. So, from the moment Joan learns that her sister has been kidnapped (on page 14), the plot moves into high gear. The balance of the first act is spent getting Joan to Cartagena and pushing her to deal with dangerous and unpredictable forces. But, because the writer devoted a substantial amount of time setting up the "B" and "C" stories, these subplots are not left behind at the gate when Joan gets off the plane. Instead, her movements, mannerisms, dialogue, and even wardrobe conspire to portray a woman for whom every step is a scary, uncomfortable, unwelcome venture into the great *unknown.*

The first turning point in this film consumes almost ten pages. It occurs in stages that continually grow more tense and unpredictable. When Joan first gets off the plane, she encounters utter chaos. Instead of heading to the Cartagena Hotel, where she can simply give the kidnappers the map, take her sister, and go home, Joan is *unknowingly* put on the wrong bus that will take her high into the wilderness of the Andes Mountains.

When she finally realizes that she's going the wrong way, Joan tries to stop the bus, but manages instead to cause the driver to crash dangerously close to the edge of a mountain road. At this point it's clear that the story is now going in a new and unpredicted direction, but the most important condition of a turning point has not yet been met. It's still possible for Joan to simply hitch a ride back into Cartagena, where she can fulfill the plan and take her sister home. The story needs substantial jeopardy at this turning point to block Joan from achieving that goal.

So, as the peasants leave the bus and start trekking down the mountain, Joan is *unknowingly* persuaded by the very man who murdered her apartment superintendent to just wait for another bus to come along. But the moment the other passengers disappear from view, he pulls a gun and demands the treasure map.

NOW, Joan not only has to save her sister's life; her own life has been put in jeopardy as well. The stakes have soared, and resolving the problem in the "A" story just became a whole lot more difficult and complicated. However, this turning point serves an even greater function because it also substantially complicates the "B" story. It serves to validate all of Joan's worst fears about venturing out into the unknown. It *is* a dangerous place and she wants nothing more than to run back to the lifeless prison cell she calls home—where, at least, she can *feel* safe. But that option has become impossible.

As strong as this turning point is, however, it still lacks momentum from the "C" story. How will Joan learn to follow her heart if nothing happens to nudge it along? SO, just when all seems lost, the (Jesse-like) silhouette of her rescuer appears on the horizon, and with perfect aim he easily wipes out the bad guy, never breaking a sweat…. Well, not exactly. This hero gets off about five rounds and never even wings the bad guy, who easily manages to escape.

Hiding under the bus, Joan catches a glimpse of her rescuer and quickly realizes that he's no Jesse. He's rude, crude, and not the least bit interested in aiding a damsel in distress. In fact, the only reason he agrees to help Joan get to safety is that she offers to pay, and since he is the only way out she is now forced to follow wherever he leads.

There's an important aspect to the first turning point in the "C" story that bears attention. Because the romance in this film primarily occurs in the subplot, the emphasis must be placed on Joan's internal issues of learning to trust love and follow her heart. Therefore, the primary purpose Jack Colton (Michael Douglas) serves in the story is to bring out these issues of faith and trust. This is why it isn't necessary to actually meet him until page 25, when he appears at the first turning point. Up until then it is his alter-ego, Jesse, who defines Joan's relationship conflict. In fact, Colton is able to make a stronger entrance because the comparison between him and her fantasy man, Jesse, is a major reason she isn't getting the love she desires.

2) *Lethal Weapon*

As an action film, it's no surprise that *Lethal Weapon* begins with a beautiful, drugged-out woman taking a nose dive off the balcony of an L.A. high-rise. What is surprising, however, is that this event is **not** the focus of the first act. Instead of pulling the audience into the story in the traditional way, using explosive, plot-oriented, high-intensity action sequences, *Lethal Weapon* opts instead to develop the first act around the subplots—the *inside story*.

The filmmakers took the gutsy and non-traditional approach of putting the emphasis in the first act on character development rather than plot development. And it paid off. As action films go, the original *Lethal Weapon* wasn't just successful, it was highly memorable. Riggs and Murtaugh have become two of the most recognized and imitated characters in the action genre. But if you want to write a movie that is just as successful, don't try to replicate just the buddy-buddy banter or the yin-yang characterization that it's become known for. Imitate instead the depth to which the fatal flaws of the co-protagonists are exposed in the first act. This character development sets the story on a course that makes meaning out of all the action and mayhem that ensues in the rest of the film. Most importantly, it establishes a very strong arc of character.

Lethal Weapon is set up so that the audience gets to *know* these two cops and understand their vulnerabilities. It is, therefore, the "B" story—which introduces the fatal flaw of character—that first captures our attention.

"B" STORY	RIGGS AND MURTAUGH
(INTERNAL SUBPLOT)	LEARN TO TRUST LIFE

We first meet Roger Murtaugh luxuriating in a bathtub on the morning of his fiftieth birthday. His reverie is interrupted by the intrusion of his adoring family, who ply him with cake and merriment, completely disregarding the fact that he is soaking in his "birthday suit." This is not exactly the image of the hardened, tough-as-nails cop we're used to seeing. Instead, we're introduced to a guy who has it all: a nice home, great family, loving spouse, and comfortable lifestyle. *He's a cop who has a lot to lose.*

Our first encounter with Martin Riggs is a stark contrast. He lives alone in a ramshackle trailer, slugging down beer and choking back cigarettes for breakfast. He's so far to the extreme end of the image of a hardened cop that when we first meet him we're not even sure if he's one of the good guys or the bad guys. But this is the writer's *intention* and he uses this uncertainty in the next scene to take us into the heart of a drug deal, where Riggs is buying cocaine off the back of a Christmas tree truck. When the bust finally goes down and Riggs flips into cop mode, he's so outrageous and cavalier that even the drug dealers don't take him seriously. Big mistake. As they try to escape, Riggs turns into a tough, aggressive pit bull who refuses to back down even when he's taken hostage. He screams at his backup team to shoot, but there's a taunting edge to his demand that seems to be goading the drug dealer to kill him if he dares. *Clearly, he's a cop who's got nothing to lose.*

It's important to remember that it's not enough to just set the fatal flaw into motion. If the audience isn't given any sense of what a character's vulnerability *relates* to, his behavior can come across as merely an affectation or an exaggerated mannerism. The next scene with Riggs is the film's most memorable moment because it establishes why he has a death wish. Sitting alone in his trailer with annoying Christmas cartoons playing in the background, Riggs tries to do what the drug dealers failed to accomplish—put a bullet in his brain. Next to him is his wedding photo, and when he tearfully apologizes to the portrait of his bride for not having the courage to pull the trigger so that he can join her, presumably in death, the source of his pain becomes very clear.

However, if someone in the audience still doesn't get it, there's a *defining moment* in the following scene, where the precinct psychologist warns that Riggs is a basket case because he's still mourning the loss of his wife. In no uncertain terms she cautions that he's a danger to himself and others. Her superiors pay no attention to her concerns—but we do.

Now the stage is perfectly set for the development of the "C" story.

"C" STORY	RIGGS AND MURTAUGH MUST
(RELATIONSHIP SUBPLOT)	CONNECT AND FORM A TEAM

Murtaugh is introduced to his new partner, Martin Riggs, whom he first mistakes for a deranged gunman. Riggs' turning out to be a cop, not a criminal, gives Murtaugh very little comfort as the new team heads out to solve the mystery of why the dead girl dove off a balcony.

In the first twenty pages of this script, the audience is given only a scant amount of plot information and none of it includes a clear indication of what the central conflict is in the "A" story.

"A" STORY	RIGGS AND MURTAUGH MUST
(PLOT)	STOP THE DANGEROUS DRUG
	CARTEL

Therefore, in the first act, no external goal is provided for the protagonists in the "A" story. All we are told is that the girl who dove off the balcony is the daughter of Murtaugh's old war buddy and that the drugs she was on would have killed her even if she hadn't jumped. Although this means that the suicide has escalated into a murder investigation, this *inciting incident* is not yet of very great consequence to the co-protagonists. The story would have been stronger had the plot been better developed in the first act, *but* what's important to note is that the movie didn't really suffer for it either. You will see as we progress with the analysis of all three case studies that none of them are "perfect." They all have structural shortcomings, *but* because they also have strong arcs of character, those deficiencies somehow don't diminish the story. On the other hand, without a strong character arc, any misstep in the development of the "A" story can pretty much render the film illogical, un-involving, clumsy, and (in the words of my son) "just plain stupid."

It is not my advice to underwrite the plot ("A" story) in the first act, especially when you are dealing with the action genre, but as we discussed with *Rocky*, it can work. However, also take note that one reason films like *Rocky* and *Lethal Weapon* get away with a lack of strong plot development in the first act is that there is a lot of action and activity surrounding the development of the subplots. These are action films and they need to be set up as such. Just as a comedy needs to be set up with humor and a thriller needs an undertone of caution and tension, an action film does need a lot of action.

At the first turning point in *Rocky*, Apollo Creed gives the unknown fighter a shot at the heavyweight title. Whatever may have been lacking in the setup of the first act is more than compensated for with this huge turn of events. But in *Lethal Weapon*, the turning point only introduces the antagonists—the General and Mr. Joshua—as a very frightening and deadly set of characters. No direct link is made between solving the girl's murder and a big drug deal that the General and Joshua seem to be planning. So, technically, Riggs and Murtaugh are not yet in the loop (they *don't know* what is really going on). But the story still holds together at this point because several other compelling things are taking place.

Murtaugh meets with the dead girl's father, who demands that his old army pal catch and kill the men who murdered his daughter.

Although it's made clear that Murtaugh has no intention of killing anyone, he acknowledges to Riggs that Hunsaker did save his life in Vietnam, and that he does owe him something. So finally, on page 26, there is a *call to action*. There is also an explosive turning point in the relationship subplot between the new partners when they respond to a random police call to assist in getting a suicidal jumper off a tall building. Riggs volunteers to bring the jumper down, but Murtaugh's apprehension of his new partner becomes more than justified when minutes later both Riggs and the jumper fly off the building handcuffed together into a police net.

Murtaugh is furious with Riggs and confronts him about his recklessness, only to realize that this is not part of an act he's putting on to get disability—*Riggs really is nuts.* We are now at a turning point in the "C" story, and the jeopardy is reinforced when Murtaugh calls the police psychologist and is told that his new partner has a death wish.

Even though the conflict of the plot itself isn't yet putting the protagonists in any real jeopardy, there is still plenty at stake to keep the audience strongly connected to the outcome of the story. The heightened danger that closes out the first act is coming from within Riggs and Murtaugh and that's definitely enough to hold our attention as we are pulled into the second act.

3) ORDINARY PEOPLE

It takes awhile for the dialogue in *Ordinary People* to clarify the issues that set the conflict of this story into motion. For many movies, this would indicate that the setup is slow and perhaps even un-involving. However, that is not the case here. What the dialogue does not communicate directly in the text, it communicates even more powerfully in the SUBTEXT. **The subtext of a character's speech is not just a literary device; it's an observation of the natural way in which most human beings tend to communicate.** How often have we all heard the phrase, "It's not what you say, but how you say it"? Our tone, inflection, mannerisms, and body language tend to reveal much more about the meaning and intention of our words than any well-developed phrasing ever could. Because this is a story about a family that represses emotion, the eloquence of the dialogue often comes from what isn't said, rather than from what is.

In addition, a great deal of the dramatic tension in this story is set up through the use of imagery. In the first few minutes of the film, idyllic autumnal images waltz across the screen, leading us into a quite upscale community, where the local high school choir is practicing Pachelbel's Canon in full voice. As the camera pans the fresh, energetic faces of these privileged youth, it finally rests on a young man, Conrad Jarrett, who doesn't seem to fit in. Although he sings as boldly as his classmates, he is ill at ease, his skin is sallow, and his eyes are distant and tense; it seems as though he is lost in another world. Indeed, as the song reaches its climax, the movie jumps to the next scene, in which Conrad awakens in a cold sweat from a terrifying nightmare.

The juxtaposition of these contrasting images provokes a sense that all is not what it appears to be. In the next few scenes, as we enter the lives of Conrad and his parents, we can feel the desperation pulsating behind their well-polished veneer of normalcy. This pulls the audience beneath the surface of this family, where the real drama of their lives is unfolding. While the dialogue in the first twelve pages reveals very little of what is really at stake, the parents' delicate and self-conscious encounters with Conrad signal that his stability is the desired goal. As his parents talk about mundane things, what they really seem to be saying is, *"If he could just be normal again then the family would be okay."* But the *subtext* behind their words is not lost on Conrad, and we can see that he is struggling to *act* normal to please them. However, this only serves to aggravate his mother and further distress his father.

On page 7, a revealing scene clearly sets up the conflict in the "C" story.

"C" STORY	THE FAMILY MEMBERS MUST
(RELATIONSHIP SUBPLOT)	LEARN TO VALUE EACH OTHER

When Conrad doesn't immediately respond to a call to breakfast, his father becomes instantly anxious and worried. His mother, on the other hand, remains disengaged and continues to cook. A few moments later, when Conrad ambles down the stairs, she plasters a broad smile on her face and presents him with his favorite morning fare: French toast. Conrad tries to react "normally" to the delicacy, but can't even seem to wrap his mind around the idea of being hungry. Dad attempts to cajole him, with the reminder that breakfast is the most important meal of the day, but Mom snatches the plate from the table and dumps it down the garbage disposal before anyone can stop her.

> BETH
> (surprisingly upbeat)
> You're not hungry, you're not hungry.

> CALVIN
> Wait a minute Beth, hang on a second, he'll
> eat it. Come on. It's French toast.

Beth impassively tosses the French toast into the garbage disposal.

> BETH
> There's fresh fruit for you when you get
> home from school, Conrad.

>   CALVIN
>   (shocked)
> What are you doing, Beth? What are you
> doing?
>   BETH
> You can't save French toast.
>   (turns to leave)
> Listen, I've got to run, I'm playing at
> nine. Will you please call Mr. Herman about
> the shutters? I can't get anywhere with
> that man.

Beth exits, Calvin calls after her.

>   CALVIN
> You have to charm Mr. Herman. Did you charm
> him?
>   (returns his attention to Conrad)
> You have to eat, Con. We just want you to
> keep on getting stronger.
>   CONRAD
> Dad, I'm not hungry.
>   CALVIN
> Are you okay?
>   CONRAD
> Yeah.
>   (gathering his things)
> Well, I've got to go, Lazenby's picking me up.
>   CALVIN
> Oh, is he? Great.
>   CONRAD
> Why is it great?

                    CALVIN
        Oh, I don't know. I don't see the old gang
        much anymore. I kinda miss them. Why don't
        you bring them around -- Bill and Don and
        Dick Van Buren. We'll play touch football
        on the lawn.

In its understatement this scene strongly reveals just how encased in pain this family really is. Ironically, for all his awkwardness and discomfort, Conrad seems to be the only one who has any touch with reality. But he, like the rest of the family, is suffering alone. None of them appear to have the capacity to share their own pain or to acknowledge it in each other. Dad wants the old days back, Mom wants to pretend that nothing ever happened, and Conrad just wants to disappear.

It's difficult to establish the exact moment when the fatal flaw or internal conflict of the "B" story is set up in this film.

"B" STORY	THE FAMILY MEMBERS MUST GET
(INTERNAL SUBPLOT)	HONEST ABOUT THEMSELVES

The more we get to know this family, the more we are able to read between the lines of their conversations and realize that no one is being very honest about themselves. Calvin pretends to be interested in a play that he and Beth are attending, but it's clear he's bored to tears. Conrad refuses to admit that he's having difficulty sleeping, and he seems to be far more deeply troubled than anyone realizes. In nearly every scene with Beth, she either changes the subject or walks away when she doesn't like what's being said, especially when the conversation gets emotional. What no one in this family is conscious of or will admit to is that they are already lost. Their system of survival has broken down; the family is falling apart, and if nothing changes, they will never find their way back to each other again.

Hope arrives when Conrad goes to see a psychiatrist, who properly diagnosis what is ailing them all. Bad feelings don't just go away, and they can't be "controlled." In fact, if they aren't expressed and given proper attention, the suppressed feelings will end up controlling everything. Up to this point in the story all of the other scenes rely on subtlety and subtext, but this scene with the psychiatrist is very direct and unambiguous. It is the *defining moment* in the setup of this film, because it clarifies for the audience the exact nature of the conflict and what it will take to resolve this family's crisis. Dr. Berger's dialogue summarizes the facts: that Conrad has attempted suicide and that his brother has drowned in a boating accident. He asks Conrad to commit to therapy at least twice a week, which is the young man's *call to action*. Since Conrad is only one of three co-protagonists, he cannot solve the family's problems completely on his own, but as he begins to get honest about himself and his own needs his actions will lead the way for Mom and Dad to follow. It's as if they are all lost in the woods and Conrad has come upon a way out. Whether or not his parents choose to follow him is beyond his control. But this new path of honest self-reflection is the only course that can lead to the family's *true* survival, which is the central conflict of the "A" story.

"A" STORY	THE FAMILY STRUGGLES TO
(PLOT)	REMAIN A FAMILY

There is no doubt that Conrad is entering treacherous territory; therefore, no one in the family is eager to go willingly, especially Mom. But all it ever takes to change a family dynamic is for one family member to step out of sync with the status quo. This throws the existing equilibrium out of balance. For an unstable family this is particularly precarious, and it doesn't take much to knock the Jarretts off their game.

At the first turning point in the "A" story (plot) of *Ordinary People*, it becomes apparent that as Conrad begins to let go of his need to please everyone, his mom is losing control over the family. But she is not someone who will give up gracefully. At a dinner party, Calvin mentions to a friend that Conrad is seeing a psychiatrist. While this may not appear to be a very big moment, it causes a serious breach in the battlement that Beth has built around her idyllic family structure. It even causes her to have an emotionally charged exchange with Calvin—something she is not accustomed to doing.

These incidents close out the first act, and while there are no car chases or shootouts involved, it's clear that the battle lines in this family have been drawn. Mom is fortifying herself with righteous indignation, Conrad is building up internal strength, and Dad is playing both ends against the middle. The biggest problem in this family is that no one is yet clear on what they're really fighting for. The greatest jeopardy they face is that as long as they all believe that Conrad is the problem, they are moving away from, not closer to, resolving the real issues that are destroying the family.

CHAPTER EIGHT

ACT II—PART ONE
What Goes Up...

Life is a series of diminishments.
The self is lightened, is held on earth
by a gram less of mass and will.

~ COLEMAN DOWELL

The Dreaded Second Act

Let's be honest—*nobody's* favorite part of screenwriting is the second act. Our inspirations begin with great ideas and can take us to amazing conclusions, but our creative juices seldom get turned on by all that cumbersome story development found in the vast, dark, empty regions that lie somewhere between the beginning and the end of a story. This part of the writing process is just plain hard work—for both you and your protagonist—and, quite frankly, there's no way around it. However, what the transformational arc reveals is that the second act is not a barren wilderness, but a place of remarkable potential—once you get the lay of the land.

To gear up for the journey, let's check our compass and set our bearings.

At this point in the story, the protagonist has just been cast out of the land of **Unknowing** and has entered into the steep terrain that leads to **Exhaustion.** At the borderline between these two territories a very high toll was exacted, which came in the form of a harsh **Awakening.**

If all of this sounds pretty ominous, it is—but in a good way. Again, *a conflict is a conflict because we don't know how to solve it*. We have to *exhaust* everything we know, or think we know, in order to get to someplace new. The first half of the second act is the region of the arc where old values, ineffective ideas, and distorted perceptions are challenged. Anything that doesn't serve either the external or internal needs of the

protagonist may be broken apart, or shattered altogether. **Transformational change is, in fact, a process that demands exhaustion. It isn't until a person gets so tired and worn out from holding on to or fighting for what is outmoded and unnecessary that his or her resistance is finally low enough for something new to break through.**

> ### FATAL FLAW
> A survival system that has outlived its usufullness.

Notice in the following illustration that the shape of the arc in this portion of the story suggests that the protagonist is in for an exhaustive climb out of his or her problem.

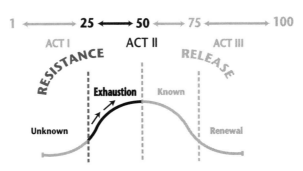

In the first half of the second act of *The Fugitive*, Dr. Kimble is on the run from Gerard and his relentless band of U.S. Marshals. In this part of *Tootsie*, Michael Dorsey chases after success at any cost, while in *Rocky*, the hard-luck fighter spends his time dodging and weaving to avoid success altogether. Henry Hill in *Goodfellas* thinks he's hit the lottery at this point in the story because he's running with the fast crowd. Yet most of his energy is consumed running to keep up, to get ahead, and to keep the wolves at bay. George Bailey, on the other hand, spends the first half of the second act in *It's a Wonderful Life* chasing after everyone else's needs and desires, putting his own dreams on indefinite hold.

It is likely that the protagonist's actions in the first half of the second act are not leading toward a resolution of the conflict (especially internally), because he or she is still *stuck* making decisions that feel safe, familiar, and easy. Therefore, even if the protagonist is headed in the wrong direction, he or she will stay committed to running that course, and we in the audience will usually run right along with him or her. We root for Doc Kimble to make his escape—*Run, Jack, run!* We cheer for Tootsie to strut her stuff—*You go, girl!* And we applaud George for his selfless acts of kindness—*Make us proud, kid!*

But there is something in the back of our minds and, hopefully, in our hearts that just doesn't *feel* right. Where's Jack running to? Michael's becoming famous for being something he isn't—a woman. And will poor old George ever see Paris? Nothing is ever going to feel resolved if these characters can't reach a greater goal for themselves. But, for the moment, aw heck...*Run Jack! Go Girl! Attaboy, George!!!*

Three's Company

In the first act, three storylines were developed: A) an external problem, B) an internal conflict, and C) a relationship issue. As the script moves forward, never lose sight of the importance of keeping these plotlines traveling in threes. In the first half of the second act, it's important to keep pushing the protagonist toward the point of exhaustion in all three storylines. This means that attempts to solve the external problem in the "A" story will be thwarted, misjudged, ill conceived, poorly timed, and so on. For example, in a police drama, this is where the killer slips through the police net, or false leads are followed, or no lead can be found to follow at all. Frustration, false hope, disappointment, and even chaos are the order of the day.

In terms of the internal conflict in the "B" story, denial tends to reign supreme. The *awakening* may have brought about the dawning of new consciousness, but it's still early and the protagonist is in a deep fog as to what's really going on. This denial especially impacts the relationship subplot, because the protagonist lacks understanding and the ability to connect to real inner emotions, which makes *relating* to what he or she wants and needs nearly impossible.

This doesn't mean that relationships can't be formed or developed at this point in the story. Actually, this is an excellent place for the relationship subplot to be expanded upon and explored. Just be very careful not to resolve it here or there will be no more story to tell.

At this point in *Tootsie*, for example, Michael is beginning to fall for Julie (Jessica Lange), but in the old way. He may be effective at portraying a woman on camera, but he really has no idea how to sustain a real relationship with one. Everything is play-acting for Michael, and even though he treats Julie well, it's only because she's the *femme de jour*. In this section of the script, we can see from his selfish and thoughtless behavior toward Sandy (Teri Garr) that eyeliner and heels are not yet enough to make a sensitive man out of him.

While it feels like Michael is achieving success in his career at this point, bear in mind that it's not sustainable. As his character claws his way to the top of the arc, he is creating a mountain of lies and deceptions that are going to have to be dealt with if he's ever going to truly succeed at life, love, and career.

One feature of this portion of the transformational arc is that the protagonist is usually quite entrenched in his or her belief that all problems can be solved by human will alone, which means that the ego is still very much in charge. In the first half of the second act, hubris is often the guiding force. For Michael Corleone in *The Godfather*, we can see the tragedy of his life beginning to fall into place as he, too, trudges up this dangerous slope at the beginning of the second act. Even though Michael has some insight in Act I that the family business will not lead him where he wants to go, he can't keep himself from getting drawn in when his father's life is threatened. Mistakenly, Michael believes he can control his involvement and get out anytime he wants. But power can be habit forming, and Michael easily becomes addicted.

In the "C" story, relationships need to be kept in resistance as well. Be very careful, however, because **"resistance" doesn't mean resistance in general, but resistance to the goal of the plotline.** Therefore, if two people are meant to fall in love by the end of the story, at this point in the development of the arc they usually can't stand each other, can't find each other, don't know each other, or are developing a relationship that is counter to their goal of falling in love.

For example, in *Moonstruck*, Cher's character, Loretta Castorini, is a young widow intent on marrying a man she doesn't love so that she won't become cursed by caring for someone she might someday lose. This, of course, leads to disaster, because, as fate would have it, she meets and falls for her fiancé's depressed, ill-tempered brother. By the end of the story, Loretta will decide that love is worth the risk. But if she were capable of doing that at the beginning of Act II, the story would have no place to develop.

When Harry Met Sally offers up a different sort of resistance. At the first turning point, the two title characters meet and become friends by commiserating over their respective broken hearts. In the first half of the second act, their friendship blossoms and they delight in each other's company. This hardly feels like they're in resistance to each other—because they're not. But they are in resistance to falling in love at this moment in their lives, which is their ultimate goal by the end of the story.

If the goal of a plotline has to do with ending a bad relationship, then at this point in the story everything may *appear* to be going rather smoothly for the couple. For example, if this is a story about a woman who is married to an abusive man, then during the first part of the second act she will be doing everything she can to produce harmony in the home so that he won't have an excuse to hit her. Or, if he has beaten her at the first turning point, he might be the one who's doing every-thing he can to keep from erupting again. Their actions must tell us that they are in resistance to the truth about the abuse. As a result, this section of the story may even *feel* like a honeymoon, except that we *sense* a real discomfort and tension that the couple is holding in.

It doesn't matter if your protagonist is withdrawn and shy, like Ada in *The Piano*, generous and caring, like George Bailey, or funny and self-effacing, like Alvy Singer (Woody Allen) in *Annie Hall*. There must be a willfulness about the protagonist at the beginning of the second act that is keeping him or her in *resistance* to achieving either the internal or external goals—if nothing else changes.

But, of course, something always does…

Make Way for the Midpoint

As things continue to worsen and become more frustrating, the ego strength of the protagonist will begin to break down. This is part of the essential function of exhaustion: **Where there is a breakdown, there is potential for something new to break through.**

Exhaustion is what brings about the next structural element that the protagonist encounters on the journey through the transformational arc. Although this element is commonly referred to as the **MIDPOINT** because it does occur at or around the middle of the story, its real func-tion is to create a **breaking point** in the dramatic tension. Imagine a rubber band being stretched to the point of snapping apart; that is the sensation of reaching the midpoint of a story.

Despite willful attempts to make things turn out the way the pro-tagonist wants, something happens, usually in the "A" story, that rips the sense of control from his or her exhausted clutches, causing a dramatic shift in the course of events. The more forceful this incident, the more powerfully your protagonist will react.

One of my favorite midpoints occurs in *The Fugitive*. After being chased *exhaustively* through watery catacombs, Dr. Kimble finally can run no more. He stumbles out onto a precipice, where he is cornered by his dogged pursuer, Marshal Gerard. This is the first time the men have come face to face, and there is no sentimentality in the confrontation. Gerard demands that Kimble drop his gun and surrender even though the doctor pleads with him that he didn't kill his wife. Gerard responds with indifference; he doesn't care whether Kimble is guilty or not.

As Kimble looks behind him at the deadly 100-foot drop down the cement-walled dam, he realizes that his options are used up (exhausted). So he does as he is told. The gun hits the ground and his arms are raised cautiously over his head. But then there is a moment's hesitation, and suddenly Kimble realizes that he still has one more option he never considered (the new thing).... To Gerard's astonishment, his cornered prey turns and dives, headfirst, down into the unknown, unfathomable waters below.

In the first act, Kimble is presented to us as a victim, and it really doesn't seem fair that such a bad thing should happen to such a nice guy. As are most of us, he is a decent, honest person who follows all the rules to have a happy and successful life. So why is he being persecuted and hounded? Gerard's answer to this is that he *doesn't care*; it doesn't matter whether or not Kimble is innocent. But how can that be? Gerard is the voice of *justice* in this story, but what kind of justice can be so indifferent to a man's guilt or innocence? This is the big thematic question of the story. Does the response that he doesn't care merely relay personal indifference or, at this crucial moment of decision for Kimble, does it carry much greater symbolic value? Perhaps the thematic insight conveyed here is that **true** justice in life answers to a higher source than our human sense of correctness. Hardship and suffering is as much a part of the natural order of life as is abundance and plenty, and there's no evidence that you can have one without the other. Difficult, unfair things happen to everything in nature. The real question when it happens to us is: *What am I going to do about it?*

In the beginning of the film, when Kimble's wife is murdered, he is indignant and outraged. He demands of the authorities that they go out and catch the man who did it, but his plea to be rescued from this terrible fate is ignored. Next, Kimble turns and runs away. Who wouldn't? But how long and how far can he run to ever be truly safe? Finally, when Kimble is caught and cornered, he is forced to decide his own fate. Will he go backward into bondage, or forward toward the new place? Both directions feel dangerous, but there's only one course that offers hope. So he literally takes a *leap of faith* and jumps into the dark, watery *unknown*.

This is never an easy choice, and like Kimble we, too, can expect to be bashed and battered around a bit before we land on our feet again. But once Kimble has made this decision, his courage is rewarded with guidance that takes him out of this place of darkness (unknowing, unconsciousness, exhaustion) and illuminates the path that will guide him into the future. After miraculously surviving the plunge into the icy reservoir, Kimble manages to make it to the shore. In a state of utter collapse (surrender), he falls asleep and dreams of the life he and his dead wife once shared. But as the dream turns into the nightmare of her death, he hears the refrain: "You catch that man!" Only now the inflection of that phrase points inward instead of outward. No longer the victim, Kimble gets up, dusts himself off, and heads toward Chicago, where he now intends to *catch the man* himself.

The nature of the transformational arc is that it will rise or escalate as the tension to resolve the conflict intensifies. But no conflict can go on forever unabated; it requires too much energy. So when the protagonist is stressed to the breaking point, a shift occurs that allows something new to enter the picture. That new thing usually comes in the form of new information or a new perspective that changes the outlook or perception that the protagonist holds. I refer to this shift as the **MOMENT OF ENLIGHTENMENT** because it does, in effect, cast a new light on the problem and allows the protagonist to begin to see how the conflict might be resolved. This is the point in the story when the conflict is shifted out of *resistance* and *released* in the direction of the resolution.

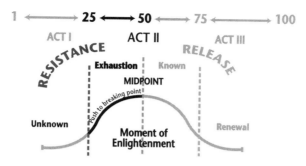

Looking Inward

At the midpoint of the "A" story, something happens that shifts the external action out of *resistance* and points the protagonist toward resolving the conflict of the plot: the police get an important clue that tells them where to find the killer; a map to a treasure is discovered; something or someone who was lost is found. However, it is in the internal subplotlines that the midpoint has the biggest impact on the outcome of the story.

It is not the physical action but the internal reaction to the midpoint that opens up the new idea or new thought that allows the protagonist to move forward toward resolving the conflict. At the midpoint in *The Fugitive*, Kimble turns, shifting the physical direction in which he is traveling. Instead of running away from the authorities, he chooses instead to run toward catching the man who murdered his wife. He makes this decision based on a new inner awareness that motivates him to take action in a new direction.

This new self-awareness, or *enlightenment*, comes about because the protagonist has begun to see how his or her own behavior (fatal flaw) impacts resolving the conflict. Since the fatal flaw of character comes directly out of the writer's thematic point of view, it is that thematic content that is specifically expressed at the midpoint. This is the *truth* that the protagonist begins to understand.

In *Casablanca*, the midpoint is the place in the story where Rick learns the truth about why Ilsa didn't show up at the train station in Paris. Now, for the first time, he begins to see that his own selfish and self-absorbed perspective kept him from ever considering what Ilsa may have gone through. This begins to reopen his heart and dissolve the barriers that have kept him so alone and isolated. As a result of this new awareness, there is an internal shift in Rick that will eventually lead to his selfless and heroic actions to help get Victor and Ilsa out of Casablanca—hence, to resolve the goal of the plot.

In *Tootsie*, it is at the midpoint that Michael begins to earnestly fall in love with Julie, which motivates him to start looking for some way out of his false career as a woman. But because it is not yet time to reveal who he really is, the story takes an interesting and comic twist that demonstrates a larger aspect of the theme. When a person begins to sincerely open his or her heart to love, love begins to open itself to that person as well. Therefore, because Julie can't know at this point that Michael is a man, she can't yet begin to form a romantic attachment to him. But her father, who believes Michael is a woman, can fall in love with him/her—and he does.

When Harry Met Sally has a similar predicament. At the midpoint in this story, the two friends are dateless on New Year's Eve, so they accompany each other, just as pals, to a big, rollicking party. But just before the clock strikes midnight, a slow dance begins to play, and as they dance in each other's arms the camera catches the undeniable look of love that is dawning in their eyes. But the sensation is so new, and so daunting, that neither is yet ready to admit to themselves, or to each other, just how they're feeling. However, there is a definite shift at this point in their relationship, as they cautiously watch for a signal or an indication that their growing romantic affections are going to be returned. But because love is now in bloom in this part of the story, and as the protagonists are not yet fully able to express it, the writer has developed a surrogate love affair between their two best friends, who've also fallen in love. This helps demonstrate the thematic principle that lovers can be friends.

For Thelma and Louise, the midpoint of their story brings about a true initiation into their own sense of personal power. Louise's world of control and limitation broke apart at the first turning point, when she shot the man who was attempting to rape Thelma. As the script heads into the midpoint position, Louise is overcome and disoriented, unable to reestablish any sense of equilibrium. But along with this weariness (exhaustion) comes a vulnerability, which allows the man she's been pining over for years to give her something she was never able to receive before: love and support. However, instead of clinging to it as a lifesaver, she is empowered by it and given the strength to face the rough road that lies ahead.

Thelma, who likewise has been accepting the absolute minimum from her relationship with her husband, has her first sexual encounter with another man that, she claims, wasn't completely repulsive.

It doesn't matter that the new object of Thelma's affection turns out to be a sociopath, liar, and thief who runs off with all their money. She wasn't meant to trade one jerk for another anyway, and what she gets out of the bargain is worth the price. From this point forward in the story, Thelma is finally able to stand on her own two feet. In fact, when Louise breaks down upon learning about the missing money, Thelma does the unthinkable—she takes charge. She even yells at Louise to keep moving!

Another very interesting shift occurs at the midpoint in a story with a co-protagonist structure; both of the central characters tend to swing in the other's direction. Louise moves from a condition of being too controlling to a position where she needs to be taken care of. Thelma, on the other hand, moves from being a helpless victim to becoming headstrong and willful.

Returning to the premise that all conflict results from some sort of imbalance, it's essential at the midpoint for the protagonist to move toward the opposite position from the one he or she has been holding. However, an encounter with an opposite force can be so powerful and intoxicating that the protagonist is likely to get swallowed up in it for awhile.

A great example of this can be seen in *Sea of Love*. At the midpoint Pacino's character, Frank Keller, dives headfirst into a potentially dangerous love affair with a woman who may be the serial killer he's been assigned to hunt down. Because Keller has lived his life on a diet of only masculine bravado, he is empty and alone at midlife, starving for any morsel of feminine contact. Therefore, this encounter with an opposite force—a "dangerous" woman—is so energizing that it feels as though it could consume him if he doesn't find his equilibrium. Hence, the conflict that moves the story along in the second act is greatly intensified. (It also allows for very heated and passionate love scenes!)

The midpoint is also an important place for a heroic story to become more fully distinguished from one that ends in tragedy. Since the midpoint reveals the writer's thematic value, the heroic protagonist will begin to comprehend and embrace it while the tragic character is more likely to ignore or disregard it.

Approaching the midpoint in *Goodfellas*, the net tightens around Henry yet he continually chooses to ignore the obvious.

> HENRY
>
> For most of the guys, killings got to
> be accepted. Murder was the only way that
> everybody stayed in line… You got out of
> line, you got whacked. Everybody knew the
> rules. But sometimes, even if people didn't
> get out of line, they'd get whacked. I
> mean, hits just became habits for some
> guys. Guys would get into arguments over
> nothing, and before you knew it, one of
> them was dead.

The chickens are coming home to roost at this point in the story. The murder that Henry witnessed in the opening of the movie is now drawing heat. So Henry is forced to help Tommy dig up the six-month-old corpse and relocate it. On the home front, there is also a great deal of tension between Henry and his wife, complicated by his taking on a mistress, who brings her own set of troubles into the situation. Emotionally, however, the scene that really turns the story toward its tragic conclusion seems, at first, relatively small in terms of plot development.

As Henry and his pals enjoy a typical poker night, psycho Tommy pulls his gun on the young kid, Spider, who's serving drinks. Tommy "playfully" urges Spider to move his feet faster, like they did in the old western movies. "Come on, dance, you varmint," he jokes, and then shoots the poor boy in the foot. However, this isn't even the shocking part. Two scenes later, we return to a similar poker night where Spider is once again passing out drinks, now with a bandaged foot. When Tommy starts hassling him again, young Spider tries to stand up for himself. "Go fuck yourself," he tells his tormentor, and all the men laugh at the kid's bravado. Then Tommy pulls out his gun and simply shoots Spider three times in the chest.

The scene *hits* very close to home. Spider was making his way up the bloodstained mob ladder exactly the same way Henry had. His only misstep was that he demanded a little respect. Isn't that what tough guys are supposed to do? Up to this point, everything has been fun and easy in this gangster tale, but from here on the hidden costs of this treacherous lifestyle begin to take their toll. Henry, however, still foolishly believes that anything he wants in life is free for the taking.

The Moment of Truth

Whether a story is told heroically or tragically, or whether it uses a linear or non-linear structure (e.g., *Pulp Fiction*), the midpoint not only reveals the truth to the protagonist, but it also reveals the writer's truths to the audience. Through the protagonist's actions and reactions, the writer's thematic values are clarified and defended at the midpoint. In fact, if you ever feel inclined to have your characters give a speech, tell a story, tell someone off, or demonstrate a principle regarding the thematic value, this is the place where you can usually get away with it. In order to comprehend what's going on around him or her, the protagonist will often need to be lectured to, scolded, or taught a lesson.

At the midpoint in *Dead Poets Society*, Keating inspires his students to see themselves from a greater perspective. Quoting Thoreau, he warns the boys to not resign themselves to leading "lives of quiet desperation." He reiterates the theme, challenging them to break away from the safe confines of conformity and complacency by accepting the quest to find their own voice and discover their authentic nature.

At the midpoint in *A Few Good Men*, written by Aaron Sorkin, Navy lawyer Corporal Kaffee (Tom Cruise) is rebuked by his co-council, Jo (Demi Moore), for not having the courage to stand and fight for his clients in a murder case.

> KAFFEE
>
> Tomorrow morning I'll get them a new attorney.
>
> JO
>
> Why are you so afraid to be a lawyer? Were Daddy's expectations really that high?
>
> KAFFEE
>
> Okay, please spare me the psycho-babble father bullshit. Dawson and Downey'll have their day in court, but they'll have it with another lawyer.
>
> JO
>
> Another lawyer won't be good enough. They need you. You know how to win. You know they have a case. You know how to win. You walk away from this now, and you have sealed their fate.
>
> KAFFEE
>
> Their fate was sealed the moment Santiago died.
>
> JO
>
> Do you believe they have a case?

> KAFFEE
>
> You and Dawson both live in the same dreamland. It doesn't matter what I believe, it only matters what I can prove. So please don't tell me what I know and don't know. I know the law.

JO looks at him, shakes her head, and turns to walk away. She turns back.

> JO
>
> You know nothing about the law. You're a used car salesman, Daniel. You're an ambulance chaser with a rank. You're nothing... Live with that.

But Kaffee can't live with that, and in the next scene he not only decides to go to trial with his clients, he also comes to a rather humbling understanding about why he was chosen to represent them—it looks as though he is being used as part of a cover-up.

> KAFFEE
>
> Why does a lieutenant junior grade with nine months experience and a track record for plea bargaining get assigned a murder case?
> (beat)
> Would it be so that it never sees the inside of a courtroom?

As a result of coming to greater self-awareness, Kaffee gains new insight into the case on which he is working. This internal shift leads him to an external shift in the action, which moves the story out of resistance and pushes it toward resolving the conflict. From this point forward, Kaffee no longer resists defending his clients in court. In fact, he no longer resists becoming a real courtroom lawyer. He also stops resisting the advice and better instincts of his straightlaced (and beautiful) co-council. Most importantly, he no longer resists his own better judgment, which tells him that there's a lot more to this case than meets the eye.

At the midpoint in *The Fisher King*, written by Richard LaGravenese, Parry (Robin Williams) lies naked in the center of Central Park and tells Jack (Jeff Bridges) the story of how the wounded king was healed by a caring fool who brought him back in touch with the Holy Grail (his inner spirit).

                    PARRY
…Now as this boy grew older, his wound
grew deeper until one day life, for him,
life lost its reason. He had no faith in
any man, not even himself. He couldn't
love, or feel loved. He was sick with
experience. He began to die. One day, a
fool wandered into the castle and found
the king alone. And being a fool, he was
simple-minded. He didn't see a king, he
only saw a man alone and in pain and he
asked the king, "What ails you, friend?"
The king replied, "I'm thirsty; I need
some water to cool my throat." So the
fool took a cup from beside his bed and
filled it with water, and handed it to
the king. And as the king began to drink,
he realized his wound was healed. He
looked at his hands and there the Holy
Grail; that which he sought all of his
life. He turned to the fool and said with
amazement, "How could you find that which

my brightest and bravest could not?" The
fool replied, "I don't know, I only knew
that you were thirsty."

Jack sees the reflection of his own wounded spirit in this legend and becomes inspired to do something kind for Parry. Up to this point in the movie Jack has been looking for an easy fix to redeem his life. But from this point forward he begins to put genuine passion into his efforts, and this caring is what ultimately brings about his salvation.

This speech, in its entirety, is over four minutes long, and at any other point in the film it would have stopped the action and hindered the momentum. However, the climb to the top of the arc has been arduous and exhaustive, so this is a very good place for both the protagonist and the audience to rest and be reminded of the value and importance of the quest itself.

Because the midpoint generally divides the story in half, it can be used as a point of demarcation from which to tell the tale from two different perspectives. *A Beautiful Mind*, written by Akiva Goldsman, brilliantly uses the midpoint as the place in the story where the fiction of John Nash's extraordinary life becomes separated from his severe schizophrenia. Through the entire first half of the film, the audience is unwittingly drawn into the protagonist's increasingly delusional world, where we believe, along with him, that his exceptional mind is being exploited by a treacherous underworld spy network. But as this experience causes Nash to spin out of control, his internal and external realities literally collide with each other at the midpoint of the script, and the *truth* of what is really happening to him begins to break through.

Always look for there to be a midpoint in the plot and in each of the primary subplotlines. Sometimes these separate midpoints will intersect each other, but it's not essential that they all occur at the same time and in the same scene. It also doesn't matter in which order they fall. In our own lives, sometimes events occur that make us rethink who we are and what we stand for in the world. At other times we begin to see the need for change and that, in turn, influences the choices we make. For example, a woman might decide that she's been dating too many losers and that if she wants a real relationship she must hold out for someone who is real. This will influence her encounters with men, especially when she meets someone special. On the other hand, she may need to have a really terrible encounter with a man to suddenly realize that she doesn't have to settle for men who don't truly value her.

Because the midpoint is so heavily thematic, writers themselves can look to it for inspiration. If you are having trouble understanding your theme, examine what's happening in the middle of the story. Ask yourself what is physically shifting the action toward resolution; then try to understand what is internally motivating the protagonist to take that new course. If nothing is motivating him or her, this may be a pretty good indicator that your theme is underdeveloped. Use this as an opportunity to explore motivational possibilities, and then work backward into understanding your theme through what the protagonist is coming to understand. This is also a good place to see if the theme you think you are developing is the same theme the story actually wants to communicate. As I've said, I believe writers are called to write what they don't know, not what they do know. Therefore, as you work with the development of your protagonist around the midpoint, open yourself to the possibility that the "new thing" may be breaking into consciousness for you as well as for the characters in your story.

This is why I always pay special attention to the midpoint when I'm analyzing a script. Even if the story has a very underdeveloped arc of character, somewhere around the midpoint I often find clues that help me understand what the writer's conscious and unconscious intentions might be. In Chapter Five, I discussed *Don Juan DeMarco*, pointing out that the theme of the film and the development of the protagonist didn't seem to match up. While the story expresses the need for passion in life, this message falls flat because the protagonist, Dr. Mickler, doesn't really lack passion. Yet, in a confrontation at the midpoint between Don Juan and the doctor, whom he calls Don Octavio, Don Juan accuses the doctor of being all dried up. He tells him that his heart is closed and this has turned his blood to dust. He says the reason the great doctor is so interested in his case is that he needs his passion as a transfusion.

Finding dialogue like this at the midpoint of a script that so clearly states what the story is intended to be about is where the rewrite process needs to start. As eloquent as Don Juan's diagnosis of the good doctor is, it doesn't carry a lot of weight in this story because it isn't true. We've seen no evidence that Dr. Mickler's heart is closed to love or that he is devoid of passion. However, if the doctor were redesigned around the descriptive idea that his heart is closed and his blood has turned to dust then the story itself would begin to come alive.

Case Studies

1) ROMANCING THE STONE

The first half of the second act of *Romancing the Stone* is a classic example of how resistance works in the romantic comedy genre. In the first act, Joan is very clear about what she's looking for in a perfect man. In the second act, however, she's stuck with a guy who's completely the opposite of that fantasy. This opposition keeps the situation tense and unpredictable, which is a great source to draw upon for comedy and romantic entanglements.

As Joan begins the second act, she is forced to trudge through the jungle on foot to find and rescue her sister. This makes the going rough and uncomfortable, but if that's all there is to it she will eventually get to her sister and simply complete the mission. However, things get worse after the first turning point because her attacker returns with backup troops and they aggressively pursue Joan through the jungle with bayonets and machine guns. This forces her to move faster, harder, and not necessarily in the direction of her sister. Keeping the protagonist in resistance to achieving the goal is the most important thing for a writer to focus on in this section of the story. Not only does it significantly add to the dramatic tension, but it also effectively *exhausts* the protagonist physically, mentally, and emotionally. This serves to make way for the midpoint, where something new can break through—especially on the internal level.

For Joan, the lack of control over her external world in the "A" story is causing a high degree of emotional instability that affects the "B" and "C" storylines. In the "B" story, Joan begins the second act by being forced into an adventure that she didn't sign up for. It is one thing to have to pack a suitcase, don her linen traveling suit, and fly halfway around the world to bring back her wayward sister. But to have to deal with the dangerous wilds of the South American jungle on foot, while being shot at, is something that will test her courage and ability to face the unknown in ways she never imagined, even in her most tempestuous adventure novels.

As Joan makes the arduous climb up the steep face of the transformational arc at the beginning of Act II, her resistances are wearing down. Because she is set up as a woman who hides from life and love, she is challenged at this point in the story to overcome her fears. The more Joan physically weakens, the more she is forced to survive by drawing on inner strengths she didn't know she had.

Also, keep in mind that all of this adventurous activity really serves a higher function in this story because it services the metaphor through which this writer is exploring the nature of romantic love. Therefore, it's in the "C" story, or relationship subplot, that the real jeopardy for Joan must take place. She has maintained her distance from true love by idealizing men, but this adventure seems to be pinning her chances of survival on a man who *appears* to be anything but the swashbuckling hero of her fantasies.

The dichotomy between Joan's expectations and the reality of who Jack Colton is provides the most powerful stimulus for the action in the first half of the second act. It is, in fact, their *resistance* to each other that provides the most comedy, character development, and plot development in the story. Unlike the selfless heroes in her novels, Jack has a mercenary mentality and only agrees to guide Joan down the mountain for a profit. He likewise refuses to make any gallant efforts to assist in carrying her suitcase, and doesn't hesitate to toss her "baggage" down a ravine when she has trouble lugging it along. Jack thinks he's calling all the shots until very real bullets start flying over their heads. Then he begins to realize that this easy and lucrative gig is going to cost him a lot more than he bargained for. He'd like to dump Joan, but she's not so easy to get rid of.

In this part of the story, they both resent being stuck with each other in order to make it out alive. However, their need for survival is greater than their mutual dislike and this brings out qualities in each of them that the other begins to admire. Joan is becoming less uptight and Jack is behaving less like a cad. The real breakthrough in their relationship occurs at the midpoint when they stumble upon the wreckage of an old airplane, presumably used by drug runners. In it they find a safe hiding place from their pursuers and a contraband shipment of marijuana, which they use to stoke a fire for warmth. Needless to say, the smoke from the fire loosens their inhibitions and the two opposites begin to attract.

In a love story, the midpoint is the perfect spot for love to bloom. Even if a couple finds themselves attracted to each other in the first act, something needs to keep the lid on their growing affections until the midpoint. This is where the shift of consciousness occurs and the awareness of real feelings, real attraction, real love, and real connection begins to form. In *Romancing the Stone*, there is a definite shift in the relationship between Joan and Jack, but when he finds the treasure map in her satchel, it becomes hard to tell whether it's her or the hidden treasure he really lusts after.

If you recall, the core internal issue of this story is *trust*. Joan needs to learn to trust the adventure that leads to love. Therefore, creating a love interest for her whose loyalty is questionable is an ideal situation.

When Jack finds the treasure map, our attention returns to the plot. It, too, needs a midpoint shift if the external goal is eventually to be attained. When the story began, a rather benign set of kidnappers demanded that Joan trade the treasure map in her possession for her sister's release. Now, however, a second set of bad guys has entered the picture and they are only interested in retrieving the map at any cost, which clearly may include Joan's life. This means that if Joan wants to achieve her goal, she's going to need a new strategy—which Jack presents to her. He convinces Joan that the only way out of this mess is for them to go after the treasure themselves. If they find it first they will then have a position of power from which to negotiate. Joan really wants to *trust* Jack, so she agrees. But we in the audience are not so sure about him. However, this new approach to achieving the goal of the plot pushes the story over the crest of the arc and points it toward the resolution.

Keep in mind, however, that it was a long, high climb up to the midpoint, which means that there is nowhere to go from here but down.

2) LETHAL WEAPON

When developing a co-protagonist structure, it is necessary for the central characters in the story to find at least part of their resolution by coming into *balance* with each other. Because the first half of the second act is on the opposite side of the arc from the resolution, it's a safe bet that this is the point in the story when the co-protagonists are most out of balance and out of sync.

Lethal Weapon perfectly illustrates this principle of finding balance. In the last chapter, we saw that most of the action surrounding the first turning point dealt with the questionable pairing of this unlikely couple. But now that they are thrown together to solve the crime at the beginning of the second act, the fun really begins. As they pursue a routine lead, Murtaugh can't keep from mumbling to himself about his great misfortune at being partnered with a wild man who will surely facilitate his premature demise. Riggs makes a feeble attempt to reassure Murtaugh, but manages instead to add to his insecurity. This sharply increases the tension in the "B" storyline.

Hostile banter between the two cops continues as they approach the lavish Beverly Hills home of the man they believe to have been the dead girl's meal ticket. Murtaugh cautions Riggs not to "damage" this

H reaches higher & higher, height is
self deserved, lying to others he
begs to cover the he he works
he himself (? that women are seen first
worthy? that they don't deserve the talk...
Where is it going to be enough?
It's dying. He has to lie more & more to
have women. Though guys like these,
they don't include them in their group
...for how he gets women away from them...

and/or his sisters exclude him from
parties because he's bad news for their
female friends.
(we/Julia don't know anything about H. weed
to know more)

refuses to listen or even bother

those brothers asleep/ ester.. asleep

zone ice SR
You can't buy want the present
HUNTER PLEADS
side of the car - does Diane ?? ACP3

guy because he's the only suspect they have and they need him for questioning. Riggs tries not to shoot anyone (he really does), but the bad guy opens fire first. Murtaugh attempts to merely wound him, however, the suspect pulls out a second gun and is about to shoot Murtaugh when Riggs finally takes aim and fires.

With their prime suspect dead, the protagonists are now further from their goal of resolving the plot ("A" story). However, Riggs did save Murtaugh's life, so this incident manages to bring the two closer and they start working as a team. This means that the relationship subplot ("C" story) is moving toward the midpoint.

In gratitude, Murtaugh takes Riggs home to dinner, and the loner is instantly enveloped into the warmth of his new partner's family. For the first time in the entire story, Riggs begins to laugh and relax a little. This is an indication that the internal arc of character ("B" story) is also moving toward the midpoint, where he will begin to find purpose and meaning in his life again.

Sometimes the conditions of the plot will move the protagonist(s) toward an internal shift, but in this story it's the other way around. Because Murtaugh and Riggs finally start to trust each other, they begin to act as a team. Even though it appears that the man they killed was behind the young girl's death, Riggs especially feels that something much worse is going on with this crime. Together the partners reassess the clues and realize that there was another woman on the scene of the girl's death who may have been more than just an eyewitness. However, just as they arrive at her home to investigate, the house is blown up. In the burned-out rubble, Riggs and Murtaugh gather evidence that points to something very big going down. The clues indicate that some Vietnam-era mercenaries may be involved. This leads Murtaugh to speculate that his old war buddy Hunsaker was the real target, and that Hunsaker's daughter's death was meant as an intimidation.

The truth about what is really going on in the plot ("A" story) is now finally taking shape for the protagonists and the audience. Murtaugh's hunch proves correct and he gets to Hunsaker, who confesses that he is part of a very powerful drug ring, just before he too is murdered.

The story is now at the apex of the arc because the conflict in all three plotlines has shifted out of resistance and is headed toward resolution. In the "A" story, Riggs and Murtaugh finally know who they're fighting and why. They've also begun to develop a plan for catching the drug dealers. In the "C" story, they are starting to trust each other and work as a team, and this has helped put their personal fears in perspective, which is what is needed to help them resolve the "B" story. One very important thing to notice about this particular script is that as these co-protagonists move out of resistance to each other, they start to form a unit. This will be necessary in the second half of the story, because the antagonists are so powerful it will take the unified force of these two men to stop them.

3) ORDINARY PEOPLE

As *Ordinary People* enters the second act, the biggest issue facing the family is their denial of (resistance to) the idea that the family itself may be in trouble. They will admit that the death of their son/brother was catastrophic, and they will admit that Conrad has big personal problems, but they don't have a broad enough perspective to see the enormity of the crisis that they, as a family, are actually facing. None of them, including Conrad, understands that his suicide attempt was not just an expression of his own pain; he also feels responsible for carrying the weight of the entire family's pain.

Therefore, the purpose of the first half of the second act is to push this family to a *breaking point*, where the depth of their collective grief and inner turmoil can become clear and undeniable to them. The family cannot begin to heal itself until they can acknowledge that they have a problem. At the first turning point, their wall of denial is finally breached. It begins with Conrad's visits to a psychiatrist and is further cracked apart when Beth overhears her husband confiding this personal and *unseemly* information about their son to a friend. But the assault on their façade of normalcy does not just come from Beth's feelings of betrayal; it also comes from Calvin's dawning realization that his wife is trying to cut the family off from their own reality.

The second act begins with several poignant scenes. The family members seem to sense that they are experiencing the calm before a terrible storm, so they make awkward attempts to reconcile their differences. Beth and Conrad share a quiet moment in the backyard, but can find no common ground on which to communicate. Later, when Conrad tries again to open up a personal dialogue with his mother, she becomes easily diverted by a frivolous phone call, leaving Conrad feeling deeply wounded by her indifference and inattentiveness.

As the story moves up the arc, the rift between mother and son deepens and Dad becomes more perplexed and distant. He is clearly caught in the middle and doesn't know how to cope with these issues because he can't yet see what's really going on. His blindness translates into ambivalence, which causes the dramatic tension to intensify greatly as the film nears the midpoint range. This is where the battle lines finally begin to clarify themselves. At a family photo session, Conrad explodes at his mother when she can't even muster the patience to pose in a picture with him. Beth's reaction to his outburst is to rethink sending him away to school, so that the "problem" of Conrad can be put out of sight and out of mind. Calvin reacts as if he's shell-shocked. He's confused and confounded by his wife and son's behavior, but it's beginning to sink in that something significant is happening to his family.

Conrad's reaction, on the other hand, is one of great *release*. He's never stood up for himself before because to do so would have meant standing against the family. However, with his doctor's help he begins to realize that he's not personally responsible for the success or failure of the family. The lifting of this great burden begins to liberate Conrad, and for the first time we see him acting like a happy-go-lucky teen. His character arc has just crested and he is now heading in the direction of resolving his personal issues that once drove him to suicide.

The family's problems have not yet hit the midpoint, but Conrad's new attitude is just the sort of thing that will force this to happen. Within a few scenes, Beth learns that Conrad quit the swim team months earlier and has never told them. She is infuriated, and Calvin is surprised. However, the real difference in their response is that Dad asks Conrad why he did this; Mom only wants to know how he could do this to *her*. At this point, Conrad is incapable of withholding all of his pent-up anger and resentment toward his mother and unleashes a torrent of thunderous expletives. Later, when his father tries to talk with him in his room, Conrad finally utters the unbearable truth: "She hates me." Dad still wants to deny this, and maybe it isn't literally true, but he and the audience *know* that from this point forward the spell of "normalcy" that Beth has cast over this family is finally broken. They aren't ideal; they're real— their pain is real, their grief is real, and they really do need each other. This is what will make them a *real* and whole family. It is here, at the midpoint, that the story shifts out of resistance to this truth and heads toward resolving whether or not they will become a *real* family.

CHAPTER NINE

ACT II—PART TWO
...Must Come Down

Thy fate is the common fate of all;
Into each life some rain must fall.

~ HENRY WADSWORTH LONGFELLOW

Amazing Grace

A few weeks ago, a friend invited me to join her for a little hike. Not being much of an outdoorsy type, imagine my surprise (and ire) when our little afternoon hike actually turned out to be a *hike*. "C'mon, you can do it," she kept yammering—way too cheerfully. "It's beautiful at the top." Frankly, I didn't care if we were on our way to Shangri-La—my back hurt, my ankles throbbed; I was thirsty, sweaty, and not very happy about our differing interpretations of the word *hike*. An *hour* later when we finally reached the summit, I was sure I was going to have to be airlifted out. (I was also sure of one name I could cross off my homemade basil vinaigrette Christmas gift list.) Gulping for oxygen, I was barely able to lift my thorn-ravaged torso over the last boulder before I collapsed. "Take deep breaths," my friend admonished, "or you'll get leg cramps." That was the least of my worries; I hadn't felt my legs for the past twenty minutes.

When I was finally able to breathe again, something quite astonishing happened: I started to feel light (which is always a surprise in middle age). It wasn't a feeling of light-headedness or vertigo, just a sense of buoyancy, as if I wasn't quite earthbound. It took awhile for my pulse rate to slow down, but the crushing throb in my chest seemed to melt away. And then I saw it; I looked down and saw the path I had just climbed and couldn't believe what I had achieved. Then I looked out over the horizon and couldn't believe what Mother Nature had achieved either. I have to admit that I was awestruck by the beauty of it all....

As we ate our little lunch I was amazed at the surge of energy I suddenly felt. My poor, tired old legs not only came back to life, but they also seemed unusually agile and sprightly for the return trek down the mountain. Of course, the next day my body wasn't quite so euphoric (and I was back to questioning my Christmas list), but at that moment I felt completely invincible.

This blast of energy produced by my arduous (if not foolhardy) climb is probably the simplest way I can describe what occurs following the midpoint of a story. The nature of climbing, in general, relies on a huge expenditure of energy; *the steeper and harder the climb, the greater the amount of energy used.* Reaching the summit of a climb provides a natural place to rest, and this brings about a renewal of energy.

Additional energy can also come in the form of anything that refuels the body, mind, or spirit. Obviously, food and rest help with our physical renewal, but things such as inspiration, awe, insight, and ideas can revive our exhausted souls in even greater ways. From this sort of energetic boost we are able to tackle what lies in front of us with renewed confidence and vitality.

In great stories, I often find a reflection of this restoration process in the phase of the script that follows the midpoint. I refer to this as a **PERIOD OF GRACE.** Once *enlightenment* has entered the protagonist's consciousness in the form of a new idea, a new understanding, or a new perspective on the problems or issues of the past, he or she will be inspired and motivated to face what lies ahead with renewed vigor, strength, and resolve.

Consider the moments in your own life when you emerged out of the darkness of a troubled period, and try to remember how you felt.

Did you feel lighter? Did the world appear brighter and filled with more promise? Was it easier to get out of bed in the morning? Did you find yourself engaging more significantly with those around you, and did people even comment that you looked better? Most of us not only feel healthier and have more energy and stamina once the storm passes, but our aspirations toward career, fitness, wealth, creativity, and relationships seem to fall into place with more ease and *grace*.

The period of grace is not an exact point in a story, but a nonspecific *period* of time in which the protagonist tends to thrive instead of strive. It can be as long as eight pages or as short as a single scene. In fact, it is not even a mandatory part of a story's structure. But I do find that scripts that have it tend to be much stronger for several reasons. To begin with, it just *feels* right. If the first half of a script pushes the protagonist to face higher and greater resistance to the goal, then it is quite natural to experience a break in the tension at the midpoint. It is also natural for there to be a sensation of rest and rejuvenation in the period that follows the arduous climb to the top. The period of grace also helps a story find a natural *rhythm*; music itself tends to take a rest after an especially strong escalation of notes before it moves to another phase. Further, if the dramatic tension in a story is strong, the audience will welcome this rest before being thrown into the turmoil and upheaval that leads to the climax.

The most significant reason a period of grace improves the quality of a story is that the shift of consciousness experienced at the midpoint fills the protagonist with new and greater potential. This potential is required to open up possibilities for resolving the conflict and achieving the goal of the plot. As a result, we often see in the grace period a glimpse of what life might be like for the protagonist *if* he or she can ever reach the goal.

In love stories, for example, a couple may resist each other up to the midpoint, where they finally realize they have genuine feelings for each other. What follows this moment of connection is a *period* of falling in love and getting to know each other. Very often we, in the audience, are somewhat hoping the story will end here, where everybody's happy. But we are also aware that there is too much still unresolved.

Again, *Casablanca* is an excellent case in point. Once all the truth about Paris has been revealed at the midpoint, Rick and Ilsa find their way back into each other's arms, where the fit is so perfect we feel as though they're now free to love fully and forever. Except for poor old Victor, the leader of the Resistance, who needs a little help liberating France. Alas, this great love between Rick and Ilsa is still not right. Even though they've reclaimed their love for each other, the story is propelled onward by their need to resolve the problem of Victor, France, the Nazis, the transit papers, and so on....

In *An Affair to Remember*, it is at the midpoint that the depth of Nickie and Terry's feelings toward each other is revealed. A funny, joy-filled, romantic sequence, or period of grace, follows in which we not only see their love develop, we also see that these two people have the capacity to bring out the best in each other. Both Nickie and Terry have been heading down roads that will lead them only to false, inauthentic lives. But now that they've found each other they can get back to the things that mean something to them, including their art. However, they both still have the entanglements of other fiancé(e)s that have to be dealt with. This means that, even though they're in love, the story is not yet over.

Because the grace period feels so good, it can give the false impression that all is well and the conflict has abated. Many good thrillers and action films take full advantage of this misimpression and intentionally lure both the audience and the protagonist into a false sense of safety and security. In *Basic Instinct*, for example, the grace period functions as a time when we think Detective Nick Curran (Michael Douglas) is out of danger or at least on safer ground. Even though we've had serious suspicions about Catherine Tramell (Sharon Stone), we're beginning to think that she might be innocent and that her feelings of love and passion for Nick might be real as well. Nick would like to believe this, too, but unfortunately Catherine still likes to play with knives.

In good thrillers this is an excellent place to allow the tension to ease in a way that causes the protagonist to lower defenses and even become too sure of him- or herself. At the midpoint in *Sea of Love*, for example, Frank so badly wants Helen to be innocent that he wipes her fingerprints off a coffee mug, which implies that he won't be able to test her prints against those of the killer. Following the midpoint in this story there is a period of grace in which we see Frank fall so much in love with Helen that he sets up a special date in order to ask her to move in with him. When the evening doesn't turn out the way he plans, she goes home angry and alone and he goes to a bar to cool his heels. But in the middle of the night Frank shows up on Helen's doorstep and tells her he can't sleep without her, he's so madly in love. While she goes to check on her daughter and mother before leaving with Frank, he notices a newspaper clipping with personal ads stuck to her refrigerator. All the names circled are of men who died at the hands of the serial killer he's been trying to catch. This can't be a coincidence.

Or can it? The writer very effectively plays with our emotions at this point in the story. We've come to care for Frank and even for Helen. But, like Frank, how can we ignore the obvious implications of those personal ads stuck to her refrigerator?

In a heroic story, the most important use of the grace period is to show us the protagonist's *potential* of whether he or she can ever achieve the internal and external goals. In the external plotline, this is the place where an illusive killer is identified, the map to a treasure is found, and the weakness in an opponent's strategy is exposed. But more importantly, this is the moment in the story when you want to explore what is shifting *inside* the protagonist that will lead him or her to transformational change. This shift may eventually open the door to true love, creativity, healing inner wounds, growing up, facing loss, and so on. But it also must be evident that there is work still to be done because transformational change cannot be achieved without commitment, hard work, courage, and a lot of *letting go....*

The Fall

Another reason I believe a period of grace strengthens a story is that it can feel like a gift or reward one receives for having struggled to achieve greater self-awareness (enlightenment) at the midpoint. The true benefit of this gift of self-knowledge is that it increases access to the realm of **CONSCIOUSNESS.** What was once unknown, both externally and internally, is now becoming **KNOWN.**

But higher consciousness alone is not enough; it must be acted upon before it can be transformed into something greater within us. This is the nature of the challenge that still lies ahead for the protagonist. When an alcoholic finally acknowledges that his or her drinking is out of control, that person has crossed an important threshold opening the door to sobriety. But just recognizing the problem is not enough to actually get sober. Sobriety demands action—continuous, consistent action—especially when the going gets tough. Likewise, it's not enough for an artist to wake up in the morning with a great idea. Unless significant action is taken, there will never be any tangible evidence that he or she has actually created anything. The act of love also involves more than just acknowledging deep feelings for someone. Only with consistent, committed involvement and interaction in good times and bad can there be any possibility of real intimacy.

In storytelling, this principle must be evident or the arc of transformation will feel false or incomplete. Because the moment of enlightenment is so powerful, there is a tendency to feel that the work with the internal storyline is complete. In reality, the midpoint is only the gateway to transformation; given proper attention, the inner story will really catch fire from this point forward. While life may finally seem pretty good for the protagonist after he or she crosses the midpoint and enters into the period of grace, there are still unresolved complications that will eventually cause a great undoing. Therefore, what follows the grace period is some sort of a **FALL** that sets relationships, ambitions, aspirations, and achievements into a decline or even a tailspin.

You can see in the shape of the arc itself that there is a slight plateau at the top, which is where we encounter the grace period. But once the protagonist moves past the plateau, he or she will begin a clear downward free fall, and this is exactly what the story should feel like in the last part of the second act.

Things will begin to slip and slide for the protagonist. This is the place in the story where lies and half-truths are about to take their toll. For example, at the midpoint in *The Graduate*, Benjamin Braddock (Dustin Hoffman) finally begins to fall for Elaine, the girl his parents have been trying to get him to date ever since he came home from college. Up to the midpoint, he resists having anything to do with her and instead succumbs to the seductions of her mother, the infamous Mrs. Robinson. When Benjamin finally gets to know Elaine (at the midpoint), he finds himself falling in love (during the grace period). But the truth about what he's done with her mother casts a very dark shadow over any future they might have together (the fall).

The fall is also the place in a story where miscommunication and misjudgments occur, leading to bad timing, bad advice, and bad planning. The result is often a sense of betrayal, unfaithfulness, duplicity, and treachery. True or not, the effect will be the same. Things are about to *fall* seriously apart for the protagonist.

In the horror classic *Carrie*, the title character (Sissy Spacek) is a naive, awkward teenager who is horribly taunted by her classmates. As a punishment for how they've treated her, a group of girls are not allowed to attend their prom. While this leads most of them to resent Carrie even further, Sue, one of the students involved in the hazing, is genuinely remorseful and convinces her boyfriend, Tommy, to take Carrie to the prom in her place. Most of Carrie's awkwardness is due to the influence of her mentally unbalanced mother, who has tried to suppress her daughter's natural feminine and sexual instincts with fanatical religious teachings. But once she is invited to the prom, Carrie begins to emerge as a beautiful young woman. At the dance, she and her date are even chosen as king and queen. The cheers and good wishes of her classmates are very real and it would be great if the story just ended as Carrie is being crowned. But unfortunately that isn't the case. There are still those other nasty classmates running around, who resent Carrie and want to get even. As the story develops, they devise a terrible and humiliating trick to play on her. Just as she is being crowned, they let loose a bucket of pig's blood held in the rafters over her head. But what Carrie doesn't realize as she is doused with the red, gooey stuff is that the other students are as horrified as she is. To her, it seems that this terrible prank is something the whole school is in on and that they are all laughing at her. This misunderstanding leads to very tragic consequences, where Carrie lets loose her own terrifying brand of retribution and nearly everyone and everything in the school is destroyed.

Often the biggest reason for the fall is that, despite the enlightenment that is achieved at the midpoint, the ego won't easily let go of old perceptions and values. This creates a conflict between the old self and the new self that is struggling to emerge. As a result, protagonists can become ambivalent, indecisive, and even disengaged from the very goal they've been struggling toward. In other words, they are often directly or indirectly responsible for the fall itself.

At the midpoint in *An Officer and a Gentleman*, Zack (Richard Gere) is literally pushed to the breaking point by his commanding officer,

Sergeant Foley (Louis Gossett Jr.). Foley physically and mentally exhausts Zack in an effort to get him to drop out of the flight academy because he has been unable to make Zack a team player. But when all of his resistances are broken down, Zack finally admits the truth to himself and to Foley: "I got nowhere else to go." At last he can see and feel just how empty and isolated his life is (midpoint). As a result of this break-through, Zack opens himself to Paula (Debra Winger), the woman he's been dating, and they begin to fall in love (period of grace). But at this point Zack still fears intimacy and is, therefore, incapable of making a complete commitment. He stops calling Paula and makes lame excuses to avoid seeing her. Even though some of the events that follow are out of Zack's control, his fall from grace is really by his own hand.

Things will fall apart if the new consciousness the protagonist acquires at the midpoint is more than he or she can handle. While the young students in *Dead Poets Society* respond enthusiastically to Mr. Keating's teachings about embracing their own value and "sucking the marrow out of life," they have neither the ability nor the wisdom yet to temper their enthusiasm with patience and prudence. In effect, they get a little drunk on their newfound personal freedom. This leads to poor judgment, inflated egos, and irresponsible behavior. After one of the boys foolishly mocks the headmaster at a school assembly and nearly gets himself expelled, Keating takes him to task. He stresses that it's important to learn how to moderate self-expression, and that a wise man knows how to mediate between daring and caution.

Of course, wisdom isn't something that most sixteen-year-olds have yet acquired. It is generally achieved over time as we mature and learn to process our experiences in order to find meaning in them. This is especially true of our encounters with hardships, disappointments, and loss. As a teacher, Keating is only able to hold a mirror to his students so that they can catch a glimpse of their own greater potential. Creating value from that potential is something each boy must do for himself. It's important to recognize that, as the story plunges into the fall, Keating has pretty much taken the boys as far as he can go with them. The final phase of transformational work is something each student must do on his own. It takes a lot of strength of character to proceed from this point forward, which is why the fall will lead to the greatest test a protagonist has yet to encounter.

The Death Experience

It would be great if transformational change was merely a matter of coming to a new understanding in life. If this were true then all of those self-help books and seminars would really be worth the money. As soon as we comprehend that we're overeating to nourish our starving inner child, or that we never have enough prosperity because we don't feel we're worth anything, or that we can't hold on to a relationship because we're afraid of intimacy, then all of those problems would instantly go away. But they don't. In fact, once we begin to see the truth about ourselves, life will often get a lot more difficult before it gets better. (I really hate that.)

Maybe there's a Tibetan monk somewhere who knows how to bypass this next step in the transformational process, but change only seems to come through a very unwelcome experience: our own undoing. The hardest thing for most of us to let go of is the desire to control the outcome. As long as we hold on to that agenda, we're still holding on to our old value system. Transformational change is, in fact, the *death* of an old system of survival (the fatal flaw) and the *birth* of a new one. Therefore, it's extremely important that the protagonist has what I refer to as a **DEATH EXPERIENCE,** one that challenges him or her to let go of what is obsolete and surrender to the part of his or her nature that is struggling to be born.

Remember, the fatal flaw is a survival system that has outlived its usefulness, and this is precisely what is falling apart at this point in the story. Therefore, it is essential that the writer force the protagonist into a situation that will bring about his or her undoing, which is how we arrive at the **SECOND TURNING POINT** at the end of the second act.

Like the first turning point, the second turning point tends to throw a very big obstruction into the wheel of progress for the protagonist.

The greater the magnitude of this obstruction, the greater the *death experience* will be and the stronger the momentum for the story as it moves into the third act.

When you are determining the death experience at the second turning point, the most important thing you want to ask yourself is: *What's the worst thing that can happen?* By **worst thing** I am not referring to the biggest external disaster imaginable, such as the moon falling out of its orbit and crashing into our planet, destroying all life as we know it. Granted, that's a pretty terrible thing, but in terms of the transformational arc the worst thing *must* always relate directly to the **internal struggle of the protagonist.** The internal struggle is *always* the thing that determines the development of the **external conflict.** As with every other decision a writer makes, determining the worst thing that can happen at the second turning point must relate to the thematic goal of the story. Whereas at the midpoint and throughout the period of grace the protagonist has begun to make substantial internal progress as it relates to the thematic value, at the second turning point something happens *externally* that creates a major challenge to this *internal* achievement.

For example, in *Dead Poets Society* the worst thing that can happen at the second turning point is *not* the suicide of Neil Perry, the boy whose father won't let him perform in the school play. Granted, that's an awful death experience, but the worst thing that can happen to these boys is the loss or *death* of the personal power they've been struggling so hard to acquire. To surrender their emerging sense of self-worth back to the institution and parents who want to assume absolute control of their futures is far more tragic.

In this context, the death of Neil Perry as a second turning point in the "A" story is an excellent choice. It is an ideal external crisis that will force the remaining group of students to make an important internal decision about the direction their own lives will take. While their newfound freedom has been fun and thrilling, they neglected to read the fine print when they signed up for it. Independence can only be achieved by demonstrating responsibility to ourselves, to others, and to that which we value. If the boys can stand up for themselves against the power structures that are trying to dominate them, they will achieve their internal goal of being true to their nature. Neil Perry's death is the perfect external incident to provoke such a confrontation.

It's important to notice which part of the development of the second turning point comes first. Even though the suicide is the lynchpin that turns the "A" story in a powerful new direction at the end of the second act, its real purpose is to force the boys to grow up and take responsibility for their own lives. Understanding this principle gives writers crucial information about how to develop an effective turning point. Too often writers focus their creative energy at the second turning point on what will make the biggest boom and they neglect the internal demands of the story. However, if the second turning point is approached from the inside out, the action will not only conform more naturally to the movement of the transformational arc, but it is also by far the most inspirational source for creating the best *big boom* ideas.

Think of the second turning point or death experience as the moment when the protagonist *feels* he or she has lost everything—especially all the gifts that came with the internal shift of consciousness at the midpoint. In *When Harry Met Sally*, the theme has to do with how essential it is for lovers to be friends. Therefore, the worst thing that can happen at the end of the second act is the loss or death of their friendship, which was on the verge of blossoming into true love. Knowing this single piece of information can help a writer avoid poking around and randomly trying to come up with some sort of disaster for the second turning point. All that really needs to be considered in this story is: *What would cause a break in their friendship?* There is no single, right answer to this question, and there are a lot of interesting choices to play with: one of the characters moves away, one of them marries someone else, they become too possessive of each other's time, they take up other interests and develop other best friends, and so on. Any one of these ideas has potential, but the writer of this film came up with her own unique idea: They *do* become lovers and it scares them so much that they run away from their friendship.

Fear is what has kept these two people (and most of us) from becoming intimate. In the beginning of the story, when they were young, Harry and Sally made only safe choices in determining who they would give their hearts to, but it never yielded love—only the pretense of love. Now that real love is close at hand, fear is the beast that challenges their internal progress. If they have what it takes to do battle with this monster and conquer it, they will win the prize—each other. If they lose, it is love that is defeated.

On the other hand, *Sleepless in Seattle* exemplifies how the lack of an internalized second turning point greatly diminishes the impact of the action in the third act and climax. As discussed in Chapter Three, this film seems to be about the need to take a great risk to find true love. At the second turning point, the young boy in the story runs off to New York, by himself, to meet Annie, the woman he wants his dad to marry. The dad, naturally, runs after his son. While Dad is very worried about his kid, it's unlikely that in the middle of this crisis he's going to give much thought to what Annie (Meg Ryan) is doing that evening. His son may risk a lot for his dad to find love, but the dad risks *nothing*. Therefore, in the climax, when he happens to meet Annie while in the process of reclaiming his son, we can be happy for him, but it really doesn't mean very much to us in terms of what this story has to say about love.

The *death experience* at the second turning point must be a real experience of loss, but it doesn't have to be the actual death of someone. *Death* can be used metaphorically to imply deep sorrow, extreme disappointment, great failure, and/or a sense of profound disconnection. It symbolizes dispossession, forfeiture, sacrifice, defeat, and devastation. Consider your own emotional response to the experience of loss; there can be an unbearable sense of disillusionment, anger, and betrayal. Difficulties and supreme hardships are inflicted upon everyone's life at some point, but that doesn't keep any of us from taking these setbacks very personally. How can we open our heart to love, only to have it stomped on again? If we follow our bliss and invest all our energy in becoming a great writer, painter, or actor, how can we tolerate another rejection?

How can we put all our faith in God or surrender our will to a higher power only to get cancer or lose a loved one in a car accident? Especially if we feel we've done the internal work to get sober, trust love, take risks, and have faith—it can seem like a cruel trick of fate that our lives aren't working out the way they're supposed to. So we rage at God, condemn the opposite sex, fall off the wagon, and withdraw from love.

Throughout all of the loss and devastation the protagonist encounters at the second turning point, the one thing that can never be taken away is the enlightenment or new consciousness that was gained at the midpoint. However, this greater self-awareness can be unwanted, un-trusted, and despised because it is now attached to the loss. This makes the threshold at the death experience a place of profound internal crisis. Whereas during the grace period the new consciousness felt like a gift, at the second turning point it can feel like a great burden.

An excellent example of this is found in *The Fisher King*. In the setup of the story we meet Jack Lucas (Jeff Bridges), a pompous, ego-driven radio shock-jock, whose late-night rantings inspire an unbalanced listener to pick up a rifle and randomly shoot at a yuppie couple sitting in a bar. This horrific deed so completely knocks Jack off his self-ordained pedestal that were it not for the love of Anne (Mercedes Ruehl), a kind but taste-challenged woman, he would have ended up a derelict on the street. In fact, on one of his nightly self-loathing benders, Jack is mistaken for a vagrant and nearly set ablaze by teenage vigilantes. He is saved at the last moment by Parry (Robin Williams), an eccentric, reality-challenged homeless person who believes Jack is a noble knight-errant sent to help him rescue the Holy Grail. Jack, of course, wants nothing to do with this "nut job" until he discovers that Parry is the husband of the woman who was murdered in the bar. Apparently, this horrific incident pushed Parry over the edge and he has been unable to recover his sanity. Jack, therefore, decides to make it his mission to rehabilitate Parry as a means to achieve his own salvation. The only problem is that Parry doesn't seem very interested in being saved. As noted in the last chapter, at the midpoint in this film, Jack finally has a breakthrough, but it is *he*, not Parry, who undergoes a dramatic shift of consciousness.

With Parry's help, Jack sees that he's the one who has been a fool. With this insight, his actions become kinder, more caring, and he even learns to use his great vitality and showmanship in the service of others, not just for his own gain. Although he's not sure if Parry will ever be the man he was before his wife was shot, Jack wants to at least help him find love again and get his life back on track. This leads to a very joyous and funny period of grace where Jack manages to make Parry's romantic fantasies come true.

Again, it would be great if the story could just end here, but there is too much left unresolved. Though he's in love again, Parry is still delusional and Jack's ego still has him believing that he's running the show. In fact, Jack becomes so inflated by his achievements with Parry that he resolves to return to radio and reestablish his high-powered lifestyle, which means leaving behind Anne and all the people he met who helped him rebuild his life while he was out on the street. It also means he's going to become the same pompous ass again that he was in the first act.

To find the second turning point in this film, it's important to focus on the dilemma of Jack's ego. The question isn't how to destroy or crush it, but how to bring it into balance so that it serves Jack instead of serving the illusion of his own supreme self-importance. In the beginning of the film, Jack is completely ignorant (unconscious) of just how monstrously arrogant he has become, until his actions indirectly create a disaster. As a result, his life falls into a hellish tailspin, but it also delivers him to a place of greater self-awareness (consciousness) and a deeper connection to others.

As Joseph Campbell writes, "It is by going down into the abyss that we recover the treasures of life."[1] In order for Jack to hold on to his new-found *treasure*, he must learn to *let go* of his control over it. At the first turning point he believes he is responsible for Parry's grief. At the end

---

[1] Joseph Campbell, *The Hero With a Thousand Faces* (New York: MFJ, 1949), 24.

of the second act, he also believes he is responsible for Parry's happiness. Both of these assumptions give Jack the false impression that he has godlike powers. In order for Jack to complete the arc of transformation, these omnipotent illusions must undergo a profound death experience. This is the best *worst thing* that can happen to him. He must learn that he cannot control the world; he can only control his *relationship* to it.

In this regard, Jack's attempt to make Parry "normal" again must not succeed or Jack will hold on to the illusion of control. So at the second turning point, his triumph must turn to ashes, which is exactly what happens. When Jack tries to reawaken Parry to love, he inadvertently reawakens his new friend to the horror of the love he lost. Parry's delusional world that had protected him from fully experiencing the nightmare of having his wife's brains blown out before his eyes is shattered and he becomes catatonic. This not only leaves Parry unable to communicate with Jack, but it also indicates that Parry cannot guide Jack any further on his journey of transformation. Jack is devastated, and like the rest of us, he doesn't understand why things went so bad when he tried to do so much good. At this point, goodness, kindness, consideration, and connectedness all feel highly overrated to Jack and he begins to revert to his old, selfish ways.

While it may feel to the audience as if all the internal development Jack has gained is now lost, this isn't the end of the story. The audience also knows that it's not too late for Jack to get it all back—if he's willing to fight for it. This is the challenge of the third act that now lies in his path.

A Tragic Turn

In the first half of the transformational arc, tone, innuendo, foreshadowing, and attitude are the primary tools used to help distinguish the setup of a heroic story from one that turns tragic. In other words, both heroic and tragic characters have to overcome a fatal flaw. Therefore, they are both subject to similar challenges, the kind that beset anyone who is at a point where his or her survival system is breaking down. The biggest difference is that even though heroic characters may greatly resist the need to grow and change, at some point they begin to "get it." Tragic characters, on the other hand, remain stuck in old patterns of survival, and even if they see the need for change they continue to resist. They don't "get it."

Heroic and tragic characters become most conspicuously distinguished from each other at the midpoint. Whereas a heroic character will come into new consciousness, the tragic character will miss or avoid the opportunity altogether. This, of course, sets a very different tone for the second half of the second act in a tragedy, because there can be no real period of grace. Instead, the fall sets in almost immediately. The second half of the story becomes an unrelenting downward spiral, and even if there are moments when the protagonist wants to change, it's usually too late and too poorly motivated by his or her own selfish needs.

The tragic story of Henry Hill in *Goodfellas* is an excellent example of this principle. As described in the last chapter, Henry is so caught up in the gangster lifestyle at the midpoint that when his relationship with his wife begins to sour, people around him are being shot for no reason, and he ends up in prison for one of his gangland escapades, he remains oblivious to the reality that his life is careening out of control. There is no period of grace for Henry, just more and more of the same. He is on a high-speed treadmill that will only stop when his luck runs out—which it finally does at the second turning point. After most of his friends and associates have been murdered and there is no one left to trust, Henry is finally caught by the Feds for dealing drugs. He's a mess, his marriage is a mess, his life's a mess and yet he sees no way out except to dig himself in deeper.

Getting More Than You Bargained For

Whether a story is told heroically or tragically, notice how energized it becomes from all the upheaval that occurs in the second act. This is not a vast wasteland, as many writers believe, but a place of incredible heights and devastating depths. It is also a place where much is gained and much is lost. If you can see this portion of the story as a well-defined landscape that presents rigorous, necessary challenges for the protagonist, instead of allowing it to be a dumping ground for random pieces of plot development, the second act will become the strongest, most interesting part of your story. It can also be very gratifying for you, the writer. In order to get the protagonist through this awesome ordeal, it is necessary, on some level, for you to engage in the experience as well. It is in the second act that the story most clearly reveals what you are *really* writing about.

TRANSFORMATIONAL ARC

1 ⟷ 25 ⟷ 50 ⟷ 75 ⟷ 100

ACT I   ACT II   ACT III

RESISTANCE   RELEASE

EXHAUSTION KNOWN
MIDPOINT
Unknown   Push to breaking point   *Grace*   FALL   Renewal
1st Turning Point   Moment of Enlightenment   2nd Turning Point
Awakening   Death Experience

Case Studies

1) *ROMANCING THE STONE*

As *Romancing the Stone* climbs toward the midpoint, the exhaustion of running for safety and battling with each other lowers Joan and Jack's defenses to the point where they finally begin to talk. Talking leads to sharing, which leads to the discovery of common ground. It becomes clear that they're not really so different after all. Joan hides from love in the fantasy pages of her romance novels, but Jack hides too. Even though he's a robust adventurer, his heart is no less isolated than Joan's. *His* fantasy is to buy a sailboat and sail around the world. But, as Joan points out, there's no one else onboard that fantasy vessel with him.

> JOAN
>
> So you're just gonna sail away? All by yourself?
>
> JACK
>
> Yeah.
>
> JOAN
>
> Sounds lonely, Jack T. Colton.

As they share their hearts with each other, a real attraction begins to develop. This is a clear signal that the relationship subplot ("C" story) has crossed the meridian of the arc. Joan has moved out of *resistance* to the goal of finding true love and is now *released* or pushed toward that very real possibility. But the only way Joan can move out of resistance to love is if she has an *inner shift of consciousness.* In other words, in the internal subplot ("B" story) she begins to find the courage to **trust** the possibility of love even though Jack is nothing like her ideal and there is no guarantee that things will work out. But Joan's newly acquired trust encourages her to have **faith** in Jack, which is why she agrees to go along with his plan for them to find the treasure themselves and use it to leverage her sister's freedom. Instead of running away, Joan is now proactively moving toward the goal of saving her sister. This indicates that she has also moved out of resistance to the goal of the plot ("A" story) and is now firmly on the side of the arc that *releases* or sets into motion her ability to resolve the conflict.

As a result of this new perspective, Joan's *fear* has turned into *confidence*, her *trepidation* has turned into *daring*, and her *constraint* has become *desire*. All of these attributes bring with them a substantial amount of energy that gives Joan's quest renewed vitality and optimism. Before the midpoint, she had been ready to quit, but now she's ready to fight. She had also distrusted Jack, and now—even though she's not completely sure of his motives—she's willing to follow him on his crazy scheme to get the treasure. Therefore, in the period of grace, Joan is becoming the fun, confident, and even sexy woman we always knew she could be. Jack can't stop himself from falling in love with her, despite his original plan to use romance only as a means to get to the treasure. What he's beginning to figure out is that Joan *is* the treasure.

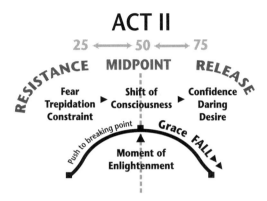

ACT II

Often, during the period of grace, the protagonist begins to receive help and support, especially from unexpected sources. As long as the protagonist is in resistance to the goal, it's likely that even if support is offered he or she can not or will not accept it. But after the midpoint, things start turning in the protagonist's favor and doors that were previously shut begin to open. This is the one place in a story where coincidence feels natural, and can be accepted easily by the audience as good luck or even divine intervention. And perhaps, in symbolic terms, that's exactly what it is.

In the grace period of *Romancing the Stone*, Joan receives just this type of unexpected support. In one of the funniest scenes in the film, she and Jack find themselves staring down the barrel of a gun belonging to a very menacing-looking drug lord. All seems lost, and Jack says off-handedly, "Okay, Joan Wilder, how would you write us out of this one?" Before she can respond, the drug dealer brightens, "Joan Wilder?... Joan Wilder? *The* Joan Wilder, the novelist? I read all your books!!!" He lowers his gun, embraces her, and invites them into his splendid hacienda. Later he helps the couple elude their pursuers and even drives them to safety.

While this is truly a ridiculous coincidence, not only does it get a big laugh, but it also serves an even greater symbolic function in the story.

At the beginning of the film, Joan had so lost herself in the fantasies she wrote that they were destroying her potential for real love and romance. However, now that she's found the courage to venture into the real world and take a chance on finding real love, her writing has become an ally.

The grace period is also essential for setting up what's at stake in the rest of the script. By now the audience is not only invested in having Joan get her sister back, but they also want Joan to hang on to this great love that she has spent a lifetime trying to find.

While the period of grace crests gently across the apex of the arc, it is moving in the direction of a steep, unrelenting descent or fall. As much as we'd like for Joan and Jack to just live happily ever after at this point, there is too much left unresolved. The bad guys really are *bad* and they're not about to give up until they have the treasure, which means that Joan and Jack still have quite a lot of danger to face before they can resolve the conflict. Also, Jack may be falling for Joan, but it's impossible to know if his feelings for her will outweigh his desire for the treasure once he has it in his hands. So, we sense that Joan may be headed toward her biggest challenge yet. Love is only true if it can stand up to the bad times as well as the good, and there is no way to know if it's true until it is tested—which is right where the story is headed.

The drop-off in the arc in the second half of Act II can occur very quickly and dramatically. Just as Joan and Jack are solidifying their plans to get the treasure, the "really" bad guys track them down and the couple is forced to make a quick getaway through the back window of their hotel. Out of desperation they steal a car that just happens to belong to Ralph (Danny DeVito), one of the comic bad guys, who is sleeping in the back-seat. Now that they are acting as a team, Joan and Jack make quick work of finding the treasure, which turns out to be a huge, brilliant emerald. But their prize is just as easily jeopardized when first Ralph and then the other villains show up. From here, as you might expect, the chase is on.

Because this particular script is strongly invested in the adventure metaphor, the plot twist at the second turning point could have been taken right out of the pages of one of Joan's novels. The getaway car she and Jack are driving crashes into raging rapids, then careens downstream headed straight for the rim of a 500-foot waterfall.

But is this the worst thing that can happen to Joan? As dire as it may appear, taking a nosedive off a sheer wall of water is not the worst thing for her. The worst thing would be surviving the waterfall and returning to her old life, where no love is possible.

Joan and Jack have had a very romantic interlude that's been exciting and remarkable, which made following her heart pretty easy. But love isn't always easy and Joan must be able to maintain her courage and belief in love, even when it's not fun, when it feels dangerous and uncertain. So, the worst thing that can happen at the second turning point is for Joan to experience the dark side of the adventure of love—where her trust and faith will be greatly tested.

On an intuitive level, I think the writer understood this, but unfortunately she never let that dark side really develop—and this becomes one of the weakest moments in the film. Joan and Jack do survive the plunge, but they end up on opposite sides of the raging river with the emerald still in Jack's possession. This makes Joan furious, and she rails at him with accusations that he must have planned for things to turn out this way, which is so preposterous that it's obvious even she doesn't really believe it. Jack promises her that if she just follows the river she'll end up in Cartagena and he'll meet her at the hotel where her sister is being held. Jack really seems sincere, so even if Joan says she doubts him at this point, the audience doesn't.

While the split between these two is effective to a degree, there is no real jeopardy attached. For the arc to be complete, Joan needs to fight her way back through feelings of loss, betrayal, remorse, anger, and so on. She needs to have a death experience; otherwise, how will we ever know if she's capable of letting go of those false ideals that have kept her from experiencing love? If Jack is simply her uncompromising hero from this point forward, the theme of the story will be greatly undermined. There is still a lot of action left and even a little uncertainty between Joan and Jack in the third act, but, as we'll discuss in the next chapter, the lack of a real death experience for Joan greatly diminishes the dramatic tension in the last part of the story.

As an exercise, try to come up with some ideas for how this problem could have been fixed. Remember: The more the protagonist feels all is lost, the more the audience will need to see Joan fight her way back to love.

2) LETHAL WEAPON

As discussed in the last chapter, several events occur at the midpoint in *Lethal Weapon* that bring clarity to the conflict of the "A" story and harmony between Riggs and Murtaugh in the "B" and "C" storylines. The huge shift of consciousness that occurs at the midpoint not only impacts their ability to get along with each other, but also provides Riggs and Murtaugh with an understanding of who they are actually fighting and why. This effectively moves the co-protagonists into a period of grace, where they start working together as a team. Now that they have stopped fighting each other, they can start directing their energy toward defeating the real enemy.

One of the first big clues they unearth in the grace period reveals that the bad guys have a strong military background and were part of a Special Forces unit that served in Vietnam. Riggs happens to recognize their military insignia because he was once part of that same elite group. Therefore, he now *knows* just how well trained and deadly these men can be. Of course, this also indicates to the audience that Riggs is just as well trained and equally as deadly. More clues reveal that their adversaries, who once served their country with distinction, are now serving themselves by running a highly profitable heroin operation.

Since Riggs and Murtaugh have finally gotten past their animosity toward each other, the film can shift gears and concentrate more sharply on resolving the goal of the plot, which is to stop the drug dealers. This results in a very brief grace period. However, because the first half of the film had so much humor and relationship development, the writer made a smart choice to get back to the action as quickly as possible. I bring this up because it reinforces the point that there is no fixed or formulaic way to work with the transformational arc. If all of the natural elements are present—including an awakening, a moment of enlightenment, a period of grace, and a death experience—then there can be a great deal of creative latitude with the shape the arc will naturally want to take. This film, for example, puts an enormous amount of focus on the development of character and relationships in the first half and then emphasizes the conflict of the plot in the second half. This works well because there is a sense of *balance*. Viewers have gotten to know these two detectives individually and now they really do want to see what they can accomplish together.

Because of the shortened grace period, the fall comes about rather quickly and leads to a very precipitous descent. In the third act there will be a lot of violent *mano-a-mano* confrontations, but in this portion of the script Riggs and Murtaugh are more involved in a cat-and-mouse game as they and their opponents size each other up. Bear in mind that because the story is moving toward the second turning point and the death experience, the bad guys are going to increasingly gain the upper hand.

Even though this section of the script focuses on the action of the "A" story (plot), note that the "B" and "C" storylines are not completely ignored. There remains a subtle edge of doubt between Riggs and Murtaugh; they're still not sure how much they can trust each other. This keeps the audience connected to their personal stories and also lets us know there is still room for unpredictability in the outcome.

As *Lethal Weapon* approaches the second turning point and the death experience, the best *worst thing* that can happen to the co-protagonists is a true encounter with death itself. Because the theme of this story is about the need to value life, they must be challenged to *fight* for it. In the "A" story, the challenge is very direct: Murtaugh's daughter is kidnapped by the ruthless drug dealers, who already proved at the beginning of the story that they have no problem executing the beloved daughters of their enemies. In most of today's action movies this would be all that is needed to launch the story into the third act, where the protagonist fights to the death for what is right and moral. But because this film has a well-developed character arc, the co-protagonists are fighting for a great deal more.

As they prepare to go after the men who kidnapped Murtaugh's daughter, Riggs firmly tells his partner that if he wants to defeat the enemy he's going to have to "get bloodied." Normally in a relationship storyline ("C" story), the second turning point is where the relationship itself is put into jeopardy, but in this film something else occurs. Because these two men are opposites, they each have the ability to guide the other toward resolution. Whereas in the first half of the film Murtaugh was the guide who led Riggs back to the civilized realm, it is now Riggs' turn to guide Murtaugh back to the wilder, more untamed side of his nature. Getting bloodied, of course, refers to the need to stop the enemy at all costs, but blood also has a very symbolic and primal (unconscious) meaning to us: *Blood* is a vital part of our essence. Therefore, Murtaugh is being guided back to his essence or spirit.

Had the story ended back at the midpoint when Murtaugh realizes that his life was saved only because Riggs didn't hesitate to use a gun, he (and we) would only have been led to an intellectual understanding of the idea that sometimes we do need to defend ourselves. At the second turning point, however, Murtaugh is being challenged to actually use his own gun in the service of a noble cause—to save his daughter. This means that he is being called upon to embody what it means to *kill to live*.

This is not a simplistic "kill or be killed" notion. It goes to the core of what Riggs and Murtaugh are really fighting for. They each have been so caught up defending and fighting for only one side of their nature that this experience now challenges them to fight for the *other*. By getting bloodied, Murtaugh is being forced to embrace his shadow side, to acknowledge and value the other part of his nature that *can* kill. Remember, the theme of this film is about valuing life, and death is very much a part of the life experience. Don't get caught in the trap of only dealing with the part of a theme that feels comfortable and reassuring, or you'll miss the most important gift a story has to give. Also, try not to literalize the meaning behind every action a character takes. When Murtaugh uses a gun to go after his enemy in this story, consider what that enemy symbolizes. Also, ask yourself: Is the action the protagonist takes leading away from or toward a greater sense of personal wholeness?

Sometimes the act of killing in a story is regressive, in that it represents the more thuggish part of the protagonist's nature that has no ability to connect with others except by domination. Sometimes, however, the act of killing has a very different meaning, which is why an otherwise non-aggressive audience will cheer at the sight of the villain's death. Action-filled epics have been with us since humans first began to paint on cave walls. The heroic stories directly express our deep desire and need to relate to the soul's hunting experience, which is the hunt for the "other" parts of our true nature with which we have not yet made a conscious connection.

Therefore, as the second turning point pulls Riggs and Murtaugh into an action-packed third act, they are not just being called to obliterate the enemy, but symbolically they are also being challenged to go down into the hellish underworld or underside of their own being. Granted, this film has neither the depth nor the poetic scope of the action-filled classics of Homer or Shakespeare, but it does serve a similar function. When the transformational arc is utilized, it will carry a story far past anything most writers ever even imagined.

3) ORDINARY PEOPLE

Ordinary People has an exceptionally strong and well-needed grace period. The first half of the film contains so much tension and uncomfortable behavior that it's a welcome relief to finally see some smiling, cheerful faces for a few moments. In the internal storyline, Conrad hits new emotional territory at the midpoint, allowing him to tap into repressed feelings of anger and rage that have nearly destroyed him. As a result, he has a confrontation with his mother where he releases some of this long-pent-up hostility. In the aftermath, having directed his anger outward at her instead of inward at himself, Conrad starts feeling less guarded and more social than he has in a long time. He flirts with a classmate, invites her on a date, sings boisterously, and enthusiastically helps his dad put up a Christmas tree. These few moments of grace allow us to see who Conrad can become if he can work his way through the rest of the conflict.

However, dark clouds quickly reappear on the horizon when Beth comes home and confronts Conrad for not bothering to tell her that he quit the swim team a month earlier. She has no concern for why her son did this, only for how his actions make her look to her friends. Conrad's new sense of personal power enables him to fight back, and he slings some rather venomous accusations her way, reproaching his mother for doing the unspeakable: not loving him the way she loved his dead brother. This leads to a midpoint moment of clarity for Dad, who finally begins to see that maybe Beth does harbor resentment toward Conrad after all.

This film demonstrates the importance of treating all characters in a co-protagonist structure both as individuals and as part of the collective. How each character personally faces the challenges of the conflict informs what will become of the whole group. For example, it is necessary for Conrad's shift of consciousness to come first in this story because he is the conscience of the family. His changes are in the vanguard because they force everyone else to take action. Dad may not fully agree with Conrad that Beth doesn't love him, but a veil is lifting that allows him to finally see that there is something in this mother-son relationship that isn't right. As the story progresses and Dad gains even more understanding of the family's dynamics, he is the one who will eventually lead the way toward resolving the conflict of the plot—which is to make this family whole.

Beth, on the other hand, is trying her best to lead the family in the opposite direction. She is fighting as hard as she can to defend the status quo. Whereas Dad is coming into a greater understanding of things, Beth can't open herself to any new possibilities. Her character has no moment of enlightenment at the midpoint, and this is a clear indication that she is set on a very tragic course. Her inability to change enhances the central conflict and draws the audience deeper into the story by posing a real dilemma: Will Beth's tragic behavior undermine or overwhelm Conrad and Dad's heroic efforts to change and make the family whole?

As mentioned in an earlier chapter, this film is really structured like a war story. There are skirmishes and battles, advances and retreats, triumphs and losses. At the midpoint and into the grace period, Conrad's side scores some major victories. Not only does he stand up to Beth, but he also begins to win Dad over to his side. In addition, Conrad has a very poignant visit with his therapist where he comes to another significant realization: Maybe the problem isn't that his mother doesn't love him; maybe she just isn't capable of loving him *enough*. This insight begins to significantly change Conrad's perspective and will eventually allow him to forgive his mother and get on with his own life. Instead of waiting around for her to change, he will find validation within himself. If Conrad's side wins, this is the foundation on which the newly transformed family will begin to rebuild.

But at this point in the story a fall is inevitable because Beth has no ability to surrender to the changing attitudes of either Conrad or her husband. In fact, for every victory scored against her, she can be counted on to come back swinging twice as hard. The irony is that Beth has the instincts of a mother bear, defending her family at all costs. The problem is that she is clueless (unconscious) that what she is fighting for will actually destroy them.

As the script nears the second turning point of the "A" story, the *worst thing* that can happen is for Beth to force her family into a retreat. If they return to the *safety* of their old behavior, there will be nothing left for them but a disingenuous, superficial connection to each other. After having a particularly insightful experience of his own with Conrad's therapist, Dad comes home and tries to break through Beth's tough, unemotional veneer by getting her to talk about her son's death. Beth, of course, resists any attempts to bring up unpleasant matters and categorically refuses Calvin's heartfelt plea for the whole family to talk with the therapist together. Instead, he is the one who capitulates and agrees to take her on a vacation, leaving Conrad at home to fend for himself. Even though Dad has begun to see the lifeless road his family is headed down, he's not much of a fighter. Instead, he wants to be the peacemaker, and Beth uses this vulnerable quality to get him to back down and take her side again.

Meanwhile, Conrad is certainly feeling more self-assured than when we first met him, but he has not yet built up enough inner reserve to withstand an external assault. That assault (fall) first comes from old boyhood friends who have no ability to recognize that Conrad is struggling to become a self-reliant young man. It's not uncommon in life that when we are undergoing a powerful transformational experience, one of the most difficult things to deal with is the criticism and judgment of old friends and family members who resist our need to change and grow. In fact, this can be one of the toughest tests of all, because even if we reject their overt and covert attempts to undermine our progress, they still have a powerful influence over how we see ourselves.

Conrad reacts with increasing hostility toward these old pals and even toward his new girlfriend, the one person who really does support him. But as his storyline nears the second turning point, there is so much upheaval and change swirling around him that he begins to lose the ability to cope. Therefore, the *worst thing* that can happen here is for Conrad to give up and retreat back into his old self-perception that devalues all the emotional progress he has made.

At the second turning point, Conrad learns that a friend he met while in the psychiatric hospital has committed suicide. Her death reactivates all the feelings of guilt and shame associated with his brother's drowning. He feels that he wasn't strong *enough*, brave *enough*, or clever *enough* to save his brother. Now he wasn't good *enough* to save his friend either. But only by going through this type of a death experience will Conrad finally be challenged to either make peace with himself and move on— or just end it all and take the easy way out of his pain.

Notice that as both Conrad and Dad's storylines hit the second turning point all seems lost and it is not a foregone conclusion that what is broken in this family can ever be repaired. Everything seems to be returning to the way it was at the beginning of the story when they were all dominated by Beth, and it was highly doubtful that Conrad would survive. However, one thing is very different now: Conrad and Dad see their world more clearly. Once new consciousness is acquired, it can't be unlearned. Even if we try to avoid it or ignore it, our perspective has shifted. This is what opens up the drama for the third act. Conrad and his father have each lost a big battle, and only they can decide if it's time to give up or find the courage to fight on.

CHAPTER TEN

ACT III
Down and Dirty

Things fall apart; the centre cannot hold;
Mere anarchy is loosed upon the world,
The blood-dimmed tide is loosed, and everywhere
The ceremony of innocence is drowned;
The best lack all conviction,
While the worst are full of passionate intensity.

~ W. B. YEATS

Let the Chips Fall Where They May

Although it can be complex and challenging to come up with a great idea for the *worst thing* to happen at the second turning point, the hardest part for many writers is what lies ahead. Often, when terrible things happen to the protagonist, a writer's instinct is to jump in and rescue their main character as quickly as possible. DON'T DO THAT!

It's clear to see by the shape of the arc that what follows the second turning point is a distinct, downward slide that should have been well in progress ever since the midpoint and grace period. Therefore, the conflict has picked up a lot of momentum and velocity. In fact, the more unstoppable this downward trend feels, the more urgency your audience will feel as well. After all, the third act is leading toward a climax, and this is definitely not the time for things to slow down.

Everything the protagonist has been struggling for, both internally and externally, is at stake in the third act. If you begin to resolve any piece of this tapestry of interconnected plotlines too soon it will cause the other strands of the story to lose their texture and strength.

Under-developing the jeopardy attached to the second turning point is an especially common problem in the relationship subplot. Within two pages of a breakup, writers often feel compelled to have the lovers make up. If real life were this easy, Oprah would be out of a job. **The second turning point is not the place where cute little tiffs occur. It is the realm where our darkest fears are met head-on.**

In *When Harry Met Sally*, the lovemaking scene at the second turning point marks the beginning of a descent that almost instantly dissolves all of the progress toward intimacy that has been achieved throughout this couple's twelve-year friendship. Fear overrides their ability to talk things over, stay in the moment, and let the relationship flow naturally and spontaneously. After Harry and Sally awake from their first sexual encounter, he has one foot out of the bed and she already has images of china patterns and bouffant bridesmaid dresses dancing in her head. Their friendship had taught them to be vulnerable and trusting with each other, but the sexual act broke through to a new barrier of intimacy, reconstituting old fears and illusions of what it means to be in a romantic relationship with someone.

The setback that protagonists experience at the second turning point will often feel like a validation of their old way of perceiving things:

> *See, women can't be trusted!*
> *You men are all alike.*
> *I'm better off alone.*
> *People will always let you down.*
> *It's every man for himself.*

Any of this sound familiar? I hope it does because, more than ever, the story needs a writer's honesty and emotional integrity in the third act. How *you* feel when love lets you down, when dreams are smashed, promises are broken, and trust is violated is what you are really writing about. This is the part of the story where the protagonist will *feel* the most disillusioned, disheartened, cynical, angry, betrayed, and vulnerable. These emotions are very real and they are what will make your characters most human—most like you and me.

If the second turning point is going to effectively push the protagonist toward a transformational experience before reaching the climax, then it is critical that the third act be the biggest challenge yet. Whereas the period of grace offered the protagonist a respite from the conflict and an opportunity to experience what life might be like if he or she could change, the **DESCENT** that follows the second turning point has just the opposite effect. It is generally a time of pain, disappointment, and unhappiness that reveals to the protagonist what life will be like if he or she refuses to change and grow. As a result, this is also a time when the protagonist will feel most acutely alone. In earlier parts of the story, even when the protagonist was in complete resistance, there were usually people and other influences around that offered help and support. However, once the threshold at the second turning point is crossed, the protagonist is pretty much left to his or her own devices. Ultimately, transformation comes only through making a personal, conscious choice (*to be or not to be*), and because no one else can make this kind of decision for us, it is necessary to experience a time of real aloneness.

By "aloneness" I don't mean that the protagonist will necessarily be alone. Sometimes when we are at our lowest point we surround ourselves with a lot people and activity in order to avoid the emptiness. But it doesn't work.

After Parry falls into a coma at the second turning point in *The Fisher King*, Jack tries desperately to forget him by returning to all his past indulgences. He swiftly reclaims his old lifestyle as a high-powered DJ, living in an expensive Manhattan high-rise with a very classy, high-maintenance girlfriend. But none of this makes him happy. Jack's high-flying new lifestyle only succeeds in showing him just how low he's sunk as a human being. In the middle of contract negotiations for his own weekly sitcom that pokes fun at the homeless, Jack is suddenly startled back to reality. He walks out of the meeting and runs back to Parry's bedside. There he angrily confronts his comatose friend:

```
                    JACK
                (sarcastically)
    Everything's been going great. Great.
    I even have my own cable talk show. With
    an incredible equity, I might add. I've got
    an incredibly fucking gorgeous girlfriend.
    I'm living an incredible fucking life. So
    don't lay there in your comfortable little
    coma and think I'm going to risk all that
    because I feel responsible for you. I'M NOT
    RESPONSIBLE!!! And I don't feel guilty.
    You've got it easy. I'm out there every
    day. Every fucking day trying to figure out
    what the hell I'm doing. But no matter what
    I have it feels like I have nothing. So I
    don't feel sorry for you. It's easy being
    nuts, try being me.
```

The region of the story following the second turning point is perhaps the most treacherous for the protagonist and it cannot be crossed without extracting a great amount of effort and self-sacrifice. Ironically, the terrible experiences of *death, sacrifice,* and *descent* are the toll that must be paid to gain entry to the land of **RENEWAL: the place where new life begins.** Just as the fresh blossoms of spring burst forth from the dead wood of winter, so, too, are we revitalized and enabled to grow anew from our own death experiences. However, we must first go through the deathly process of undoing that is brought on by experiences of loss, failure, betrayal, abandonment, and diminishment.

The death process pushes us to the point of **SURRENDER, where all our ego systems fail and we are forced to engage the world in a new way.** Therefore, this is the place in a story where the protagonist will be pushed to surrender those aspects of him- or herself that don't work anymore: willfulness, selfishness, fear, anger, resentments, and so on. But a surrender of this type seldom comes easily or without a fight. This is why the period of descent that follows the second turning point tends to reengage some of the most negative traits that the protagonist has been trying to overcome.

Following the suicide of their classmate in *Dead Poets Society*, the schoolboys not only feel betrayed by Mr. Keating—the teacher who was trying to help liberate their spirits—but they also allow the fear and intimidation he was helping them outgrow become the very weapon that will be used against him by the school administration. In the beginning of the story, the co-protagonists were mere boys who were unaware (unconscious) of how their authentic nature was being manipulated and co-opted. Now, in the third act, even though their eyes have been opened, they cower and are unwilling to *surrender* their boyhood dependencies so that they can stand and be counted as men.

One of the biggest self-deceptions in our culture is the belief that transformation is *free* for the taking. As a result, we often feel shocked and victimized when a toll gate appears and a great **SACRIFICE** is demanded of us. This is why the death experience at the second turning point will usually cause the protagonist to go through an emotional, moral, and even spiritual collapse. Thus the second turning point becomes the gateway leading into a perilous Underworld journey, where the protagonist must fight like never before to reclaim his or her life.

In *The Odyssey*, Homer's wayward protagonist, Odysseus (Ulysses), struggles for many, many years to find his way home after the Trojan War. He survives terrible trials that would have destroyed a lesser man, but the final test seems to be more than he or anyone can bear. He is told that he must journey to the Underworld and speak with the dead seer Teiresias, who is the only one who can guide him homeward. In order to get to the Underworld, Odysseus is instructed to sail to the "Ocean's utmost ends," where he must sacrifice rams and let their blood flow into the earth in order to awaken the spirits of the dead.

While this might seem like a wildly fantastic exploit that is reserved only for a hero who occupies the mythic realm, it is in fact a very powerful symbolic description of exactly what is demanded of anyone who has embarked on the transformational journey.

There is no way to get to the new place within us until we have sailed to the outermost reaches of our own known world—of who we *think* we are. This is the true nature of the death experience; it pushes us beyond what we believe we can tolerate. Therefore, the outermost edge of our known realm is always a place of suffering, and the degree to which we believe our needs and wants are not being met determines the intensity of the suffering. The sacrifice of the rams represents the **BLOOD SACRIFICE** that we, too, must make in order to gain access to the Underworld. This Underworld is not a place of hellfire and damnation, but it is the *underside* of our own being, the dark fringes of our existence where the unwanted and unknown parts of us have been hidden away. It is the place where we send our hurt, our shame, our ugliness, our sorrow, and our loneliness. But if we want to be whole, we have to resurrect those pieces that have long been denied and bring them home with us, back into the light of a new day.

The experience of going down into this shadowy Underworld is most often felt as a period of depression, despair, rage, sorrow, or hopelessness. It is certainly not a desirable place to be, but for those who have sailed to their outermost edge, fallen into the Underworld abyss, and found their way out again, it is not an experience that most would give back. When we say that a person has depth or soul, it is usually in reference to someone who has been to these depths and has retrieved the lost pieces of themselves. Their lives have been enriched with meaning and purpose because in their darkest hours, when the rest of life was silenced, they were able to hear the whisperings of their inner spirit, the wise old sage Teiresias, who told them how to find their way home again.

Jane Campion's award-winning film, *The Piano*, perfectly illustrates the importance of this Underworld descent. In this story, her 19th-century Scottish heroine, Ada, is literally forced to travel to the edge of her known world—the wilds of New Zealand—to marry a man she has never met. But this is not the final act of Ada's story; it is only the beginning. In her inner world she has not yet reached the edge. In fact, she is locked firmly inside a steep-walled battlement of her own design that she erected to shield her independent spirit from the repressive constraints of Victorian society. But what once served as protection now serves as a prison, where she resides in mute defiance. Communication with the outside world is made only indirectly, through her daughter's voice and the enigmatic music she composes on her piano. But upon arriving on the primordial shores of her new home, both begin to fail her. The daughter increasingly misinterprets Ada's sign language to suit her own growing need to break out of her mother's isolated fortress, and the cumbersome piano is abandoned by her new husband on the beach where she landed, then it is traded to a local settler without Ada's consent.

As harsh as her husband's actions are, they serve to *awaken* Ada to the desolation and isolation that has become her existence. Without her piano she has no means of self-expression, leaving her to feel completely unseen and unheard. So when George Baines, the boorish neighbor who bought the piano, offers to let Ada have it back in exchange for piano lessons that come with unspecified sexual favors, she barely hesitates. But what begins as need quickly explodes into desire, and Ada and Baines start a torrid affair that nearly destroys both their lives.

Ada now wants to be part of the world—as long as Baines is in it. His love topples the mighty fortress that had both shielded her and held her captive. But as the walls fall away, leaving her open to love, she is also vulnerable to its attendant darker side. Feelings of jealousy and outrage take possession of her husband, who tries to rape and then imprison her in their house. However, Ada's spirit can't be contained at this point, and he soon realizes that the only way to hold on to her is to throw open the doors and windows and just trust her to stay away from Baines—which, of course, she can't.

Ada wrenches a key from the piano and inscribes it with words of love, which she sends to Baines, letting him know that he is even more important to her than her music. But Ada's love is so consuming she doesn't see that it has made her daughter feel as irrelevant as the dismantled piano. Therefore, when Ada orders her daughter to take the key to Baines, the resentful child delivers it to her stepfather instead. He reacts with predictable rage and marches home, ax in hand, determined to punish Ada for her betrayal. Taking her by surprise, he pulls his wife from the house and hacks off her forefinger. The *bloodied* piece of flesh is then exchanged for the piano key and he has Ada's traumatized daughter deliver it to Baines with a warning that he'll continue to chop off all of Ada's fingers if Baines doesn't stay away.

Now, Ada has reached the outermost edge of her known world, where she is left with nothing that makes her life tolerable. Her finger is literally the blood sacrifice that had to be paid, because without it she can no longer find solace or safe harbor in any known place, including her piano. As cruel as this may seem, it's not until Ada's defenses have been exhausted and she is rendered powerless that the new thing growing inside her has any real opportunity to be born. Up to this point her passion for Baines is nothing more than another place to hide from the world. But after her finger is severed, Ada is only able to stagger a few more steps before she collapses into the earth in complete surrender.

Later, when her husband tries to minister to her wound, he becomes sexually aroused and clumsily attempts to mount her. This awakens Ada from a fitful sleep, but she is neither surprised nor frightened by him. The war is over and her eyes are bottomless pools of serenity. As she stares at her husband, he too is drawn into her unfathomable depths.

He cocks his head as if to hear her better, but Ada still hasn't uttered a word. Later, he describes the experience to Baines. Touching his forehead he says that he heard Ada's voice inside his brain. Her lips didn't move and yet he could understand clearly what she was saying.

In the deep Underworld caverns, where all the truth of life is known, Ada discovers the wisdom of Teiresias and is told how to find her way home. Somehow she manages to communicate this to her husband. She tells him that her will is too strong and that if she is going to survive, she has to let go.

This silent communication slices open her husband's heart, helping him to let go as well, and he allows Ada to leave with Baines. As a result, her world is no longer an empty, isolated fortress, but through her love for Baines she makes a deeper connection to the rest of her spirit.

Obviously, not all stories will take the transformational process to these depths, but, in truth, not all of our real-life transformations will go there either. The death experience and the blood sacrifice are symbolic of a natural process that the writer must design in proportion to the depth of the internal conflict. It also must be appropriate to the genre in which the story is told.

There's a great sequence in the romantic comedy *Something's Gotta Give* where Diane Keaton's character, Erica, falls into an emotional abyss following her breakup with Jack Nicholson's character, Harry, at the second turning point. Erica is utterly defeated by love and purges a lifetime of disappointments and frustration in an extreme crying jag. She sobs, weeps, blubbers, whimpers, wails, and sniffles her way through the next eight scenes. Ironically, within the content of these same scenes, she is also blasting her way through the third act of her own play, which had been in a creative sinkhole up to this point in the story. As her pent-up emotions become dislodged, they unleash a torrent of creative juices. Even though this crying episode is played for laughs, the humor hits home because this is how big and awful our own pain can feel when love lets us down.

To achieve this emotional honesty, it is neither required nor always necessary for the third act to throw the protagonist into a complete emotional breakdown. But something must occur at this point that allows him or her to see—and above all feel—the depth of the emotional loss suffered at the second turning point. If the protagonist doesn't experience such feelings, then the turning point isn't strong enough and/or the loss isn't great enough.

If this part of your story is weak, it's important to look within yourself; you can't write the protagonist's pain if you don't honestly feel it. This doesn't mean that you have to understand it; sometimes our pain runs so deep that the only part of it we can touch is the sense of fear, anger, and confusion surrounding it. But if you're at least honest enough to show us the fear, anger, and confusion, we will still be able to connect with the story's emotional reality.

On Shaky Ground

It's not just feelings and relationships that take a hit in the third act; the goal of the plot itself must be falling apart as well. Nothing is a sure thing at this point in the story. The more the protagonist feels as if the ground is slipping out from under him or her, the more the tension will build toward the climax.

In genres that are strongly plot-driven—such as action, suspense, and caper—the goal of stopping the bomb, catching the killer, or getting away with a heist must be completely unraveling at this point. In the first half of the story, the protagonist has difficulty putting things together and making progress. In the middle range of the story (midpoint and grace period), real advancement toward the goal is achieved, but then is seriously thwarted at the second turning point. Not only does progress fall apart in the third act, but the protagonist experiences the highest level of personal jeopardy he or she has yet encountered.

By the middle of *Basic Instinct*, Detective Nick Curran foolishly believes he can outwit and outmaneuver the psychotic femme fatal Catherine Tramell, the prime suspect in a growing list of unsolved homicides. Even more foolishly, he believes he can bed her without any serious side effects (such as ending up with an ice pick between his eyes or, even worse, falling in love with her). By the third act, events have spun so far out of control that other Catherine-inspired femme fatales seem to be coming at Nick from every direction. One tries to run him over and (possibly) another murders his partner. Catherine has, indeed, outplayed him. The action in the third act is riveting because Nick is caught in a spiraling descent from which there seems little possibility of escape.

This feeling of plummeting into the depths of despair, ruin, confusion, anarchy, chaos, and so on is not limited to action films. After the breakup at the second turning point in *When Harry Met Sally*, things not only worsen between the two, but it also seems like any effort to salvage their relationship only backfires. Attempts at civility completely fall apart at the wedding of their two best friends, when Sally's true feelings of disappointment and hurt are exposed and then battered even further by Harry's lame defense of his actions.

In this part of the third act, the trajectory of the arc is pointing distinctly downward. Of course, this implies that if nothing changes this story is headed for *tragic* consequences.

In films like *Basic Instinct, Goodfellas*, and *The Godfather*, that is indeed the outcome. The protagonists in these stories ultimately can't differentiate right from wrong, good from bad, truth from lies, and/or they never develop the strength of character to stand and fight for what is right.

In contrast, the ending of a story takes a *heroic* turn when the protagonist is able to pull him- or herself out of this descent by making choices and taking actions that not only resolve the external conflict but also revitalize his or her inner sense of purpose and value.

Moment of Decision

Things will continue to fall apart for the protagonist until and unless something intervenes to stop this downward, calamitous momentum and shift the story toward a successful conclusion. This intervention may occur passively for the protagonist, wherein an outside source swoops in to save the day. Or, it will occur proactively, meaning that the protagonist will take decisive action to resolve the conflict.

Obviously, you want to be careful with the first option because it can easily render all of the efforts of the protagonist up to this point meaningless. Classically, this is referred to as the **DEUS EX MACHINA**, which means that the solution to the conflict comes from some unexpected outside source. This usually provides a very contrived ending. Keep in mind that if the protagonist is relatively inconsequential in achieving the goal of the plot, then what's his or her purpose in the story? On the other hand, it may be precisely the protagonist's passivity that is required to bring about the desired results. This would be particularly true in stories where he or she needs to learn to let go and trust destiny or come to believe in miracles. It's also true in stories that are about the protagonist learning to let go and let others help, such as *It's a Wonderful Life*. As discussed in an earlier chapter, the town is saved from the destructive grasp of Mr. Potter not by George battling the old tyrant, but by the townspeople rescuing themselves.

Most commonly, our stories tend to have a protagonist who becomes proactive, and there is a point toward the end of the story where we will see him or her make a *conscious* decision to take action toward achieving the goal of the plot. This is especially true in stories with a strong transformational arc, because the primary function of the arc is to demonstrate the direct relationship between the inner development of character and the ability to resolve the conflict. The hardships and obstacles a protagonist has had to overcome throughout the story will serve to bring about a new sense of inner purpose and personal resolve. Ultimately, this is what enables a protagonist to stand up against the crushing downward spiral of events in the third act and decide not to give in, but to stand and fight for what he or she wants and for what is right.

This leads to a **decision** by the protagonist that is the pivotal event of the *entire* story. I refer to this as the **TRANSFORMATIONAL MOMENT,** because this is where the protagonist decides his or her own fate. Even though it is in the climax that the protagonist takes physical action toward resolving the conflict and achieving the goal of the plot, it is this internal moment of decision that marks the true transformation of character. Most often, in fact, the transformational moment is also the climax of the "B" story, because it is the showdown between internal forces that leads the protagonist toward making this decision. Victory or defeat in this arena will define the true nature of his or her character—whether he or she is heroic or tragic: moving toward life or running away from it. If the internal goal is met, the protagonist reaches the highest point of consciousness in the story and thereby makes the decision to do what must be done to resolve the external conflict.

Transformation is *always* a conscious choice.

A lot has happened to the protagonist since the beginning of the story. People, events, and circumstances have pushed, pulled, and even hammered at him or her to try to facilitate the *movement of spirit* that is required for personal growth and development to occur. Now, as the final moments of the story approach, the ultimate decision belongs solely to the protagonist. He or she can certainly be reminded and encouraged by others (this is where the symbolic voice of Teiresias is heard), but in the end the choice—*to grow or not to grow; to be or not to be*—is a personal decision.

While the voice of Obi-Wan Kenobi may remind Luke to *trust* a force greater than himself, the ultimate decision is Luke's alone. The destruction of the Death Star means the resurrection of hope for him and for the Rebellion. But that hope rests not on Luke's actions, but on his *choice* of what actions he will take.

By the time we get to the final scene in *Dead Poets Society*, the wrongful firing of Mr. Keating has already occurred due to the boys' cowardice, and it cannot be undone. But the ultimate question of *How shall I live my life?* is still in play. This is the choice that must be made. So when Todd—seemingly the weakest of the group—decides to defy authority by standing on his desk and saluting his teacher, he creates the possibility of greatness not only in himself but in all the other boys as well.

Likewise, in *When Harry Met Sally*, the decision of a future with or without Sally and with or without true love and intimacy is what inspires Harry to literally stop in his tracks and turn and run to her.

Tragically, at the end of *The Godfather*, Michael doesn't have the courage and the quality of character to make the same decision. After extracting a bloody revenge on everyone who ever crossed his family—including his sister's husband—he is given the opportunity to be truthful with his wife. Symbolically, this would have indicated that there was still the possibility that he could someday grow in the direction of love. Instead, he not only chooses to lie to her, but the door is literally closed on her, effectively sealing Michael's fate of isolation that will lead to his ultimate downfall and destruction.

There is no definitive placement for the transformational moment in a story. Most often I see it occurring just prior to the climax, setting the final showdown into motion. However, sometimes it occurs during the climax itself. This is especially true in modern action films, where the climactic sequence can last for as long as ten to fifteen minutes. The ultimate battle between the protagonist and the antagonist may parry back and forth for quite awhile before the protagonist makes a final, critical decision that brings about victory. Luke and his fellow fighter pilots engage in the deadly battle to destroy the Death Star for quite some time before Luke hones in on the target and makes the decision to trust his own intuitive radar.

Even though there is some latitude in the placement of the transformational moment, if it occurs too early, especially before the last act, the story will lose its potency. Because we make a strong emotional connection to the internal movement of character in a story, if the protagonist makes this inner shift too soon it tends to deflate the dramatic tension that is pulling us through to the climax. But any transformational moment is better than none at all, because it serves to complete the arc of character. If it is missing, chances are your arc is either weak or non-existent, indicating that your theme is underdeveloped as well.

All Good Things Must Come to an End

The dramatic tension in a story is the result of something or someone opposing the resolution of the conflict. In *Casablanca*, the Nazis stand in the way of Victor getting safely out of Africa. In *To Kill a Mockingbird*, a bigoted white court stands between an innocent black man and his freedom. In the comedy *Tootsie*, the lie about Michael Dorsey's gender stands between him and his acting career and the woman he loves. Therefore, to resolve the dramatic tension, the thing that stands in the way must be beaten, outsmarted, overcome, knocked out, killed, destroyed, won over, or in some way neutralized if the dramatic tension is going to be resolved. However, in a good story, this is not so easily accomplished because the stronger this opposing force, the greater the dramatic tension, and the harder it is to stop.

To understand what happens in the climax of a story, it's important to first understand more about the nature of the **antagonist** or the **antagonism**—that is, **the someone or something that opposes the resolution of the conflict.** On the surface of many stories, the antagonist comes across as merely the bad guy, or the bad institution, or the bad behavior that is trying to thwart the good guy from winning. Nazis, bigots, and liars are pretty much a slam-dunk in this category. But if nothing else is going on in a story, then in the end only goodness, righteousness, and honesty will prevail. However, real-life experience has a lot more complexity to it—and so does a great story.

For example, Ada's husband in *The Piano* doesn't really fit the description of the traditional bad guy. In fact, he seems to be quite ordinary and even somewhat benign. What makes him antagonistic to Ada is that he's been acculturated to see her only as property. This is what Ada's been fighting against her entire life and it's probably a good part of the reason she stopped talking at the age of six. It's also the reason she's built steep walls to defend herself against becoming nothing more than someone else's possession. But as with all fatal flaws, there comes a time when the very survival system that was used to help a person endure becomes a death trap. Therefore, the husband's function in the story is to provide the means for Ada to escape. He's the thing that stands in the way, blocking the doorway out. All Ada needs to do is find the *key* that will win her her freedom.

Throughout Ada's life she has used the strength of her will to protect herself. But in this final battle, following the dismemberment of her finger, what transforms in her is the understanding that her will has become the real enemy. Having sailed to the edge of her known world and made the blood sacrifice, what Ada must retrieve from the dark recesses of her Underworld depths is the other side of her nature— which is the ability to *surrender*. When she awakens and sees her husband staring into her eyes, it is this surrender that greets him. As a result, he sees something he has never seen before—he *sees* Ada. She is real to him, she is not a piece of property, and he *now* knows he cannot own or possess her. He has been neutralized.

- **A great antagonist must represent the darkest side of the protagonist's shadow.**
- **The antagonist is the physical manifestation of the internal conflict that besieges the protagonist.**

In *Basic Instinct*, the reason Nick Curran's life is failing has nothing to do with the ball-busting machinations of Catherine Tramell. He's an ego-driven loner who relies solely on the brutish masculine side of his nature to survive. As long as he disregards the feminine part of himself that holds his instincts, his intuition, and his ability to relate, he will suffer at the hands of this dark, feminine force. In Hindu mythology, one of the preeminent deities is the dark goddess Kali, who wields the sword of destruction as a means to break through the limited boundaries of the ego in order to unleash our greater potential.

Antagonists often carry this destroyer/creator energy. What they break down in us is a means of pushing us to new heights and greater consciousness. Understanding the antagonist from this perspective can help in determining the essential action that must take place in the climax. If the climax is the moment in the story when the protagonist must stand up and fight, it's necessary to understand what he or she is really fighting for. This, of course, harkens back to the importance of the theme, because it must ultimately be that value that is at the center of the fight.

In the climax of *Casablanca*, Rick kills the German officer who is about to alert the authorities that Victor Laszlo is escaping. On the surface, this is no great act of heroism. He merely pulls out his revolver and shoots the guy. But behind this action is a symbolic indication that Rick is willing to take sides again and fight for what he believes in— *that the actions of every individual do make a difference.*

Be extremely careful in the climax to avoid endings that relate to anything other than the theme that's been established. Because the theme represents your point of view and what you value, applying any other significance to the ending will tend to confuse the audience and negate the relevance of the theme altogether.

For example, there's been some controversy over the ending of Clint Eastwood's Academy Award–winning film *Million Dollar Baby*, because it brings up issues regarding euthanasia and the right to die. Actually, it doesn't "bring up" these issues as issues; they just happen to be part of the outcome of the story. However, the reason they've become issues is because the ending doesn't flow naturally out of the thematic conflict that was initiated at the beginning of the film. Instead, it feels artificially tagged on to the script—as if it is trying to make a statement. I doubt this is the case, but it's easy to see why the audience is confused.

In the first two-thirds of this film, the conflict is focused primarily on Maggie (Hilary Swank), a young woman who desperately wants to turn her throwaway life into something of value. She dreams of becoming a female prizefighter and hitches her wagon to Frankie (Eastwood), a cranky, old trainer, whom she believes will push her to greatness (although we're never sure why she believes this). But because her ambitions seem to be motivated by something deep and authentic, it isn't difficult to buy into her heroic quest to make something of herself. The storyline is further enhanced by the evolving relationship between Maggie and Frankie. They are both very wounded people, and their struggle to win in the ring becomes an excellent context in which their inner struggles to transcend barriers of self-doubt and intimacy are fought as well.

Consistent with a well-developed transformational arc, this story shifts out of resistance at the midpoint when Frankie and Maggie form a strong union. This results in an awesome period of grace where we see Maggie becoming a strong and winning fighter. But at the second turning point a terrible blood sacrifice is extracted when she is brutally assaulted in the ring and is left paralyzed. Up to this point, the story has been about the courage and commitment it takes to become a winner, so there is every reason to believe that this dramatic shift in the action is leading to an expansion of that theme. In other words, we've seen Maggie fight to make a life, now it's reasonable to believe that in the third act, when the *worst thing* has happened, she is going to fight *for* her life.

Instead, fighting becomes a non-issue in the last twenty minutes of the film. Maggie's physical body is so irretrievably broken that she has no physical movement left in it. This leads her to the conclusion that she simply wants to die, but she needs Frankie's help.

While choosing to die is certainly a big decision for anyone to make, it's not an actual moment of decision for Maggie. Nothing transforma-tional happens to her as a result. Given the same set of circumstances, it's very likely she would have made this same choice at the beginning of the story. On the other hand, this situation forces Frankie into a very real moment of decision, which is a pretty solid indicator that it has just become his story—not Maggie's. This may be why we're confused, because the emphasis throughout the film has been on Maggie and her determination to become a successful fighter; now it's on Frankie to decide if he can let her go.

When the film first begins, it appears for a moment that this may be Frankie's story. But, in reality, he has no specific conflict to resolve until Maggie enters the picture. Then, the dominant focus of both the plot and the subplots turns to Maggie and her desire to become a great fighter by overcoming her past, where she grew up believing she was nothing but trash. While Frankie remains an important character in the story, and there are rumblings that he has issues to resolve with his own daughter, his function is always relegated to helping Maggie achieve her goal.

The uncertainty over whose story is being told is further complicated by an ongoing narration by Scrap (Morgan Freeman), Frankie's "scrappy" confidant, who likewise emphasizes Maggie's struggle to become a champion. He comments that boxing is about respect, that tough isn't tough enough, that fighters need heart, but too much heart will get you a beating, and that great fighters must fight past all endurance, risking everything for a personal dream.

This last statement, in particular, seems to strongly indicate that the theme of this is a movie about having *the courage to fight to the end—no matter what*. At the climax of this film, however, the decision that Frankie has to make is about *loving someone enough to let them go*. These are both very powerful themes and either could have made a fine story, but not at the same time because, as we see in this film, they take the story in two different, unrelated directions.

If screenwriting is to be an organic, creative process, then situations where a writer finds a whole new thematic direction at the end of a story should not be considered unusual or counterproductive. To the contrary, such a shift may be a very strong indicator that the writing experience is very much alive and evolving. This can't be a bad thing. And it isn't, *unless* this new thematic direction remains unprocessed. In other words, if a new pathway opens up for you in the end of your story, then your work isn't done. It must be integrated into the rest of the script or the story stops making meaning altogether.

To be honest, I was a little surprised by all the fuss made about the ending of this film because, even though I felt involved with a lot of the story, I wasn't left feeling much of anything in the end. I did care about Frankie and Maggie, but I couldn't participate in the ending because, even though I understood how much he loved her, his struggle to let her go was too underdeveloped to really pull me in. However, I've also observed that sometimes, when relevance is missing or unclear, audiences are inclined to add their own meaning—which may be why this was interpreted by some to be a "message" film about the right to die.

Writers have no obligation to make meaning for their audiences. A film is an artistic statement, and every individual will have his or her own perception of what a story has to say. However, the need to make meaning out of our experiences in life is a shared human trait. If a writer is ambivalent about what the story has to say, then there will be nothing available to at least guide the audience toward an understanding of his or her artistic vision.

When the transformational arc is strong, all the pieces of plot and subplot finally come together in the climax. The internal shift of character that occurs in the subplotlines ("B" and "C" stories) allows the protagonist to achieve something in the plot ("A" story) that he or she was incapable of achieving at the beginning of the film. This is the litmus test for any great story and the best place to begin the process of self-analysis for the rewrite of your own screenplay.

Has the protagonist achieved something in the end that he or she was not capable of achieving in the beginning?

If the answer to this question is *no, not really, I'm not sure,* or *maybe/sort of,* then no real transformation of character has taken place.

The protagonist began and ended the story as pretty much the same person. Therefore, what was the point of the experience?

Even though Richard Kimble in *The Fugitive* was forced to go to hell and back to prove his innocence and catch his wife's killer, what else did he really gain from all his hardships? What new part of himself did he have to access in order to achieve his goal? The action in this film demanded that he be tough, resilient, and smart—but he already had those attributes when the story began.

My Big Fat Greek Wedding was a lot of fun, but in the end what did Toula really achieve that she wasn't capable of achieving at the beginning of the story? She met a really great guy who thought she was a really great gal. No challenge there. Her family was extremely possessive, but she already knew how to manipulate and cajole them to get most of what she wanted. No real challenge there either.

In both of these films there's an insinuation that the character transformed, but there was very little in the interior lives of their protagonists that needed to shift in order for them to achieve their goals. Kimble got bolder and Toula seemed to get prettier, but in the climax there was no internal moment of reckoning that enabled them to stand up to *the someone or the something that opposed the resolution of their conflict*. What they achieved in the end they were fully capable of accomplishing in the beginning.

All the explosive action and passionate embraces in the world can't compensate for this lack of real character development. In the climax of a film like *Rocky*, we aren't just witnessing an underdog going a few rounds with the heavyweight champion; we're watching a man challenge himself to be more than he ever dreamed possible. When we see Oskar Schindler and Rick Blaine stand up to the Nazis, what we're really beholding are men who've just reconnected with the rest of humanity. When the students in *Dead Poets Society* stand on their desks and defiantly salute their teacher, we're watching boys become men. When Ada struggles to free herself from the rope that has pulled her to the ocean's depths along with her piano, we're really witnessing the birth of a free spirit.

This is the power of the climax. It is the fight for change, for liberation, for recognition, for reconciliation, and for connection. But more than anything else, it's always the fight for a *new and greater life*.

In Defense of "Happily Ever After"

Even though the climax brings the conflict to a conclusion, it is not the end of the story. The **RESOLUTION** of conflict in our own lives may bring to a close a difficult or painful experience, but what it really represents is the start of something new. In fact, when transformation has occurred, we are new—or at least it can be said we encounter life and life encounters us in a new way.

The resolution of a heroic story must give the audience a glimpse of what this new encounter with life will look like. For example, at the end of *Casablanca*, after Rick has nobly sent Ilsa off on a plane with her husband and shot the Nazi commander to protect her, it's clear that there is no turning back to his old life. Instead, he looks ahead to new prospects that will reengage him in the Allied war effort and reconnect him with the rest of his fellow human beings. He starts this new journey with Captain Renault, a Nazi sympathizer who is inspired by Rick to rejoin the "good" fight as well.

RENAULT

```
It might be a good idea for you to
disappear from Casablanca for awhile.
There's a Free French garrison over at
Brazaville. I could be induced to arrange
a passage.
```

RICK

```
My letter of transit? I could use a trip.
But it doesn't make any difference about
our bet. You still owe me ten thousand
francs.
```

                    RENAULT
And that ten thousand francs should pay our
expenses.
                      RICK
Our expenses?
                    RENAULT
Uh huh.
                      RICK
Louie, I think this is the beginning of a
beautiful friendship.

The two walk off together into the night.

Notice that even though Rick didn't get everything he wanted in the end, especially Ilsa, the cynicism and skepticism that plagued him at the beginning of the story have greatly receded. In their place is a more optimistic view of life, which signals that he now has the internal capacity to survive and thrive no matter what destiny hurls his way. Most importantly, he also has resurrected the ability to love again.

The resolution is of great symbolic value, because it tells us that there is always more life on the other side of our troubles. It also reminds us that the hardships, disappointments, and suffering we endure are worth the effort. This is not a naive or overly simplistic view of the world, but it is part of the natural order of life. People successfully traverse the arc of transformation only by growing stronger within and achieving greater consciousness. Therefore, one of the primary functions of story has always been to pull human beings toward this goal.

The final scene of *Forrest Gump* shows Forrest putting his young son on a school bus. But what this simple action really implies is that even though he may have lost his wife, the great love of his life, on the other side of all that sorrow and pain will only be more love. It may not always come in a predictable form, but the capacity to love has no limits. Forrest *will* live happily ever after, just not exactly the way he had always hoped.

In this context, the concept expressed in the phrase *"…and they lived happily ever after"* is not just a juvenile artifice, but a significant part of our collective reality that is consistently expressed throughout all variations of the human story. We *can* potentially rise above the most terrible things that life inflicts upon us and *live ever after*—not in a fixed state of contentment or complacency, but by participating in an ongoing process that continually opens our lives to deeper self-awareness, connectedness, creativity, self-expression, and balance. This may be a far more generous and expansive sense of what happiness really is than just some idealized state of bliss.

An uplifting or "happy" ending doesn't mean that it should appear as if everything in the protagonist's life is resolved forever. To the contrary, many very positive endings indicate that there are more struggles on the horizon, but that the protagonist is now better equipped to handle life's battles. In a romantic storyline, for example, a strong ending might be an indication that the couple now has the ability to face new trials together, or that even though they love each other, a lot of work still lies ahead.

Once Frank Keller has achieved the goal of stopping the serial killer in *Sea of Love*, he tries desperately to win Helen back in the final scene. But after lying to her about who he is and wrongly accusing her of being the killer, she is very reluctant to even talk to him. Gradually, with humor and tenacity, he wears her down and she agrees to at least go for a cup of coffee. Being in a real relationship may still be a long way off for these two because the trust between them needs to be rebuilt. But the resolution implies that there is genuine hope for them as long as they remain honest and stay committed to each other.

Some films have very effective endings that utilize irony and paradox to leave the audience stimulated and questioning their own values and perceptions. The Academy Award–winning film *American Beauty* climaxes on what should be a very tragic ending because Lester, the protagonist, is murdered. But that's not how he sees it.

                    LESTER (V.O.)
I guess I could be pretty pissed off about
what happened to me… but it's hard to stay
mad, when there's so much beauty in the
world. Sometimes I feel like I'm seeing it
all at once, and it's too much, my heart
fills up like a balloon that's about to
burst… And then I remember to relax, and
stop trying to hold on to it. And then it
flows through me like rain and I can't feel
anything but gratitude for every single
moment of my stupid little life…
                    (amused)
You have no idea what I'm talking about,
I'm sure. But don't worry…

FADE TO BLACK.

                    LESTER (V.O. cont'd)
You will someday.

At the end of *The Piano,* Ada and her daughter have embarked on a new life with Baines. They have moved to the city and we can see that she is happy and content and is even learning to speak and play the piano again with a metal finger that Baines has fashioned for her. But Ada also acknowledges that she is not yet fully out of the dark, and may never be. At night she still dreams of her piano at the bottom of the sea and sometimes sees herself floating above it. But this image doesn't scare her, in fact, it reassures her that she is still connected to the depths of her own soul.

Ada's life isn't perfect—that's an impossibility—but it is more *balanced.* She has emerged from her oppressive fortress and now lives a relatively "normal" existence. But she also maintains contact with and even cherishes the parts of herself that still reside in the dark, watery places outside the boundaries of the civilized realm. This is her peace, her balance—her *happily ever after*.

In Chapter Three we discussed how the nature of all conflict arises from something being out of balance with its opposing value. At the beginning of *Schindler's List*, Oskar Schindler is leading a very self-absorbed life and he is acutely unaware or unconscious of the needs of others. In order for the conflict to be resolved, he had to bring his relationship to others into balance with his own needs.

SETUP OF STORY   RESOLUTION OF STORY

SELF vs. OTHERS   SELF vs. OTHERS

Conversely, in *Dead Poets Society*, the boys began the story serving only the needs of others and undervaluing or ignoring their own needs. This gross imbalance was not only undermining their ability to mature, but it was also keeping them from connecting with their own authentic impulses. If the story had been resolved by the boys turning their back on their families and running away from the school, then they would have merely traded one imbalance for another. Instead, there was a recognition that within the boundaries placed upon them by others they could still stand up for themselves and maintain their integrity.

SETUP OF STORY   RESOLUTION OF STORY

OTHERS vs. SELF   OTHERS vs. SELF

Even a story with a tragic resolution still serves the function of informing us that if we don't work through life's challenges there will be no growth and no renewal—just stagnation and decay. There can be no peace or harmony because the opposing values that were in conflict at the beginning of the story are still out of balance, and usually even more so.

In the first two installments of *The Godfather* trilogy, Michael Corleone puts a great deal of effort into becoming a mob leader, and as a result the imagery in the resolution of each episode makes it clear that his power continues to grow. But, we also see in the end of each of these films that he is becoming more isolated, distrusting, and alone, because he has put almost no effort into developing human relationships. In *The Godfather III*, when Michael finally begins to understand how much he has misjudged what is really valuable in life, it's too late. He claims that he wants to become a legitimate businessman, but that he keeps getting pulled back into the mob world. In reality, however, Michael is only reaping what he has sown. He has created a life based on domination, control, deceit, and intolerance. The thing that is really pulling Michael back into the Underworld is a vortex of destruction that he alone has set into motion. When he dies in the final scene, he is old and alone, and there is no one left around him who really cares.

Ironically, this sort of tragic ending doesn't leave the audience feeling as hopeless and miserable as it does the protagonist. Instead, it has the opposite effect. We are left with an even deeper understanding of how our own drama will play out if, like the protagonist, we refuse to put the necessary effort and commitment into overcoming the obstacles in our own lives that challenge us to grow toward fulfillment and wholeness.

Case Studies

1) ROMANCING THE STONE

At the end of the last chapter, I posed the question: How could the second turning point in this film have been strengthened so that it would lead to a more powerful third act? The answer, as always, must involve the theme. In this story, as discussed in Chapters Four and Five, the theme requires Joan to *trust the adventure* and *learn to follow her heart*. Up through the midpoint and into the period of grace, Joan is beginning to turn her life toward this new direction. As a result, she is falling in love with a man who is flawed but real, and she agrees to follow him on a crazy scheme to get the stone. Joan's life is clearly moving away from what is safe and predictable, and she's beginning to trust the adventure that is leading her toward true love.

But Joan has yet to encounter the dark side of the adventure. So far her experiences have been exciting and remarkable; now she must face the danger and peril that are also part of the adventure of love, or it won't be a real experience—only an idealized one. Therefore, her love must be tested: What Joan trusts must appear to be *un*trustworthy. This will lead to the conclusion that her heart has steered her in the wrong direction. If she can survive this test—to stay committed to love even when it disappoints and lets her down—then she has a shot at the real thing.

To design a stronger second turning point, we must consider how to make Joan distrust love. There are always many different approaches to a broad concept such as this, but if possible try to remain consistent with what already exists in the story. Currently, this script works pretty well up to the point where Joan and Jack plummet over the waterfall and end up on opposite sides of an uncrossable river. There is a hint of betrayal here, when Joan accuses Jack of having planned this outcome, but that possibility is highly unlikely. The solution, therefore, is to either make it more plausible that Jack has double-crossed Joan, or that she—and we—at least have good reason to believe he has.

Later in the story, when Joan is about to make an escape with her sister from the hands of the comical kidnappers, the really bad guys show up with a gun at Jack's back. It's clear to see at this point that they've taken him hostage and forced him to lead them to Joan, who they believe has the stone. Wouldn't this device be stronger if it had been used at the waterfall? If Joan were to see Jack, who still has the stone, disappear into the jungle with the bad guys, she would have every reason to believe that he's swindled her. This would create a very real death experience for Joan, forcing her into a serious descent.

As the story is now written, there are indications that Joan is in a descent, but it's more image than substance. Having crawled through the jungle and made her way back to Cartagena, she enters the city in rags and tatters. People on the street stare and young boys tease her. But even though she looks quite defeated, she still manages to check into a nice hotel, where she contacts the men who have her sister and makes arrangements to meet them. She also checks to see if Jack has arrived, but he's nowhere to be seen.

Except for a few lingering looks of disenchantment, there is no real sense that the sweet, young writer from Manhattan has personally entered the dark side. She never questions why fate has so mistreated her or why she fell for someone who is obviously not her "Jesse." Because the theme of this story is about learning to trust love, it's important for Joan to completely disavow that trust. Without this descent, there is no decision that has to be made as she enters the climax. Therefore, there is no transformational moment. The fight at the end becomes just a struggle to survive; Joan isn't fighting for love, she's fighting to protect herself and her sister. This means that it is only the plot ("A" story) that is being resolved.

If you recall from Chapter Six, the "A," "B," and "C" storylines are set up in such a way that each impacts the resolution of the other. When the arc of character is strong, **the conflict of the plot ("A" story) can only be resolved if there is an internal shift of consciousness in the protagonist ("B" story). That shift is reflected in the relationship story-line ("C" story), and it is, therefore, through the relationship that the conflict in the "A" story is resolved.**

In the first and second acts of *Romancing the Stone*, this triadic relationship is working. In order to *save her sister*, Joan is forced to face the *unknown* wilds of the Amazon jungle. She survives by *following her heart*, which means that she believes in Jack Colton. However, in the third act, her ability to follow her heart has almost no impact on the actions she takes to save her sister. Even after Jack shows up with the bad guys holding him at gunpoint, his presence doesn't have much of an impact on the resolution of the conflict. There is a moment when Jack creates a diversion that lets Joan and her sister get to safety, but battling the antagonists is left almost exclusively to Joan. In fact, at the climax, while Joan is engaged in hand-to-hand combat with the ringleader of the bad guys, Jack is busy wrestling the crocodile that swallowed the stone. It is he, not Joan, who has a decision to make: whether to let go and save Joan, or hold on to the crocodile's tail and rescue the stone. He does opt to let go of the croc, but only after Joan has already saved herself.

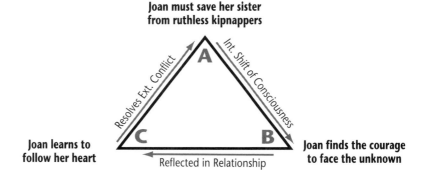

While this ending is cute, it doesn't address the theme. Instead, it makes Joan come off as a strong, independent woman who can do it all by herself. There's nothing wrong with Joan being strong and independent, but that hasn't been her issue throughout the story. The internal conflict that Joan needs to resolve is her ability to trust love, even when it's scary and uncertain. Therefore, somewhere in the climax she needed to take a huge leap of faith and trust Jack, even (and especially) if it meant risking everything.

This is a very good example of how a writer can lose track of the theme and address other values in the end that have not been part of the story. Portraying Joan as a modern woman who can take care of herself is a great idea, but if it doesn't relate to the internal conflict that has been developed throughout then it tends to make everything in the climax feel irrelevant.

The resolution of this story is further confused when the police begin to arrive and Jack jumps into the water and swims away, telling Joan that he and the Cartagena police "go way back." Joan is incredibly disappointed that he's leaving her, but he gives her a big juicy kiss and says:

```
                    JACK
  You're going to be alright, Joan Wilder...
  You always were.
```

What does this mean? That Joan is going to be alright by herself? She was alright by herself when the story began—except that she was lonely. How does his leaving her alone in the end complete her arc of character? If Jack had said, "I'll come for you, Joan. Trust me..." then his actions would have been relevant to the theme of the story. In fact, in the final scene Jack does show up—with the boat he's always wanted—and they go away together. It's a sweet ending and we're all delighted for Joan, but the third act would have been so much stronger if only the theme had been played out to the end.

2) LETHAL WEAPON

Because the theme of *Lethal Weapon* is to *choose life*, the third act of this film is where the battle between life and death must be fought. Up to the point when Murtaugh's daughter is kidnapped at the second turning point, this had been a relatively routine case for the two seasoned cops. But with the kidnapping, things become very personal—and deadly serious.

In the world of symbolism, the realm of life and death *is* a deadly serious place, and to gain access there must be a blood sacrifice of something as significant as an innocent young daughter. If this seems callous, consider how well it motivates these men to fight for life. If they can save her, the blood sacrifice will remain in the symbolic realm; if they fail, her sacrifice becomes a real death.

As these two warriors begin their descent they prepare for battle in the traditional way, but it quickly becomes apparent that they have been outmatched. Antagonists are always very powerful at this point in the story because they are the gatekeepers who guard the land of *renewal*, and they don't let just anybody in. This is where the action genre serves its highest function because it shows us how hard we have to *fight* for new life—for transformation. The heroes of these stories represent the warrior within us all, and when we see them fighting past the point of reason and endurance it reinforces just how awesome this last leg of the transformational journey really is.

In a bleak, desert landscape Riggs, Murtaugh, and the daughter are captured and brought to a cavernous, underground place (probably just a warehouse). There they are chained and manacled so that they can be tortured into submission. As important as it was to ease the tension for a few moments in the period of grace, it is equally as necessary to keep the heat and intensity on the protagonist during the descent. This is not the time for long, calm discussions. Especially if you are writing in the action, thriller, or horror genres, this is the place to push the protagonist past his or her physical threshold. Also, this is the place to use relevant Underworld images. Anything that evokes a subterranean atmosphere, such as tunnels, darkness, wetness, fire, unstable ground (earthquakes), and unbreathable air will add to the audience's unconscious connection to the fact that all of our great battles in life are fought in this Underworld place.

In fact, the tougher these scenes are, the more it feels like we, too, are being pushed past our own endurance. At this point in the story there must be nothing passive or voyeuristic about the audience's involvement. You don't just want our attention; you want our complete emotional attachment to the plight of the protagonist. As hard as it is to watch, the torture scene in *Lethal Weapon* serves to bond the audience with Riggs and Murtaugh in a very powerful way. When they break free, our own passion to catch and destroy the enemy is unleashed as well.

Entering the climax, the audience is in a free fall of pent-up, turbulent energy. As Riggs and Murtaugh chase down and tackle the soulless drug dealers, we are just as engaged in the hunt as they are. Since primitive times, great storytellers have created images like these that show us how to defeat the destructive forces that threaten both our internal and external reality. Legendary icons such as Achilles, King Arthur, and Joan of Arc or their modern counterparts, such as John Wayne, Superman, and even Xena, Warrior Princess, live in us as symbols of self-empowerment.

In a film with a strong arc of character, such as *Lethal Weapon*, the protagonists are likewise reenacting the timeless story of how to claim our own power. This film is particularly potent because it uses the co-protagonist structure to show us how our personal power must always be held in balance. A warrior must balance detachment and objectivity with compassion and relatedness. Therefore, as the story enters the climax, each of the co-protagonists must make a decision to accept and embrace the other side of his nature. Riggs is not only fighting for life; he's fighting for a life that includes a connection to others. Murtaugh, on the other hand, is fighting for the autonomous side of his nature that will not bend or yield to others when it comes to defending what he values.

The climax, therefore, must resolve these personal issues for both co-protagonists, so each is sent in a different direction. Riggs chases down Mr. Joshua, the henchman who tortured him, while Murtaugh goes after General McAllister, the ringleader who kidnapped his daughter. The final battles are tough and relentless, but, as the end approaches, each of our heroes has a transformational moment when he must decide the fate of his adversary—which will reflect his own fate as well. When the general is about to make his escape, Murtaugh picks up his revolver and blocks the path of the high-speed getaway car. With resolute calm he takes a single, well-aimed shot that causes the remorseless villain to die in an explosive crash.

Riggs takes on his nemesis, Mr. Joshua, in hand-to-hand combat. But just as he has the opportunity to strike the final, lethal blow, he backs off, acknowledging that he's not worth killing. Here Riggs decides to *choose life* at the highest level of relatedness, acknowledging his respect for life even when it comes to someone as loathsome as Mr. Joshua.

Unfortunately, Mr. Joshua isn't capable of making the same connection, and he therefore sows the seeds of his own destruction. As officers are handcuffing him he manages to grab one of their guns and takes direct aim at Riggs and Murtaugh. But now he's no match for this fearsome duo. In perfect synchronization, they each grab their own gun and fire unhesitatingly into the heart of this beast.

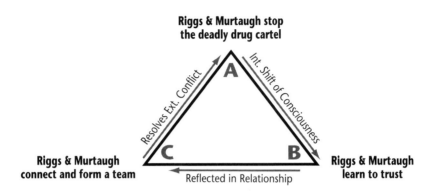

Riggs & Murtaugh stop the deadly drug cartel

Resolves Ext. Conflict

Int. Shift of Consciousness

A

C

B

Riggs & Murtaugh connect and form a team

Reflected in Relationship

Riggs & Murtaugh learn to trust

The union has been formed, the character arc is complete, and the terms of the "A," "B," and "C" triad have been met. By *learning to trust* each other ("B" story), Riggs and Murtaugh have *connected as a team* ("C" story), and through their teamwork they have *stopped the deadly drug cartel* ("A" story). The story began with an emphasis on the personal development of these co-protagonists and it is resolved in the same way. As a symbolic gesture, Riggs visits his wife's grave with an offering of flowers and tells her that he loves her. But as he walks away, we can see that he also wants her to know that he's ready to move on with his life. As a result, he goes to see Murtaugh and gives him the silver bullet that he had always planned to use to kill himself. Then he turns to leave, but Murtaugh stops his new partner and invites him to join his family for Christmas dinner.

Like the great warrior Odysseus, Riggs has begun to find his way home again.

3) ORDINARY PEOPLE

From a structural perspective, the third act of *Ordinary People* is more complex than the other two case studies. This is because the story leads each of the co-protagonists to a personal climax that then impacts the climax and resolution of the family as a collective unit. If you recall, the central conflict of the "A" story revolves around the issue of whether or not this family will survive as a family. But it is in the personal stories of the "B" and "C" subplotlines that the quality of that survival is resolved. Therefore, what is aptly illustrated in the end is that the strength of the whole (family) is defined by the quality of its parts (the individuals).

Each member of this family holds the potential to destroy and/or to create. While it's easy to see that Beth has destructive tendencies, let's not forget that Conrad is suicidal and Dad is ambivalent. If either of these inclinations is activated and becomes dominant, it has as much power to destroy the integrity of the family as does Beth's inability to be authentic. Therefore, the third act is incredibly tense because any or all of the central characters have the potential to bring down the family.

When the death experience at the second turning point is strong, it leaves open the possibility that the protagonist may not recover, which will lead to tragic consequences. In most stories, there are significant indicators throughout the course of its development to signal which way the outcome will fall—tragic or heroic. *Ordinary People* is unique in this regard because there are so many variables for resolution between these three co-protagonists that the tragic or heroic ending is not a foregone conclusion. The story itself begins with a tragedy and therefore it's very possible that the resolution will show that the family cannot rise above their circumstances. On the other hand, Conrad puts so much effort into facing his trials that he is definitely set up as a heroic character. Beth, of course, puts no effort into changing and she feels equally tragic. Dad, therefore, is the wild card. He loves his son and wants his family to be real, but he's also weak and easily swayed by Beth's manipulations. In the third act it becomes even more obvious that it is Dad's decision (transformational moment) that will be the determining factor in the outcome for the family.

Dad is ultimately guided to his decision by the actions of Beth and Conrad. Each character in this story has a second turning point experience of his or her own that leads into a descent. Conrad is the first to go, and his Underworld trials are extremely difficult. Reeling from the news that his friend from rehab has just killed herself, Conrad falls into a nightmarish vortex of panic and remembering. His breathing is heavy, the room spins, and he begins to relive with excruciating detail the events of the night his brother died. There is no doubt that Conrad has reached the farthest edge of his known world, but this is not a totally unfamiliar place to him. As he looks down at his scarred wrists and contemplates reopening the old wounds, a realization washes over him—the *blood sacrifice* has already been made. If he can just stay afloat and ride out *this* turbulent storm, he may be able to survive and find his way back home.

In this storyline, the powerful inner wisdom of Teiresias is literalized in the form of Conrad's therapist, Dr. Berger, who meets the terrified boy in his office for a late-night emergency session. Conrad is flooded with painful memories and unbearable emotions.

                         CONRAD
                       (weeping)
        Why do things have to happen to people? It
        isn't fair.
                        DR. BERGER
        You're right. It isn't fair.
                         CONRAD
        You just do one wrong thing and…
                        DR. BERGER
        And what was the one wrong thing you did?

Conrad lets out a deep, exhausted breath.

                    DR. BERGER (cont'd)
        You know…

(encouragingly)
You know...

CONRAD
(startled by this new thought)
I hung on. I stayed with the boat.

DR. BERGER
Exactly. Now you can live with that, can't you?

CONRAD
I'm scared. I'm scared.

DR. BERGER
Feelings are scary. And sometimes they're
painful. And if you can't feel pain, then
you're not going to feel anything else
either. You hear what I'm saying? You're
here and you're alive. And don't tell me
you don't feel that.

CONRAD
It doesn't feel good.

DR. BERGER
It is good; believe me.

Once Conrad has surrendered to the truth of the past and allowed his natural feelings to emerge from the pain, there is a sensation of release back into the flow of life. Early the next morning he visits his girlfriend and apologizes for having directed his anger at her. She invites him to breakfast, which he gladly accepts. This is an important symbolic gesture for Conrad because in the beginning of the film he had no appetite; the dead don't eat. But his renewed hunger signals that Conrad is now back among the living.

Meanwhile, Mom and Dad are away on their own voyage of descent, and they're having a ball! At least Mom is; she's at the top of her game—which happens to be golf. Whereas Conrad's journey was one of agonizing undoing, Beth and Calvin are on vacation. At the second turning point, Dad unwitting makes a blood sacrifice of Conrad when he allows Beth to pull him away from their troubled son during a time when Conrad is extremely vulnerable. Dad knows he shouldn't go, but it's the path of least resistance and it's easy to fall back into old patterns of self-deception and complacency. However, as easygoing as things appear, something very dangerous is rumbling just below the surface that will cause all *hell* to break loose somewhere between the 18th hole and the clubhouse. Finally, Calvin sees that he must stand up to Beth and fight for his son if his family is going to have any chance of survival. However, Beth is no pushover. She strikes back with everything in her arsenal, but it's ineffective. For the first time Calvin exposes a serious crack in her polished veneer, and what he sees inside isn't pretty.

The flight home is agonizing; the silence between Beth and Calvin is more frighteningly foreboding than all the shouting. All three co-protagonists have turned a very sharp corner in their individual lives, and it's about to lead to a big showdown. But unlike its Hollywood western counterpart, the confrontation in this film won't involve pistols at high noon. Instead, the final battle is fought with a far more power-ful weapon—real human emotion.

The climactic scene takes place on an *ordinary* night, not unlike many others. Beth and Calvin have just returned from their trip and are sitting quietly in the living room, catching up on their mail. Conrad walks in and tells them that he's glad they're home, and it's clear that Dad is relieved to be back as well. As usual, Beth acknowledges Conrad's presence with a compulsory smile. On the surface, it looks as though life is settling back to normal. Then, suddenly, from out of nowhere, Conrad brazenly takes his final shot. Awkwardly he crosses to his mother, bends down and simply wraps his arms around her in an awkward, but sincere, loving embrace.

THIS IS REALLY BIG, because with this simple, guileless gesture of love, Conrad has mortally wounded *the thing that stands in the way* of this family becoming whole. Beth's power is gone. Later that night she awakens and finds Calvin missing from their bed. Confused, she makes her way downstairs and finds him sitting alone in the dining room, crying. She asks him what's wrong.

<pre>
                    CALVIN
     Tell me something, do you love me? Do you
     really love me?
                    BETH
     I feel the way I've always felt about you.
                    CALVIN
     It would have been alright if there hadn't
     been any mess. But you can't handle mess.
     You need everything neat and easy. I don't
     know, maybe you can't love anybody. So
     much Buck; when Buck died it was as if you
     buried all your love with him. And I don't
     understand that. I just don't know, maybe
     it wasn't even Buck. Maybe it was just
     you. Maybe, finally, it was the best of
     you that you buried. But whatever it was,
     I don't know who you are. I don't know
     what we've been playing at. So I was
     crying, because I don't know if I love you
     anymore. And I don't know what I'm going
     to do without that.
</pre>

Because the balance of power in this family has shifted, Beth is lost. While the rest of the family struggled to sort out their feelings, she only pushed hers further and deeper away. Now, without access to her inner realm, she has no resources to draw upon to help her deal with this crisis. So she simply packs her bags and leaves.

Where there once were four, now there are only two. But two is all it takes to make a family. Whether or not Beth ever changes and decides to come back will not diminish what has happened. When Conrad and Calvin got honest with themselves ("B" story), they were able to value each other and even Beth in a more authentic way ("C" story). As a result, the family shed its idealized image and became something real and tangible ("A" story). In the final scene, they experience this new reality and it's not all rosy. But even though they feel some guilt and pain, they also feel joy and love. There are tears, but there are also hugs, and those who are left in the family—Conrad and Calvin—are no longer afraid to face the future *together*.

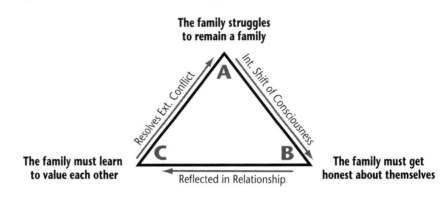

TRANSFORMATIONAL ARC

1 ↔ 25 ↔ 50 ↔ 75 ↔ 100

ACT I   ACT II   ACT III

RESISTANCE

RELEASE

UNKNOWN   EXHAUSTION | KNOWN   RENEWAL

1st Turning Point

MIDPOINT

Grace ► FALL ►

2nd Turning Point

Transformational Moment

Climax

Push to breaking point

Moment of Enlightenment

Descent

Death Experience

Resolution

Awakening

Call to Action

Inciting Incident

Defining Moment

EPILOGUE

INFINITE POSSIBILITIES

Great stories never really end; they take up residence inside us and live on in our thoughts, conversations, fantasies, and dreams. They are also a powerful influence over our beliefs, values, opinions, and perceptions. And rightly so. It's not just that we identify with Rick, Oskar, Ada, Hamlet, or Little Red Riding Hood; it's that they were already a part of us even before we ever heard their names. Their feelings of disillusionment, disconnectedness, loneliness, confusion, and fear aren't unique to the human condition; they simply give these emotions an identity. But that's not why they live in us. The characters in our stories don't just reflect our feelings; they show us how to process them—especially the painful and difficult ones—so that we can continue to evolve, moving *ever after* into a larger world of infinite possibilities.

From the first moment an idea for a story flashes into a writer's imagination, it offers up this world of infinite possibilities. Too often, however, when we receive this precious gift, we become fixated on the enticing package (the external plotline) and never bother to look inside. As a result, the story's potential is never realized and the world is poorer for it.

And so, it seems appropriate to end this book with a story of infinite possibilities. I'm sure you're familiar with the ancient tale of Prometheus, who stole food (consciousness) and fire (energy) from the gods in order to free humanity from the tyranny of ignorance and superstition. As his punishment, the gods tied poor old Prometheus to a rock where an eagle would come every day to pluck out his liver. Every night his wound would heal so that each dawn brought renewed torment. Symbolically, this indicates that the struggle to achieve consciousness is *tied* to the duality of *liberation* and *suffering*. But there's more to this story—*there always is....*

To also punish the humans who had partaken of their food and fire, the gods set up an elaborate trick. They created a spectacularly beautiful woman named Pandora. Each of the gods and goddesses bestowed gifts upon her, and she was then offered as a wife to Prometheus's brother, Epimetheus. Foremost among Pandora's gifts was a golden box that both she and her husband were severely admonished never to open. For the most part, Epimetheus was content just to admire the beautiful box, but Pandora, who'd also been "gifted" with keen curiosity by the gods, couldn't resist. So even when her husband buried the box under a boulder in the garden, Pandora arduously dug it up and lifted the lid.

I'm sure you're also familiar with what happened next. Every manner of misery flew out of the box and was unleashed upon the world: pestilence, greed, jealousy, fear, sickness, poverty, and famine.

While Prometheus, whose name means *foresight*, is viewed as a hero for courageously bringing the light of consciousness into the world, Pandora has been cast as an insipid fool, whose irrepressible passion to look inside the box has forever dimmed that light. But is this really true? Or was Pandora's unquenchable desire for *the truth that lies within* actually the fuel that has kept the flame of Prometheus alive? Without curiosity and desire, there is no motivation for consciousness to ever evolve.

As a writer, I would ask you to consider two things: What good is the gift of a great story if it is never opened and shared? And, would the world really be better off without the contents of what lies within, no matter how terrible? Only in the most childish of fantasies is life perceived as idyllic, and that perception of reality contains no hope of ever growing toward maturity and wholeness. But *hope* is precisely what was found in the bottom of Pandora's Box. And I *hope* that what you've seen in the pages of this book confirms that hope is also what is found whenever a writer has the courage to dig down into the bottom of a great story.

Every writer who is given the gift of story is, likewise, being tricked by the gods, because every story does contain the duality found in Pandora's Box: horror and beauty; awfulness and awe.... But if we sit back like Epimetheus (whose name means *hindsight*) and only admire the package, it will be too late before we realize that we never got to the true value of what the gift of story has to offer...*insight*.

So, in closing, I would like to pass on to you these final words of encouragement: Dare to be guided by your passion. Open your gift and release into the world of infinite possibilities the sacred truths that reside there—waiting only for you—*inside story*.

> *...Every man is more than just himself;*
> *he also represents the very special and always significant*
> *and remarkable point at which the world's phenomena intersect,*
> *only once in this way and never again.*
> *That is why every man's story is important,*
> *eternal, sacred;...*

~ HERMANN HESSE

GLOSSARY

"A" story – A term used to indicate the *plot* or external conflict of a screenplay.

Antagonist or the **antagonism** – Traditionally viewed as the character (human or non-human) or thing that opposes the protagonist and blocks achievement of the goal of the plot. From the perspective of the transformational arc, the antagonist is the physical manifestation of the internal conflict that is destroying the protagonist and, therefore, exemplifies the fatal flaw of character. By creating conflict for the protagonist, the antagonist creates an environment in which transformational change is necessary and relevant.

Awakening – It is the first glimmer of self-realization for the protagonist, but it is usually unwelcome because it reflects the fatal flaw of character. Therefore, the protagonist will often react with anger, resentment, rejection, and denial toward this awakening ray of consciousness that has just been forced upon him or her. It occurs at the first turning point in the "B" and "C" storylines.

"B" story – A term used to indicate a subplot storyline that exposes the internal conflict (fatal flaw of character).

Blood sacrifice – A metaphorical sacrifice that must be made by the protagonist as he or she enters the descent of the transformational arc in the third act. It indicates that transformational change is not free for the taking, but that it must be earned through great commitment and the willingness to give up or let go of the parts of ourselves that no longer serve the internal quest for wholeness.

"C" story – A term used to indicate the subplotline that exposes the relationship issues a protagonist must face in order to achieve the goal of the plot.

Call to Action – Willingly or unwillingly, consciously or unconsciously, somewhere in the first act the protagonist must be pulled into the conflict of the plot and become involved in resolving it. He or she, therefore, must be called to take action.

Co-protagonist – When two or more characters share the *same* goal in the plot and the subplots, they *share* the role of the protagonist.

Death experience – This event in the story occurs at the second turning point. As much as possible the protagonist must be forced to face the worst thing that can happen in regards to achieving the goal of the plot. The stronger the death experience, the more the protagonist will feel as if all is lost. This pushes him or her into a period of descent from which there is no guarantee of recovery. The death experience, therefore, creates the highest level of jeopardy in the story.

Defining moment – Usually a piece of dialogue wherein a character very directly clarifies the exact nature of the protagonist's fatal flaw of character. It is a very important part of the setup of the story in the first act.

Descent – The period following the second turning point is generally a time of pain, disappointment, unhappiness, and setbacks for the protagonist. The deeper the plunge into a descent, the more he or she will come to understand what life will be like if the quest for change and growth is abandoned. In a heroic story, the descent will motivate change and bring about the transformational moment. In a tragedy, the protagonist cannot pull out of the descent and the true goal of the story will be lost.

External conflict – This usually relates to the plot ("A" story). It is a conflict in the outer, physical world that the protagonist must overcome in order to achieve the goal of the plot.

Fall – Following the moment of enlightenment and the period of grace at the midpoint of the story, the protagonist is pulled back into the central conflict by unresolved issues that demand attention.

Fatal flaw of character – Resistance to change and growth can have fatal consequences. A strong internal storyline revolves around a protagonist's unyielding commitment to *an old, exhausted system of survival that has outlived its usefulness*. The fatal flaw of character indicates where the protagonist is emotionally, psychologically, or spiritually stuck at a level of consciousness that no longer supports or stimulates internal development. If the fatal flaw is not overcome, it will diminish or destroy something vital within the protagonist: the ability to love, the capacity to make a connection to others, the belief in oneself, faith in the life process, and so on. The fatal flaw of character is the source of conflict for the "B" story subplotline.

Heroic journey – This refers to the act of moving toward greater consciousness, which is the goal of the transformational arc. Achieving this goal is the essence of the heroic quest because the protagonist will be challenged by the external conflict in the plot to transcend personal limitations in order to become someone greater by the end of the story than who he or she was at the beginning.

Inciting incident – This marks the beginning of a chain of events that *must* eventually pull the protagonist into the story in the first act and call him or her to action. The inciting incident doesn't have to directly relate to the protagonist. It can be an incident (e.g., a murder, plane hijacking, or car accident) that the protagonist is not involved in and knows nothing about, but at some point in the first act it has ramifications that impact and influence the actions the protagonist will take throughout the story. The inciting incident is a major aspect of the setup of the first act.

Internal conflict – It is the struggle within the protagonist to grow and mature, and is the core around which the fatal flaw of character and the transformational arc are designed. The internal conflict defines the subplots ("B" and "C" stories).

Midpoint – This is an event or incident occurring at or near the center of the script. It shifts the conflict of the plot out of resistance to the goal and propels it toward the climax by revealing important information that helps the protagonist resolve the conflict.

Moment of enlightenment – This is one of the most significant points in the transformational arc. It occurs as a result of the events at the midpoint that bring about real consciousness for the protagonist.

The moment of enlightenment is the point in the story where the truth regarding the fatal flaw of character is revealed and causes a profound shift in the way the protagonist sees him- or herself and others. The moment of enlightenment also moves the protagonist out of resistance to transformational change and begins a process that will help guide him or her to resolving the internal and external conflict.

Period of grace – Once enlightenment has entered the protagonist's consciousness at the midpoint in the form of a new idea, new understanding, or new perspective on the problems or issues of the past, he or she will be inspired and motivated to face what lies ahead with renewed vigor, strength, and resolve. The period of grace is not an exact point in a story, but a nonspecific *period* of time in which the protagonist tends to thrive instead of strive. It always follows the moment of enlightenment on the transformational arc.

Plot – This refers to the *external* conflict that calls the protagonist to action. It *only* represents the activity of the protagonist in the outer, physical world. The plot is also referred to as the "A" story.

Protagonist – The person or being around which the primary goals of the plot and subplots are formed. The protagonist *must* carry the goals of both the plot ("A" story) and the primary subplots ("B" and "C" stories).

Release – The break in the tension at the midpoint of the transformational arc caused by a breakthrough to new consciousness. This release of tension in the second half of the arc propels the story toward resolution.

Resistance – The building of tension in the first half of the transformational arc that leads to a breakthrough in consciousness at the midpoint in a story.

Secondary characters – The primary function of all secondary characters in a story is not specifically to attain the goal of the plot, but to serve the protagonist in achieving it. Some secondary characters serve the protagonist directly, by giving assistance, encouragement, and knowledge. Others serve indirectly (antagonistically) by creating the

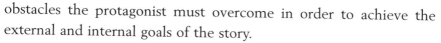

obstacles the protagonist must overcome in order to achieve the external and internal goals of the story.

Subplot(s) – The internal conflicts that form the basis of the transformational arc of character. A subplot represents the motivations and consequences for the protagonist in his or her inner, emotional, psychological, or spiritual reality. There are two primary subplots: the internal conflict that exposes the fatal flaw of character is called the "B" story; the relationship conflict is called the "C" story.

Theme – The theme represents the writer's views, values, and personal point of view. It is the single most essential aspect of a story that allows the writer to develop a strong and meaningful arc of character.

Tragic – The lethal power of the fatal flaw is activated when the protagonist fails to rise to the transformational challenge that is brought about by the story's conflict. The protagonist is thereby destroyed by his or her own inability to grow and evolve.

Transformational arc of character – This aspect of the story illustrates how a character grows and changes within the context of the external conflict that is unfolding. When the transformational arc is strong, it becomes the guiding force behind the entire drama. As a result, the transformational arc of character forms its own distinct structure inside the structure of the plot, and it reflects the natural pattern of human psychological, emotional, and spiritual development. (The transformational arc of character is sometimes shortened and referred to as *the transformational arc* or *the arc of character*).

Transformational moment – For the transformational arc to be complete, the protagonist *must* make a conscious decision to change (internally) and to take action to resolve the conflict. Even though it is in the climax that the protagonist physically moves toward achieving the goal of the plot, it is this internal moment of decision that marks the true transformation of the character, and it is therefore the climax of the "B" story. The transformational moment usually occurs just prior to the climax at the end of the third act.

Turning point – At the end of the first and second acts, an incident or event occurs that shifts the conflict of the plot and subplots in a new direction and substantially raises the stakes for the protagonist, making it much more difficult to achieve the goals of the plot and subplots.

FILMOGRAPHY

An Affair to Remember (1957)
   Written by Delmer Daves, Donald Ogden Stewart, Leo McCarey
The African Queen (1951)
   Written by James Agee and John Huston
   Based on the novel *The African Queen* by C.S. Forester
Amadeus (1984)
   Written by Peter Shaffer
   Based on the play *Amadeus* by Peter Shaffer
American Beauty (1999)
   Written by Alan Ball
Annie Hall (1977)
   Written by Woody Allen and Marshall Brickman
Apollo 13 (1995)
   Written by William Broyles Jr. and Al Reinert
   Based on the book *Lost Moon* by Jim Lovell and Jeffrey Kluger
Basic Instinct (1992)
   Written by Joe Eszterhas
A Beautiful Mind (2001)
   Written by Akiva Goldsman
   Based on the book *A Beautiful Mind* by Sylvia Nasar
Beloved (1998)
   Written by Akosua Busia, Richard LaGravenese, and Adam Brooks
   Based on the novel *Beloved* by Toni Morrison
Braveheart (1995)
   Written by Randall Wallace
Carrie (1976)
   Written by Lawrence D. Cohen
   Based on the novel *Carrie* by Stephen King

Casablanca (1942)
  Written by Julius J. Epstein, Philip G. Epstein, and Howard Koch
  Based on the play *Everybody Comes to Rick's* by Murray Burnett and
  Joan Alison
Chinatown (1974)
  Written by Robert Towne
A Christmas Carol (1938)
  Written by Hugo Butler
  Based on the short story *A Christmas Carol* by Charles Dickens
Citizen Kane (1941)
  Written by Herman J. Mankiewicz and Orson Welles
The Color Purple (1985)
  Written by Menno Meyjes
  Based on the novel *The Color Purple* by Alice Walker
Crash (2004)
  Written by Paul Haggis and Robert Moresco
  Story by Paul Haggis
Dances with Wolves (1990)
  Written by Michael Blake
  Based on the novel *Dances with Wolves* by Michael Blake
Dead Poets Society (1989)
  Written by Tom Schulman
The Deer Hunter (1978)
  Written by Deric Washburn
  Story by Michael Cimino, Deric Washburn, Louis Garfinkle,
  Quinn K., and Redeker
Don Juan DeMarco (1995)
  Written by Jeremy Leven
Dumb and Dumberer (2003)
  Written by Robert Brener and Troy Miller
  Story by Robert Brener
Fatal Attraction (1987)
  Written by James Dearden
A Few Good Men (1992)
  Written by Aaron Sorkin
  Based on the play by Aaron Sorkin

The Fisher King (1991)
  Written by Richard LaGravenese
Forrest Gump (1994)
  Written by Eric Roth
  Based on the novel *Forrest Gump* by Winston Groom
Fried Green Tomatoes (1991)
  Written by Fannie Flagg and Carol Sobieski
  Based on the novel *Fried Green Tomatoes at the Whistle Stop Cafe* by
  Fannie Flagg
The Fugitive (1993)
  Written by Jeb Stuart and David Twohy
  Story by David Twohy and characters by Roy Huggins
Gladiator (2000)
  Written by David Franzoni, John Logan, and William Nicholson
  Story by David Franzoni
The Godfather (1972)
  Written by Mario Puzo and Francis Ford Coppola
  Based on the novel *The Godfather* by Mario Puzo
Goodfellas (1990)
  Written by Nicholas Pileggi and Martin Scorsese
  Based on the book *Wise Guy* by Nicholas Pileggi
The Graduate (1967)
  Written by Calder Willingham and Buck Henry
  Based on the novel *The Graduate* by Charles Webb
Groundhog Day (1993)
  Written by Danny Rubin and Harold Ramis
  Story by Danny Rubin
Hannah and Her Sisters (1986)
  Written by Woody Allen
Heat (1995)
  Written by Michael Mann
The Hours (2002)
  Written by David Hare
  Based on the novel *The Hours* by Michael Cunningham

It's a Wonderful Life (1946)
  Written by Philip Van Doren Stern, Frances Goodrich, Albert Hackett, Frank Capra, and Jo Swerling
  Based on the short story *The Greatest Gift* by Philip Van Doren Stern
To Kill a Mockingbird (1962)
  Written by Horton Foote
  Based on the novel *To Kill a Mockingbird* by Harper Lee
Last Tango in Paris (Ultimo tango a Parigi) (1972)
  Written by Bernardo Bertolucci and Franco Arcalli
  Story by Bernardo Bertolucci
Leaving Las Vegas (1995)
  Written by Mike Figgis
  Based on the novel *Leaving Las Vegas* by John O'Brien
Lethal Weapon (1987)
  Written by Shane Black
The Lord of the Rings (2001)
  Written by Fran Walsh, Philippa Boyens, and Peter Jackson
  Based on the novel *The Fellowship of the Ring* by J.R.R. Tolkien
Malcolm X (1992)
  Written by Arnold Perl and Spike Lee
  Based on the book *The Autobiography of Malcolm X* by Alex Haley and Malcolm X
Million Dollar Baby (2004)
  Written by Paul Haggis
  Stories by F.X. Toole
Moonstruck (1987)
  Written by John Patrick Shanley
My Best Friend's Wedding (1997)
  Written by Ronald Bass
My Big Fat Greek Wedding (2002)
  Written by Nia Vardalos
Notorious (1946)
  Written by Ben Hecht
An Officer and a Gentleman (1982)
  Written by Douglas Day Stewart

One Flew Over the Cuckoo's Nest (1975)
  Written by Bo Goldman and Lawrence Hauben
  Based on the novel *One Flew Over the Cuckoo's Nest* by Ken Kesey
Ordinary People (1980)
  Written by Alvin Sargent
  Based on the novel *Ordinary People* by Judith Guest
The Pianist (2002)
  Written by Ronald Harwood
  Based on the book *The Pianist* by Wladyslaw Szpilman
The Piano (1993)
  Written by Jane Campion
Platoon (1986)
  Written by Oliver Stone
Pulp Fiction (1994)
  Written by Quentin Tarantino
  Based on stories by Quentin Tarantino and Roger Avary
Raging Bull (1980)
  Written by Paul Schrader and Mardik Martin
  Based on the book *Raging Bull: My Story* by Jake LaMotta, Joseph
  Carter, and Peter Savage
Ransom (1996)
  Written by Richard Price and Alexander Ignon
  Story by Cyril Hume and Richard Maibaum
Rashômon (1950)
  Written by Akira Kurosawa and Shinobu Hashimoto
  Based on the stories *Rashômon* and *In a Grove* by Ryunosuke Akutagawa
Rocky (1976)
  Written by Sylvester Stallone
Romancing the Stone (1984)
  Written by Diane Thomas. (Uncredited writers) Treva Silverman,
  Howard Franklin and Lem Dobbs
Saving Private Ryan (1998)
  Written by Robert Rodat
Schindler's List (1993)
  Written by Steven Zaillian
  Based on the book *Schindler's List* by Thomas Keneally

Sea of Love (1989)
  Written by Richard Price
Sex and the City (1998)
  Written by Michael Green and Liz Tuccillo
  Based on the novel *Sex and the City* by Candace Bushnell
  Series created by Darren Star
Shakespeare in Love (1998)
  Written by Marc Norman and Tom Stoppard
Sleepless in Seattle (1993)
  Written by Nora Ephron, David S. Ward, and Jeff Arch
  Story by Jeff Arch
Something's Gotta Give (2003)
  Written by Nancy Meyers
Sophie's Choice (1982)
  Written by Alan J. Pakula
  Based on the novel *Sophie's Choice* by William Styron
Speed (1994)
  Written by Graham Yost
Star Wars:Episode IV - A New Hope (1977)
  Written by George Lucas
Thelma and Louise (1991)
  Written by Callie Khouri
Titanic (1997)
  Written by James Cameron
Tootsie (1982)
  Written by Larry Gelbart and Murray Schisgal
  Story by Larry Gelbart and Don McGuire
Unforgiven (1992)
  Written by *David Webb Peoples*
When Harry Met Sally (1989)
  Written by Nora Ephron

INDEX

Dara Marks can be reached through her website at:
www.daramarks.com